Accordion Dreams

_To Mike —
Don't stop the
music
(Arrête pas
la musique!)
—Blair_

Blair Kilpatrick

Accordion Dreams

A Journey into Cajun and Creole Music

BLAIR KILPATRICK

University Press of Mississippi

JACKSON

www.upress.state.ms.us

The University Press of Mississippi is a member of the Association of American University Presses.

A portion of the author's royalties will be donated to the following organizations: Augusta Heritage Center, Louisiana Folk Roots, and Musicians' Village/New Orleans (Habitat for Humanity).

First printing 2009
∞
Library of Congress Cataloging-in-Publication Data

Kilpatrick, Blair.
    Accordion dreams : a journey into Cajun and Creole music / Blair Kilpatrick.
       p.   cm.
    ISBN 978-1-60473-101-9 (cloth : alk. paper) 1. Kilpatrick, Blair. 2. Accordionists—United States—Biography. 3. Musicians, Cajun. I. Title.
    ML419.K526A3 2009
    788.8′616241073092—dc22
    [B]   2008020370

British Library Cataloging-in-Publication Data available

For Steve, who opened the door

Contents

Acknowledgments

First, I offer love and gratitude to Steve Tabak, my partner in life, in music, and all good things. By now, he must know this book almost as well as I do.

My deepest thanks go also to our sons, who have grown into wonderful young men. They have followed their own paths—Alec into his own kind of music, Nate into journalism. I like to think their early Cajun-Creole immersion didn't hurt!

I am grateful to my mother, for her support of my music and my writing and for her willingness to let me share parts of her family history. I wish my father could see where the Cajun accordion has taken me: back to writing, an early dream he and I both shared.

And I extend very special thanks to Jane Anne Staw, a gifted writing teacher and coach. I don't believe this book would exist if our paths hadn't crossed. I am grateful beyond words for her mentoring and friendship.

My agent Barbara Braun took a chance on a new writer with an offbeat story to tell. I am thankful for her belief in this project, her wise counsel, and her hard work on behalf of this book.

I can't imagine a better home for my book than the University Press of Mississippi or a better editor than Craig Gill. He took up this project with enthusiasm, and guided me along the path to publication with wisdom and patience. He chose wonderful outside readers: Anne Galjour and Shane Bernard, two gifted Louisiana writers whose close and critical reading strengthened the book. I am deeply grateful to Debbie Self, who provided skilled and sensitive copyediting along with enthusiasm and warm support. I also thank Anne Stascavage and Valerie Jones, along with everyone else at UPM.

A few other people deserve special acknowledgment for their role in connection with this book. First is Edward Poullard, brother of my late friend and accordion mentor Danny Poullard. Early on, Ed read a key chapter in the book and offered a response I still treasure. More recently, he has clarified some details of his family history. Steve and I both thank him for the gift of his music and friendship.

Harton Firmin and Freida Fusilier, musician-writer friends, offered helpful feedback and clarification around some of our shared experiences. Joan Letendre and Denise Thompson also read a few chapters and were supportive of my efforts to write about the "old days" in Chicago. Jude Moreau, a Texas Cajun who built my beautiful red accordion, read parts of the manuscript and responded with his usual warmth and enthusiasm. Finally, California friend and ethnomusicologist Mark DeWitt offered encouragement and eventually pointed me in the direction of his own publisher.

Radhika Mathur, Randy Kasten, and Margit Stange from my writing group deserve thanks for their support, incisive feedback, and pushing when needed. I am also very grateful to Nancy Day, for her online coaching and support.

In some ways, *Accordion Dreams* is one long thank you—or perhaps a love letter—to the many people who have been a part of my musical world. It is impossible to acknowledge everyone. I don't even know the names of all the warm-hearted people I have met during my travels to Louisiana. Or everyone from music camp—the Augusta Heritage Center in West Virginia and Dewey Balfa Camp in Louisiana. So many people have made my feet and spirit dance over many years of listening to Louisiana French music.

I'll begin by thanking my band mates in Sauce Piquante—starting with Steve, my fiddler-husband. We are both grateful to guitarist Robert Richard and bass player Kathy "KP" Price for sharing this adventure with us. I offer special thanks to our son Alec, a recording engineer as well as a musician, who has played such a pivotal role in the production of our upcoming CD.

I would also like to acknowledge my teachers, many of whom appear in the pages of this book. I have been privileged to learn from them—formally, at music camps and workshops and classes, and informally, during visits in their homes and my own. First, of course, is the late Danny Poullard. I am also grateful for my time with the late Bois Sec Ardoin, Al Berard, the late Delton Broussard,

Jeffrey Broussard, Sheryl Cormier, Jim DeWan, Ginny Hawker, Craig Knudsen, Jesse Legé, the late Eddie LeJeune, Bobby Michot (and the rest of the clan!), Larry Miller, Jude Moreau, Edward Poullard, Dirk Powell, Steve Riley, Tracy Schwarz, Charlie Terr, and Goldman Thibodeaux. In big and little ways, they have left their mark on me.

I offer thanks to everyone, dancers and musicians alike, in the two Cajun-Creole music communities I have called home. The years in Chicago were shared with the Thompson-Nuccio clan (Denise, Earl, and Dennis) and the Terrs (Charlie, Lynne, and John). It is impossible to acknowledge everyone from the vibrant San Francisco Bay Area scene. I have already mentioned several California music friends. Here are a few more special people who have enriched my musical life: Andrew Carrière, Kathy Dodge, Patty Hammond, David Hymowitz, Marty Jara, Maureen Karpan, Gerard Landry, Delilah Lee Lewis, Dana Mandell, Robbie and Shirley Robertson, Suzy and Eric Thompson—and all our jam regulars. I would also like to acknowledge the community of California expatriates in Louisiana: Jim Phillips and Christy Leichty, Andrea Rubinstein, and Linda Castle.

Finally, I would like to thank a very important group of people: those who provided the photos that add so much to this book. With an assist from Suzy Thompson, I spent an afternoon with the amazing Chris Strachwitz, who generously combed the Arhoolie archives for photos of Danny Poullard. Through Ed Poullard, I found my way to the celebrated music photographer James Fraher—who graciously provided a photo of Ed and turned out to be my long-ago neighbor from Chicago! Jude Moreau directed me to David Simpson, the photographer-curator of a wonderful LSU-Eunice website devoted to contemporary Cajun, Creole, and zydeco musicians. He provided photos of Jude—as well as an offer of anything else I wished to use from his collection.

Susan Pilch, a friend from music camp, offered her wonderful Augusta photo of Danny Poullard and Eddie LeJeune. Chicago friends Denise and Earl Thompson kindly allowed me to include their photos from one of Danny's garage jam sessions. The Sauce Piquante photos were taken by band member Kathy Price and by Susan Richard, wife of our guitarist Robert. I thank my journalist son Nate for taking the author photo and for helping me unravel the mysteries of digital photo files.

In closing, I extend my deep appreciation to Marc and Ann Savoy, who have provided such inspiration to me and to countless others over the years. Their support and enthusiasm for this book mean more than I can say. I offer special thanks to Marc for allowing me to quote from a letter he wrote to me many years ago, after my first visit to southwest Louisiana. I never imagined how prophetic his words would be.

Part One   Beginnings

One Swamp Tour

Papa Joe didn't have what you'd consider a pretty voice. It sounded too life-roughened—whether from late nights, cigarettes, whiskey, or simply the passage of time, I couldn't say. And as a tour guide, he had more skill in steering a pontoon boat through the Louisiana swamp than navigating his way around a melody.

But once he was moved to sing, he didn't appear concerned about his audience—or the road ahead. He turned up the tape in the white Dodge van, threw back his head, half closed his eyes, and joined in on the rousing chorus, trying to sing through the grin that remained on his face until the song ended.

I struggled to make out the words. Not an easy task, since this was a tale told in French. I did understand one line that kept recurring: "On a trouvé un paradis dedans le sud de la Louisiane." We found a paradise in south Louisiana.

I didn't need to know much more. I could see the pride that surged through Papa Joe as he sang along with the recording, more effective than any lecture he could have given us. His words were in Cajun French, but the message came through clearly. "Listen to me. This is who we are."

The French language drew me in, but the rhythm held me there: loping and easy, but propulsive, all at the same time. Rising and falling, in and out, round and round, with that moment of hesitation in between. A lopsided carousel, an egg-shaped wheel, rising up against the pull of gravity, then falling forward, descending in a rush. I felt off balance, teetering, chasing my tail. It was an orderly sound, up to a point. But the wildness threatened to rise up, from just below the surface. I could hear it in the alternating call of fiddle and accordion, the steady roll of guitar chords, the crashing drums and ringing triangle—and in the French voices straddling the ledge between song and shout, melody and wail.

A blow to the head, a blow to the heart—something strikes you, and afterward you are never quite the same. That's how I fell in love with Cajun music: suddenly, unexpectedly, and completely. "Tout d'un coup," as the French would say.

It happened on my first trip to Louisiana, just before my fortieth birthday. The world was cold and gray back in Chicago, but New Orleans in January felt like spring. Love at first sight, I've always called it.

But that's not entirely true. It began more quietly, like a spark landing in the dry underbrush, smoldering out of sight, until the forest catches fire.

Or maybe this: a seed blows into your backyard, carried by the wind from some far off place. It takes root in your garden without your even knowing. One day, you notice a strange little shoot. The next time you turn around, your orderly garden has been over-run by a riot of fast-growing tropical vegetation, blooming flowers twining around the squash and carrots, making a mockery of the neat rows, pushing at your borders.

The music came to me at an unlikely moment: in a van, return-ing from a swamp tour, an hour outside of New Orleans. It was a prepackaged side trip with some recorded Cajun music, topped off by our guide's lusty singing. That was my improbable awakening, the point of contact, the beginning.

We had ended up in New Orleans almost by accident. Steve wanted to take me somewhere warm and exotic for my fortieth birthday. Even though he was a year younger, he figured this marked our joint entry into middle age, and he wanted us to do it in style, leaving no room for bad jokes about being "over the hill."

Originally, Steve had pictured a tropical island in the Caribbean. But the travel agent convinced him three nights wasn't enough time and suggested New Orleans instead. I wasn't overly concerned about our destination—I felt happy enough to be getting away by our-selves. Nate and Alec, our sons, were five and eight. We had never spent this much time apart from them.

"Lucky thing Dad didn't take you to Milwaukee for your birth-day," our older son pointed out, years later. "You might be playing polkas."

I had the usual stereotypes of New Orleans: Mardi Gras and

Bourbon Street, jazz bands and blackened food. The guidebook I studied before the trip deepened the picture a little, but it left me unprepared for how the city would work on me. I didn't expect to fall out of ordinary time and land in a place of mystery and unsettling contrasts, where anything might happen.

After two days of wandering the French Quarter with Steve, I felt intoxicated and unbalanced, opened up—with no need to think about the clock, the train schedule, my psychotherapy patients back in Chicago, the babysitter, or making dinner. I felt free to absorb the world around me, breathe the air, and follow the stirrings of my imagination and my senses. That was my state when I encountered Papa Joe.

I had signed up for the swamp tour at the last minute, after picking up a few brochures in the hotel lobby. The trip would be a little something extra—"lagniappe," as local people said, a chance to get a quick taste of Cajun country. I didn't expect a real person behind "Papa Joe's Cajun Swamp Tours"—or the beginning of a journey that would alter the direction of my life. I just hoped we didn't end up on a sanitized tour that felt like a Greyhound excursion.

Papa Joe picked us up late on Sunday morning in his down-at-the-heels van, collected our cash, and made the rounds of a few more hotels to gather the rest of our party—nine in all. We drove west on U.S. 90, the Old Spanish Trail, toward Lafourche Parish, an area with two advantages: accessibility to New Orleans, along with plentiful swamps and bayous.

Our guide turned out to be a weathered-looking man of about sixty. As he drove us along, he laid out his credentials. "I'm a real Cajun," Papa Joe began, "even though I live in New Orleans." He had been born and raised in Thibodaux, along Bayou Lafourche. Once he retired from the Coast Guard, he got into the swamp tour business.

Discovering Papa Joe was "a real Cajun" came as no surprise, now that we had met him. Beyond the French-sounding name, I could detect something in his voice. Papa Joe talked like a southerner, true enough, but with a hint of something else, a bite to the consonants, a certain languorous drift to the vowels. Listening to his voice felt like traveling on a river flowing in one direction, but with an original bed that remains hidden. You sense the strong currents that could alter your course in a flash and carry you off in another direction entirely.

Papa Joe talked steadily for most of the hour it took to reach Bayou Lafourche, where he docked his boat. "Let me tell you how I make catfish courtbouillon," he'd begin. Only he said it like this: "kubeeyon." Or he'd launch into a story: "Did you hear about the time Boudreaux and Thibodeaux found a gator in the back of Boudreaux's truck?" The history, tall tales, obscure facts, and recipes held my attention—more than those Cajun music tapes Papa Joe kept playing. The music served as background, creating a little atmosphere, nothing more than that.

When we reached Bayou Lafourche, Papa Joe led us onto a flat-bottomed pontoon boat, open to the elements, except for the canopy covering our heads. He kept up his steady narrative as he carried us from open waterways into the swampland, naming the trees, plants, birds: cypress and Spanish moss, blue herons and owls and snowy egrets. It was a crash course in the ecology of the wetlands.

We emerged again into more open waters. Up ahead I spotted a square white wooden building, with a Falstaff beer sign perched high above the corrugated metal roof and twin red Coca-Cola signs flanking the door. Papa Joe docked in front and we followed him into the cool darkness of the "Harvey Jr. Cypress Inn"—a bar, with a few deserted tables off to the side and Cajun dance fliers posted near the cash register. Papa Joe picked up containers of food, while the rest of the group bought beer and soda.

Back on the boat, Papa Joe opened up the steaming buckets, and dished up plates of jambalaya and chunks of French bread. "I made it myself," he announced. I wasn't certain he spoke the truth, but somehow it didn't seem to matter. I savored the spicy mixture of chicken, andouille sausage and rice, sipped my drink, and settled back to watch the swamp glide by.

The overhanging trees and moss became closer and denser the more deeply we penetrated, like hands reaching out to touch us. Papa Joe maneuvered his way between low-hanging branches from above and to the side, while avoiding the obstacles appearing in front of us, just breaking the water's murky surface: submerged stumps, cypress knees, rusty metal. We watched closely for some of the living inhabitants waiting to surprise us—water snakes and turtles, nutria, maybe even an alligator if we got lucky.

Once the boat docked for the final time, our journey continued by van. We stopped at a family alligator-processing business on Bayou Boeuf, near a half-abandoned swamp settlement called Kraemer, close to Lac des Allemands. The area had been settled by Germans, Papa Joe explained. But they were quickly absorbed into the French-speaking culture established by the Acadian settlers who preceded them.

I already knew the tragic history of the Acadians, the French people cast out of Nova Scotia by the British and sent into exile. As a schoolgirl, I had studied Longfellow's epic poem "Evangeline," and I could still recite the opening lines from memory. "This is the forest primeval" is how it starts. "The deep-voiced neighboring ocean speaks, and in accents disconsolate answers the wail of the forest" comes near the beginning, and again at the end. In between, the peaceful Acadian community is uprooted and deported, and the two young lovers, Evangeline and Gabriel, are separated. Evangeline spends the rest of her life searching the country for Gabriel, from New England to Louisiana, only to find him on his deathbed—in an almshouse in Philadelphia.

Longfellow's saga captured the American imagination—even though Evangeline and Gabriel, as it turned out, were fictional characters. I thought back to another trip, almost ten years earlier, when I had visited the site of the Acadian expulsion.

Steve and I had spent that summer traveling through Canada. I felt light and carefree, with a just-completed Ph.D. in hand and a baby growing inside me. But in Nova Scotia, the area originally known as Acadia, we saw reminders of what had happened there: homes and farms burned, families separated and deported, over ten thousand people sent into exile in 1755. "Le Grand Dérangement," they called it, the Acadian Diaspora.

Some of the Acadians eventually returned home to Nova Scotia. But the rest scattered—to other places in the Maritime provinces, to Quebec, to New England. About three thousand made their way to Louisiana, only to discover the former French colony had passed to Spanish control. The Acadian exiles settled along the bayous and swamps and eventually pressed westward into the prairies. Their area of settlement, known as "Acadiana," looks like a large triangle occupying the lower third of the state. The French language survived in these isolated rural areas, long after it had died out in the cultivated circles of New Orleans.

The Acadian settlers in Louisiana came to be called Cajuns, an anglicized version of "cadien," the short form of "acadien." Papa Joe claimed the label with pride, but for years "Cajun" had a derogatory meaning. People of his generation—and even younger—could tell stories of getting punished for speaking French at school. The resurgence of cultural pride came later. The Cajun Renaissance began in the sixties, with the resurrection of the French language—and music—at the very heart of it.

But the Acadians had done more than simply preserve their distinctive ethnic identity. Their language and robust culture enveloped outsiders, in a gently subversive embrace that produced French speakers with names like Kraemer and Miller, Riley and McGee, Ortego and Romero. Louisiana French culture gradually evolved into a complicated tapestry, a weaving together of many groups of people—with roots in France, other European countries, and beyond. There were Africans brought to the New World as slaves, Afro-Caribbeans, settlers from the Canary Islands and the Philippines, and Native Americans, the region's original inhabitants. White, black, and Creole—together, they made up a rich and complex gumbo, not always balanced or harmonious, but bound together by one key ingredient: the French language they all came to share.

Papa Joe savored the sound of French rolling off his own tongue—especially when he discovered our party included a married couple from France. They were a chic young pair of engineers, cool and contained as they stepped gingerly around the muck at the alligator farm, while the rest of us gazed at the skulls nailed to trees, admired the hanging nutria pelts, and fingered the gator teeth. They answered back politely, when Papa Joe addressed them in French, but seemed reluctant to banter.

During our final stop—a restored sugar plantation—Papa Joe stepped away from the group and one of the Americans directed a question to the French couple. "Are you having any trouble communicating with him?"

The French woman smiled slightly, then replied in her clipped, British-sounding English. "His accent is so terrible that I can barely understand his French." She cast a disapproving look in Papa Joe's direction.

Her blunt assessment startled me. I loved hearing Papa Joe speak French and blamed myself for not being able to understand more. I had studied the language for years, beginning in the fourth grade. When I finally stopped, midway through college, I had come close to fluency. My life had taken a different direction after that, with my growing interest in psychology. Still, I wondered why I had let it slip away, that beautiful language that used to feel like a part of me.

After we finished touring the sugar plantation, we boarded the van for the final drive back into New Orleans. Once again, Papa Joe turned on the Cajun music. But this time, he was inspired to sing along. He raised his voice so the sound would carry, rising above the noise of the traffic, the thrum of the van, the band playing on the tape.

This time, the Cajun music got my attention. Strange, the way it suddenly jumped from background to foreground. I tried to make sense of the words. First, I figured out one line, about finding paradise in Louisiana. After that, a little more of the story came to me, in fragments, in a gradual and incomplete revelation: "La Louisiane. Bayou. Valse. Monde."

But this wasn't just about understanding the words, or even hearing the sound in a new way. I began to feel the music inside. It all came together: the feeling of delight radiating from Papa Joe's face, the French words, the repetitive rhythms, the wailing fiddle and accordion, the insistent drums. The exuberant sounds filled me up. I could feel my chest cavity vibrating and my head shaking, keeping time.

Music always made me feel like moving. During my adolescence, I used to pace for hours around my bedroom, circling in a trance, as I listened to the nightly "Top 50 British Countdown" blasting from the radio. I grew up with rock music as the soundtrack to my life, and I'd progressed to bluegrass, southern mountain music, and the blues. Music made my spirit soar, my head nod, my body sway. But it never could carry me past the threshold of inhibition when it came to dancing.

Growing up, the idea of dancing—with a boy, or even by myself—well, the very thought could make me stumble and blush. I was left-handed, physically awkward, bad at sports, always battling my weight, and usually lost in a book or in my own daydreams. On the rare occasions when dancing became inevitable, I tried to avoid eye contact with my partner, and I prayed for no collisions and a short song. By college, when my social life finally picked up, I found it easier to sidestep the issue of dancing. And in Steve, I managed to find a man who shared my disinclination.

As I listened to Papa Joe sing along with the tape, the joyous music should have inspired me to two-step right there in the van. But it was out of the question, since I didn't dance. I didn't sing either, so I probably didn't even hum to myself. But I had started to dance inside.

"That's one of our top Cajun bands," Papa Joe informed us, still smiling, when the song ended. "That's BeauSoleil. They're playing tonight in New Orleans. Ya'll should go hear them."

Steve and I already had big plans for the evening, so we didn't pay much attention to the details about BeauSoleil. We had just one more night, and a few hours the next morning, to savor the gaudy charms of the French Quarter.

Back at the hotel, a few hours later, I squeezed myself into the shiny tube of flame-blue leather my brother and his wife had just given me for Christmas. The skirt was a foot shorter—and two sizes smaller—than anything else in my closet. "Is this a joke—or some kind of message?" I'd whispered to Steve, panicked, when I opened it. "Bring it to New Orleans. It will be perfect," he'd reassured me.

I studied myself in the mirror. Could I really go out in public like this? "Hey—looks good!" I looked up and Steve snapped my picture, grinning at me. Just like that, he made me feel like the girl he'd met on another January evening, twenty years ago, on the blind date that didn't end until dawn. He still talked about the green dress I'd worn that night. I still remembered the endearing hole in the knee of his jeans, the fetching streak of gray in his black hair, the New York accent that sounded exotic to my midwestern ears. I didn't feel middle-aged at all.

We spent our final evening as planned: dinner at Broussard's, a venerable "haute Creole" restaurant, and then a pilgrimage to hear the Preservation Hall Jazz Band in the small subterranean room where they played. Cajun music receded, once again, into the background.

We flew home the next afternoon, laden with souvenirs. On our right hands, we wore matching silver rings, slender unadorned bands from a little shop called Quarter Moon. In my ears, I had tiny gold fleur de lys studs, a present from Steve.

For my parents, we had found a pair of ceramic Mardi Gras masks in the French Market. We carried chicory coffee and beignet mix from Café du Monde, along with mugs and t-shirts for our sons. From the Italian grocery on Decatur Street, we brought back a jar of olive salad and a flat round loaf for muffulettas. We even picked up a King Cake, the traditional sweet yeast bread baked during Mardi Gras season. And we carried rolls of film, mostly undeveloped.

As for the Cajun music, we had no visible souvenirs, not even a tape or a single image of Papa Joe in those rolls of film. The white van, the Cypress Inn, the swamp, the alligators, the French couple—they all appeared among our shots. But our guide had disappeared.

We finished off the last roll of film in Chicago, back home with our sons. In the first shot, I sit between them, my arm protectively around five-year-old Nate, my hand cupping his head. I look tired and happy. I had missed them. Nate looks shyly down, half leaning on me, half sitting on my lap. Babyhood still clings to him. He clutches his new t-shirt to his chest, so you can't see it clearly. Only the single word "Monde" is visible.

Alec, full of eight-year-old expansiveness, looks boldly at the camera, his shirt unfurled like a banner. "Café du Monde" extends across the top, in large letters. Below is a drawing of a large, low building, in shades of green and beige, and underneath, in smaller letters, a promise of coffee and beignets.

The next photo shows the boys alone, flashing peace signs at the camera. You can tell Alec is the instigator of this bit of cheeky humor, since he is grinning. Nate looks more tentative, eyelids and fingers at half-mast. The King Cake, a little worse for wear, rests on the table in front of them, gaudily frosted in purple, green and gold, the traditional colors of the season, with the alternating bands of color starting to run into each other.

I study myself, that smiling mother in the photos, younger looking than I remember feeling at the time. My gaze is directed toward the camera, but I seem to be looking past it, at something in the middle distance. I search for clues. Did I know what had just happened to me, as I prepared to step back into the routine of my life? My weeks were an orderly balance of family, work, and shared dinners with friends whose lives were similar to ours. A good life, I would have said.

The following weekend, Steve had planned a big party for my birthday. We still hadn't come down from the excitement of our trip, and we wanted to keep the New Orleans spirit going. The food part was easy. We just needed some music to create the right kind of atmosphere. But nothing obvious, like a New Orleans brass band, or Pete Fountain, or the Preservation Hall Jazz Band. I wanted more of that Cajun music I'd heard on the swamp tour. The sound kept coming back to me, and I couldn't get it out of my mind. But I didn't know where to find Cajun music in Chicago.

On a hunch, I headed downtown to Rose Records on South Wabash, five floors crammed with all kinds of obscure recordings, from opera to blues. There it was: on the next-to-last floor, nestled between the "Folk" and "International" aisles, a small section devoted to Cajun music. I picked out a tape by a Louisiana band called Filé, impatient to get home and play it. And when I put on the cassette, I heard it once again—that same distinctive sound I remembered from the swamp tour. A little less percussive, maybe, but with the same infectious rhythms, the tangle of accordion, fiddle, and French, the energy that picked you up and wouldn't let you go.

The party turned into a festive affair. Steve made muffulettas and jambalaya. We served chicory coffee and pralines and draped Mardi Gras beads around the room. Our guests got into the spirit and a few even brought New Orleans-flavored gifts—a Paul Prudhomme cookbook, some hot sauce, and a tape.

I tore off the wrapping and studied the cassette. The cover showed a battered red convertible, upended, sinking into the swamp. The cover read: Bayou Cadillac. The album had been recorded by a band called BeauSoleil. I scanned the list of songs, then I spotted it: "Le Sud de la Louisiane." The rest of the selections ranged from traditional Cajun and Creole songs to the title track, "Bayou Cadillac." That wild medley included a Buddy Holly tune covered by the Rolling Stones ("Not Fade Away"); a Bo Diddley riff; a traditional New Orleans Mardi Gras tune ("Iko Iko"); and then the punning refrain "Buy you a Cadillac, buy you an old Mustang." The mix of French, English, and the smattering of Spanish turned out to be quite a gumbo, flavored with good humor and Caribbean-style rhythms.

The next week I bought a Walkman, the first I had ever owned, so I could carry the music with me. I'd slip on the earphones whenever I could—after I walked the boys to school, when I took the Illinois Central to and from the hospital where I worked, and as I passed through grocery stores and bookstores in our South Side neighborhood. I even listened while wandering through record stores in search of more Cajun tapes.

That BeauSoleil tape grew almost as worn as the battered red car on the cover. I kept trying to understand the words to "Le Sud de la Louisiane." The complete story still escaped me, but I knew just enough to realize it was about the Acadian journey to Louisiana and the new life the settlers created there.

When I found the written words a few years later, I finally understood it all. The settlers crossed water, sand, and mountains to reach the new land and discovered a colorful new life: alligators and crawfish in the marshes and bayous, ducks flying overhead, squirrels in the woods. The little Cajun women sang as they washed their clothes in the bayou, cooked up crawfish sauce piquante, and baked sweet potatoes in the fireplace. The old Cajun men had their own diversions. After chopping wood, it was time to party: a little moonshine and then on to the old-time polkas, mazurkas, and waltzes.

"Le Sud de la Louisiane" was surely no "Evangeline." This was music for dancing, not grieving, and the lyrics painted a light-hearted portrait of life in Cajun country, with little to suggest the suffering behind the journey. But I knew the song had a deeper resonance.

For Papa Joe, as he sang along in the van that day, the music provided a rousing affirmation of cultural survival. And in me, it awakened something I barely understood at the time, a faint stirring that would soon send me off on a journey of my own.

Two   Accordion Dreams

I emerged from sleep disoriented, half-awake, still wrapped in a dream. An accordion dream, once again. I could feel the nocturnal music, refusing to retreat in the face of insistent morning sounds: Steve shifting beside me, child stirring, cat scratching, city street noises filtering through the window along with the sunlight. But I kept dancing with the accordion. It was playing itself, playing me, as the bellows opened and closed. In and out, ebb and flow, no beginning and no end, with the music all around. Expanding me as far as I could go, then drawing me back in, then filling me up, and sending me out again. As natural—and essential—as breathing. And then the music, a river flowing through my fingers and onto the buttons, spilling into the air.

Now, coming to wakefulness, I held the remnants of the dream through lingering sensation more than sound. I could still feel the weight of the accordion, the heft of it, in my hands. So real, so present—and oddly familiar, this little box I had heard and finally seen from a distance, but hadn't yet touched. Its music had haunted my days and now it began to infiltrate my dreams, with a sweet and unrelenting embrace that refused to let me go.

The accordion dreams didn't come to me right away. The quiet fire I felt after my first trip to New Orleans started slowly, with few visible signs, aside from the pungent Louisiana flavors beginning to creep into our cooking.

But my new passion was brewing, right along with the chicory coffee. I sent away for catalogs featuring Louisiana foods and gifts, and I began to devour books by Louisiana writers—like Ann Rice's vampire chronicles and James Lee Burke's hard-hitting Cajun detective series, and then Kate Chopin's early feminist classic The Awakening. I watched and re-watched "The Big Easy," captivated every time by the transformation of the repressed East Coast attorney as she succumbed to the steamy ambience of New Orleans—helped along by the seductive charms of a cop whose Cajun accent came by way of Hollywood. But mostly, I fed my appetite for Cajun music—a hunger that was beginning to turn into a craving.

I started out with two tapes, a pair of cassettes in constant rotation between our home stereo and my Walkman. But I needed more. I began to haunt record stores, just as I had always lost myself in bookstores, following a twisting path that left me feeling greedy and a little dizzy, not quite sure what I was looking for, as one thing led to another and then another.

BeauSoleil, the band so proudly introduced to us by Papa Joe, provided the point of entry. Following their trail, I discovered an album called "Home Music," by a trio called the Savoy-Doucet Cajun Band. It caught my eye for two reasons. I recognized the fiddler. And—unlike all the others I'd seen—this group included a woman.

The cover was an old-fashioned tableau in sepia and blue: three musicians seated around a campfire at dusk, their figures in sharp relief against the clouds looming behind them, filling the night sky. On the left, Michael Doucet, the fiddler from BeauSoleil. In the middle, a rugged-looking man named Marc Savoy, holding a small accordion on his knees, and smiling broadly at the pretty dark-haired woman beside him. Ann Savoy looks pensive as she gazes down, absorbed in her guitar.

Their music startled me at first. The sound was so spare—just those three instruments, along with the faint metallic tinkling of a triangle or the scratch of a rubboard on a few tunes. There was no drum, no bass, and no heavy amplification. As for the singing, the two men sounded heartfelt, but a little raw, something like Papa Joe. Ann's contrasting voice had a sweet, pure tone, with an almost otherworldly stillness, especially on the slow tunes. The whole effect was unsettling, and so different from the polished, accessible music of BeauSoleil, with their rollicking Caribbean rhythms and sly humor.

Then I played the tape a second time, and something began to shift. The music didn't seem raw—just direct and passionate. As I kept listening, I realized the simplicity was deceptive. Savoy-Doucet had refined Cajun music down to its fundamental elements. Now I could appreciate the separate parts more clearly: the alternating call of the fiddle and the accordion, as each picked up the melody in turn; the persistent rhythm set down by the guitar; the contrasting timbre of male and female voices; the distinctive accent of Cajun French. Listening to the music of Savoy-Doucet was like turning a sparkling gemstone round and round, watching as the light hit each facet in turn, letting it shine with a fierce brightness. The music felt pure, deep, soulful—and a little wild, all at the same time. The longer I listened, the more the accordion began to define the music.

How can I describe the sound of the Cajun accordion? My first teacher, a young Louisiana musician named Steve Riley, would put it bluntly: "loud and crude." He had a note of bemused pride in his voice, like a father reflecting on an unruly offspring he doesn't wish to tame. I knew what he meant, but I found the sound more complicated than that.

I had always considered the accordion about as exciting as a wheezy church organ, a clutch of singing Italian waiters, or a German oom-pah band. I had childhood memories of musicians squeezing away on television shows like "Polka Varieties" and "Gene Carroll's Amateur Hour" during Sunday visits to my grandparents' bungalow in Cleveland. Accordion music was background drone: heavy, old-fashioned, and too corny to take seriously.

But the Cajun accordion had a completely different sound. Sometimes it arrived as a rhythmic assault, with sharp, punchy bursts of notes that hit me like the stuttering "rat-tat-tat-tat" of a machine gun's spray. At other times, I felt the aching pull of the melody, the notes extended like a hoarse cry hanging in the air. Anyone who has been moved by the harsh, wild skirl of bagpipes or by the moan of a blues harmonica can feel the lure of the Cajun accordion. The sound washes over you in waves, piercing your heart. You feel a crazy mix of feelings: exuberant, sad, defiant, and strangely free.

The Savoy-Doucet tape led me to another realization: this wasn't just good time music. Every other track was a melancholy waltz. The song titles—even on the fast, driving tunes—hinted at heartbreak: "Tits Yeux Noirs" (Little Black Eyes), "Port Arthur Blues," "La Grosse

Erreur" (The Big Mistake), "Chere Bassette" (Dear Little Woman), "Jongle à Moi" (Think of Me), "Quoi Faire" (Why?), "Le Pauvre Hobo" (Poor Hobo). Although I didn't understand all the words, I began to recognize simple phrases. *Tu m'as quitté pour t'en aller. You left me to go away.* Quoi faire tu fais tout ça? *Why did you do that?* Tu m'as dit tu m'aimais. *You told me you loved me.* J'suis tout seul. *I'm all alone.* The cassette sleeve didn't have much space for information. But for a few dollars, you could order notes and song lyrics, along with a music catalog, from the record company: a place called Arhoolie Productions in El Cerrito, California. An odd twist, I thought, a Louisiana band by way of California.

I pictured El Cerrito as a dusty little border town, with a few tired palm trees lining a single main street, and Arhoolie Productions housed in a post office box, or maybe someone's garage. A more likely spot for a mariachi band than those "California Cajuns" credited on one track. But my impressions of the state were hazy—I'd visited California just once, during a family vacation when I was a teenager.

When the bulky envelope with the Savoy-Doucet lyrics finally arrived, I extracted three stiff, folded pages—LP inserts—flattened them out, and began to pore over them like a road map, traveling back and forth between French and English. Now I could finally understand everything I'd been hearing.

These were sad tales, all right, mostly about lost love, abandonment—and death. In fact, nearly all the songs started out in a similar way—mistreatment by a lover—no matter how cheerful the tune itself sounded. "Eunice Two-Step," for instance, was a driving, up-tempo number, first recorded in the 1920s by a black accordion player named Amédé Ardoin, then picked up thirty years later and recorded—with new words—by the Cajun accordionist Iry LeJeune, who called it "Jolie Catin." Savoy-Doucet had come up with a combination of the two versions, which started out like this: "Hé, jolie catin, tu m'as fait des choses que je merite pas." *Hey, pretty doll, you did things to me that I didn't deserve.*

Or a haunting waltz, almost a dirge, called simply "Une Vielle Valse," described as an ancient tune of unknown origin. Sometimes called "the Balfa Waltz" after a family of musicians who recorded it. Two of the brothers, Will and Rodney, had died a few years earlier in a car accident. Marc Savoy had dedicated the song to his friend Will.

Marc sang the tale in his rough voice. "Quand j'ai parti de la maisooooooon . . ." He stretched out the final vowels so far they changed from song into moan. *When I left the house, I'd made up my mind to find you, or die trying.* The French words, translated literally, painted a starker picture: *"ou mourir au bout de mon sang"*—or die at the end of my blood. He finds his lover—with someone else. *It broke my heart—I'd rather die than see that. If I had five days left to live, I'd give up three of them to spend the rest with you. I want to die in your arms.* Those French words might sound melodious, but they couldn't disguise the meaning behind the story: love and obsession, a volatile combination.

Now the music began to paint pictures in my head: hard lives, lost loves, lonesome dangerous highways, times gone by. In some deep way these stories felt familiar—but for reasons I didn't understand, because my own life seemed so different. I was a product of the industrialized North. I hadn't known serious hardship—either as a child, or in the life I shared with Steve and our children. I couldn't really explain the pull of Cajun music any more than I could have explained why, as a little girl, I burst into tears one night at bedtime, after my Harvard-educated father told me in a kind way that no, we would probably never live on a farm. All I knew was that I felt a deep connection to those passionate, resilient country people in Louisiana—and I identified with the themes of sadness and struggle in their history and music.

Along with Amédé Ardoin and the Balfa Brothers, I read about Iry LeJeune, Lawrence Walker, Amédé Breaux, the fiddler Dennis McGee, and other legendary musicians associated with early recordings of songs that became part of the core Cajun repertoire. The background notes offered a glimpse into the history behind each song and into the folk process itself, as songs were passed along, adapted, changed, lost, and found again.

I also spent some time exploring the catalog that accompanied the Savoy-Doucet lyrics. My Cajun music quest had led me to Arhoolie Records, the legendary roots music label founded by an impassioned German-born folklorist named Chris Strachwitz. The catalog was enticing, and it had everything from blues to Tex-Mex, from

Balkan to gospel. But I remained fixed on Cajun music. It seemed exotic and familiar, very American and at the same time out of this world. It was like country western in French or folk music with an edge, or maybe just *les blues français*. I couldn't put my finger on it. But I couldn't get enough of that haunting music, with the strange mix of sounds I was just beginning to untangle.

Despite my growing obsession with Cajun music, outwardly the routine of my life hadn't changed. Four days a week, I took the train to the South Side Catholic hospital where I worked as a psychologist. We took turns walking our sons to their school, where Steve worked as a teacher and an administrator. Fridays, I attended a study group, ran errands, cooked, and had a few hours to myself.

Steve and I spent most of our free time with the boys. Our family adventures were urban ones: visits to zoos and museums or strolls through Chicago's ethnic neighborhoods. Our social life revolved around communal dinners with friends—mostly families like ours—with the occasional outing to a restaurant, film, or concert.

But then I discovered a local Cajun band, and my life began to rearrange itself.

One afternoon, as I left a bookstore on Fifty-seventh Street, I scanned the collection of fliers tacked up to a tree outside the door. A political rally. A lecture by a visiting Middle Eastern scholar. Used books for sale. Dissertations typed. Two roommates seeking a third, vegetarian preferred. A Cajun dance.

I looked again. No, I hadn't imagined it. A Cajun band was playing on Sunday, right in the neighborhood, on the austere gothic campus of the University of Chicago.

At the time, we lived in Hyde Park, near the lakefront, seven miles south of the Chicago Loop. The mile-square community had struggled for years to remain a stable, racially integrated island in the midst of the poverty surrounding it. Hyde Park meant left-leaning politics, the Great Books, urban renewal, Nobel Prize winners, progressive education, independent bookstores—and the University of Chicago, the neighborhood's anchor. The earthy strains of Cajun music didn't really fit, at least in my mind.

The campus was familiar ground. Steve and I had met as undergraduates at the University of Chicago, and he had worked for years at the UC Laboratory School, where our sons were now students. Our whole family bore the mark of this place, a serious academic community dubbed the Grey City and known for its dogged pursuit of the life of the mind.

Sunday afternoon, Steve and I—with the boys in tow—approached Ida Noyes Hall, an imposing graystone building built in the 1920s as a women's gymnasium. We joined the small crowd milling around a wood-paneled hall, waiting for the dance to begin. It turned out the dance lesson came first—our signal to retreat to folding chairs lining the wall. We resisted the brisk entreaties of a woman in her late thirties who seemed to be the teacher. She did her best to lure everyone out onto the floor.

"Dancing is just walking with attitude," she offered, trying to demystify the process. "Watch." She turned on some recorded music.

I studied the subtle movement of her hips, the sway of her short skirt, and the easy saunter of her solid legs, covered in tights. The woman seemed to glide along without effort, feet barely leaving the floor, her mass of dark curls rising and falling with the music— looking graceful, sensuous, and a little tough, all at the same time. Maybe it was the cowboy boots.

I brushed away a little ping of envy, as easy as nudging a bit of gravel out of my sandal. That dance teacher made it look so easy, and soon a small group of students had clustered around her. But she couldn't fool us. Steve and I remained firmly planted on the sidelines, hoping the band would show up soon. Alec and Nate were already restless. "Can't we leave now?" "It won't be much longer," I promised, playing for time. I watched the dance lesson—men in one line, women in the other—curious in spite of myself.

Finally, the Chicago Cajun Aces materialized, then headed over to the stage area. I looked them over. Four men, near my age, clean shaven, wire-framed glasses and neatly trimmed hair, corduroys and khakis. They had the understated look of schoolteachers or engineers—until they picked up their instruments. The accordionist sounded the first note, holding it, bringing the others to attention, offering them a half beat to jump on board. This train was about to leave the station.

I watched and listened, transported, as the music clanged to life, right in front of us. So that was how it happened, that hypnotic twining together of accordion and fiddle, guitar and triangle. The first wave of sound was fast and exuberant—the next, languorous and mournful. The songs alternated between fast and slow: lifting me up, bringing me down, and then lifting me up again.

I studied the tall man working the accordion. He appeared serious, almost impassive, and he seemed to look away from the crowd as he played—listening, gazing inward or perhaps downward, toward the accordion in his hands. It was slung low, braced against his hip, suspended from a strap across one shoulder. The accordion was small, with buttons on both sides and knobs on top, nothing like those big piano accordions. I wondered how those crashing waves of sound came out of that little wooden box, opening and closing steadily, without any wasted motion.

My attention kept shifting over to the fiddler—a small, intense, dark-haired man who bowed with abandon and did most of the singing, all of it in French. Even the impassioned shouts and wails, which sounded like a cross between a long, downward-swooping French "hee-haw" and a half-yodel: "Aaaaiyeeeee!"

No one in the band had roots in Louisiana. The fiddler came closest—he was part French Canadian. But their music sounded like the real thing. I could even recognize a few familiar tunes, music that till then I'd known only through recordings. "Lovebridge Waltz," "Eunice Two-Step," and a few others whose names I didn't know. Hearing live Cajun music for the first time was like finding myself in some faraway country, after months of gazing at postcards and daydreaming about what it might be like to visit someday. The music was so real, so suddenly present, almost too much to take in.

We had to leave early—the boys had reached their limit—but I didn't mind too much, because I had already signed up for the band's mailing list and picked up a flier for the next dance. I walked home with the music in my head and a bounce in my step, because the path ahead was clear. Now I knew where to find my music. We followed the Chicago Cajun Aces to their next venue, a North Side Irish bar called Keenan O'Malley's, where they began to play once a month.

We became regulars at the monthly dances. At first, I just wanted to listen to the band and drink in as much of that stirring music as I could. But soon I began to get the message: Cajun music was all about the rhythm that drove those dancing feet. So—like it or not—Steve and I would have to learn to dance.

Neither of us were dancers. Just once, at a big Long Island wedding on Steve's side of the family, I impulsively pulled him onto the floor. Everyone else, toddlers to grandparents, had already started to move and shake in the free form wave even bad wedding bands inspire, when they launch into rock anthems like "R-E-S-P-E-C-T," "Proud Mary," or "Light My Fire." I was feeling bold, reckless. Then Steve and I looked at each other. "I feel ridiculous," he said. That seasick look on my husband's face brought me to my senses. We sat down.

So I knew it would take some persuading to get Steve out on the floor for the monthly Cajun dance lesson. But I was insistent. Desire had overridden my innate sense of caution, and Steve was willing to be a good sport about my improbable new interest. So we began to heed the call of the dance teacher, joining the rest of the beginners who clustered around her. At least we had company.

The slow songs were waltzes. One-two-three, one-two-three, one-two-three. Good—this felt familiar. We circled slowly around the room. "Always go counter-clockwise," the teacher instructed. "It's how they do it in Louisiana."

I had to trust Steve's navigation skills, as I began to circle backward. I tried to follow him, but sometimes found myself trying to lead—offering a nudge here, a tug there. We didn't exactly glide, but we managed to waltz around the room in a more-or-less synchronized way, without any serious collisions with the other circling couples. We were actually doing it! I felt like a kid who had just shed her training wheels.

The waltzes alternated with the fast tunes, called two-steps. They baffled me. For one thing, these "two-steps" involved three steps, or maybe four. *Step-together-step-pause, step-together-step-pause.* The leader starts to the left, the follower to the right. *Right-together-right-lift, left-together-left-lift.* Steve and I mirrored each other's confusion. The confidence we'd felt with the waltz had been premature. That pause, that moment of hesitation, seemed to be the critical element.

"Don't do a polka," the teacher admonished. "Take small steps." "Feel the music." "Maintain tension in your arms, so your partner has something to work against."

"Just relax."

Easy for her to say. And easy for some of those other dancers, who traveled around the floor in a smooth circle, managing to listen to the band, look good, talk, flirt, change lanes—even throw in fancy sashays and twirls—without missing a beat.

We also had to learn the rules of engagement at a dance. I clung to Steve, feeling like an awkward girl at a junior high sock hop. When some well-meaning stranger asked me to dance, I fought back panic—because I knew it might appear rude if I declined. In fact, women often did the asking. So I'd accept—then apologize my way around the room.

"I haven't been doing this very long," I'd say, hoping neither of us had sweaty palms. "Oops, sorry," I would murmur, as our toes collided. "Oh, that was my fault," my new partner might reply. But sometimes he accepted my apology—reinforcing my suspicion he must be hoping for a short tune, so we could take polite leave of each other. As soon as the last notes sounded from the bandstand, I was poised for escape. But if the man knew the rules, he would escort me back to my original spot, safely at Steve's side.

But I didn't give up on dancing. I found myself practicing dance steps at odd moments: in the bathroom at home, as I studied my reflection in the shower door, or at work, in my small basement office at the community guidance clinic, during breaks between patients. Even the momentary privacy of a hospital elevator offered the chance for a quick two-step. Doors closing: I would begin to play a song in my head and count, stepping to the right—or was it to the left? Doors opening: I'd snap to attention, slipping on my professional face for whatever doctor, nun, or nurse might be waiting on the other side.

One way or the other, I managed to surround myself with Cajun music. At home, I played my growing tape collection, and the strains of fiddle and accordion began to filter into our family's life. Outside the house, I wore headphones whenever I could get away with it. I couldn't listen at work, since I spent nearly all my time with patients or in staff meetings. Away from work, I was usually with the boys. Mostly, I listened during my commute—on foot and by train—to and from the hospital. After awhile, I hardly needed the tapes, because the music kept playing itself inside my head.

Eventually, the music began to seep into my dreams.

But I never danced at night, during my Cajun music dreams. I played the accordion—completely at one with the instrument, the music gliding out of me with no effort at all. I'd wake up enchanted—and surprised—since it had never occurred to me that I could try to create this music myself. But in my accordion dreams, I was doing just that—and with a kind of ease and grace that eluded me on the dance floor.

As a psychologist, I was accustomed to paying attention to dreams. My own dreams usually resembled experimental foreign films—a tangle of vivid, confusing visual images, organized according to that strange logic illuminated by Freud and Jung. Sometimes recurring dreams broke my sleep, and I'd wake with a troubling recollection of standing naked in the street, crying out mutely in the face of danger, or in a panic over a forgotten term paper. Dream interpretation, I thought, meant searching for disguised meanings and hidden associations.

But my Cajun accordion dreams were different—and vivid in a way I had never experienced. I found myself completely inside them. Not watching, but occupying the experience. Long after I opened my eyes, I had a strange impression of physical familiarity, an awareness of detail—for an instrument I had never even touched, much less played. The dream spoke to me mostly through sensation—not through imagery or symbols, and not by evoking emotion or hinting at hidden meanings. I never had to wonder what my accordion dreams meant. They simply were.

Recurring dreams—especially dreams like this—have a kind of urgency. My accordion dreams kept haunting me at night and lingering in the morning, even in the face of an important development in my waking life—a job change. In late summer I moved uptown, to the university hospital just off North Michigan Avenue where I had completed my psychology internship twelve years earlier. I hadn't been looking for a new job, but a former supervisor had approached me about taking a new position, as the coordinator of one of the hospital's outpatient mental health programs.

My new role offered more responsibility and challenge than my old staff therapist position. It also required more time. When the boys were small, I had been reluctant to spend too much time away from them, and it was only in the past year that I had extended my work hours to four days a week. Now I would be working every day, and commuting to the North Side. But the change excited me. It represented a step up professionally and a chance to be part of an institution I had idealized ever since I had completed my training there.

But those accordion dreams persisted, despite the change in my professional life. The music had claimed even more territory in my inner landscape than I realized.

By late September, a month into my new job, the spark struck in Louisiana had been burning steadily, the flame growing stronger and fiercer. After nine months of listening, dancing, and dreaming music, I had to find an accordion. If I had worked up the nerve to speak to Charlie, the leader of the local Cajun band, my quest for an instrument might have been more direct. But then I wouldn't have had the same kind of story to tell.

So I was on my own, guided by a small drawing, accompanied by a few lines of text, from a Cajun music catalog: "Single row diatonic accordion, four stops, ten buttons on the treble side, two spoon-shaped bass keys. Key of C. Made in Germany, by M. Hohner. Four hundred and ten dollars, plus shipping."

I could have ordered the Cajun accordion from the catalog. But now that I had decided to act, I couldn't wait. I went to the Chicago Yellow Pages, looked up "accordion," and started calling up places like Star Concertina and Italo-American Accordion Company. "I'm looking for a Cajun accordion," I would say. And then I would pause and wait for the response.

But no luck. Most people sounded puzzled. Others offered replies that didn't make sense. One man said: "I can order you the real thing, a handmade Cajun accordion from Louisiana. But it will cost you close to a thousand dollars." I didn't listen to him.

Eventually, I tried Walles Music, a store on Chicago's far West

Side. "Yes, we have what you're looking for," said the voice over the phone. "Starting at a hundred and ten dollars." Finally—someone who knew what I was talking about. And the price was right. No point in investing too much money in an instrument I might never learn to play.

Steve and I set out for Walles Music one Saturday when the boys were visiting my parents. We drove through aging Chicago neighborhoods settled by immigrants from Eastern and Southern Europe. I looked out the window at the mix of wood framed bungalows, auto repair shops, apartment buildings, ethnic bakeries, parish halls, and liquor stores. Everything looked a little faded—and familiar. I remembered those Sunday visits to my mother's parents, during my grade-school years in Cleveland. Their Slovenian neighborhood on the city's East Side had looked something like this, I thought.

We had reached the western edge of the city when we found the place—a nondescript brick building on a North Avenue commercial strip. Inside, the store looked deserted, except for the elderly couple behind the counter. A quick look around revealed the usual assortment: guitars, keyboards, high school band instruments, and sheet music. I saw not a hint of anything Cajun.

When I approached the counter, everything started to take on a musty air. The yellowed photographs on display dated from the 1930s and 1940s. Most of them featured accordions. In one group photo, thirty shining young faces smiled out from behind their big piano accordions, little else visible besides hands and feet.

"That was our all-accordion orchestra," the small white-haired woman told me proudly, in a heavy German accent. She seemed to be the one in charge.

I admired the photo and listened attentively when she and her husband launched into a series of stories about the music school they had operated all those years ago. As they talked, I glanced around, noticing a few accordions for sale. But they were piano accordions—large, ornate instruments with pearlized finish, glitter, and day-glo colors. That was not at all what I needed.

Finally, I brought out my catalog and showed her the picture. "I called earlier about a Cajun accordion. I'm trying to find one like this," I told her. The woman directed her husband through a curtain, and he quickly obliged. He looked spry, even though his mind seemed a little cloudy. She, in contrast, was quick and shrewd, despite her physical frailty.

The old man reappeared with two or three small black boxes, which is exactly what an accordion looks like, when the bellows are closed—a squeezebox.

The woman selected one in my price range, then set it on the counter. "It's new. We got it several years ago on a buying trip to Europe. It's been in storage since then."

I studied the accordion. It was a small wooden box, ten inches high and seven inches across, less than six inches deep. Black in front, red on the sides, with a thin strip of flowered trim that looked like old-fashioned wallpaper. The centerfold of the bellows was red. On the front, printed in antique gold lettering against the black background, I could read this legend: "Eagle Brand Accordeon. Highest Quality." Silvery metal trim, with the figure of an eagle stamped in, adorned each of the four corners. Below each silver bird were raised letters that spelled out: "Eagle Brand. Trade Mark. Made in Germany."

It certainly resembled the instrument in the catalog. A row of ten buttons on one side, two metal keys on the other, two knobs on top. I thought it was beautiful—although it did have a strangely old-fashioned look.

"You can play it," the old woman said.

So I picked it up. The accordion felt so light in my hands, lighter than I had imagined. It couldn't have weighed more than two pounds. I unhooked the metal clasps holding the bellows closed, one in front, one in back, then slipped one hand into the fabric strap on the left, the thumb of the other hand into the smaller loop on the right. I pulled.

The papery bellows opened.

Silence.

I depressed one of the small white buttons and pushed the bellows closed. Then I heard it.

The sound was high and thin, different from what I was expecting. But it was the unmistakable call of an accordion ringing in my ears, sweet and piercing as it hung in the air. I pulled the bellows out, my finger on the same button, and now a different sound

The author with her antique Eagle Brand accordion, 2008. Photo courtesy of Kathleen Price.

emerged, one note higher. I moved up a button, pushed, and heard a slightly higher tone.

I knew I was just playing with sounds. But in that moment, I could hear a hint of all those waltzes and two-steps I had been listening to for the past months. Or perhaps it was more of a promise, an imperfect echo of the music in my dreams.

"This is exactly what I need," I told the old woman. "I'll take it."

Three   Charivari

At first, I felt like celebrating: I finally had my hands on a real accordion. But what I deserved was an old-fashioned Cajun "charivari"—a mocking, raucous serenade, when the neighbors gather outside the window of an ill-fated couple on their wedding night. It is a party for a pair that's mismatched or outside the bounds of propriety, like when an old man takes a young wife or a widow remarries with unseemly haste, or when an older couple gets together, second time around for both of them. Once the glow fades, there you are, stuck with the reality that falls short of your dreams.

. I remembered how excited I'd felt, when Steve and I drove away from that music store. I'd cradled my new accordion on my lap, eager to get home and unwrap it. But now, after three months, I couldn't deny the truth: this dance was not going smoothly.

My new accordion and I were definitely an odd couple. I saw the first signs the moment I got my new treasure home. I pulled the little black accordion out of the bag, extended the bellows—and sniffed. A musty smell filled the dining room. Hmm. Strange. How long had this new accordion been in storage, anyway? Or maybe I really had stepped out of time—back into the past, and then out again, with the atmosphere of that old music store still clinging to the instrument.

Even the sales receipt looked old. Yellowed paper, with the name and address of Walles Music stamped at the top, in sepia-toned ink. Below, typed in black fading to gray, I could read the details of my purchase:

-One-	"Eagle-Brand" 1 row 2 stop	$130.00
	2 basses accordion & book	
	Sales tax	10.40
	-Thank You-	$140.40

The brownish date stamp read simply "SEP 29 PAID." No year.

But I knew the sales receipt was new. The storeowner had typed it out right in front of me, laboring on her old typewriter. Besides, at the top I could see the complete date, including the year, along with my name, which had come out as "Mr. Blair Kilpartirck." Such a mysterious transformation. On paper, I had become a man, and with a new last name with a vaguely Eastern European ring. My Slavic roots were showing.

When I examined the accordion bellows more closely, I could see that someone had tried to repair the thin, papery surface with a clear lacquer coating in a few spots. And the fabric thumb strap had started to shred. It appeared that charming old-fashioned look might be more than skin deep. But I brushed my questions aside—easy to do, in the excitement of finally having an accordion in my hands.

I pushed and pulled, as I worked my way up and down the ten little white buttons on the right hand side of the accordion. It sounded like a do-re-mi scale—sort of. I pushed, then pulled—and went up a note on the scale. On to the next button, push and pull, and I continued up the scale. But then I'd hit a button where it turned around on me, and the push started to take me back down the scale. Sometimes a note appeared to be missing. A peculiar instrument, with a major catch: you got a different note when you pushed and pulled, much like playing the harmonica, when you inhale and exhale. Maybe it was time to look at the book included with the accordion.

The instruction manual reminded me of those old-fashioned music books I'd used during my couple of years of piano lessons in grade school. Simplified musical scores for popular songs, children's classics, and folk tunes—with a German twist, since the publisher was Hohner, that German company. Not very useful to an aspiring Cajun accordion player who could barely read music.

Luckily, I soon located a manual more to my taste, through one of my Cajun catalogs—"You Can Play Cajun Accordion" by Larry Miller, a Louisiana accordion builder. The straightforward title matched the booklet's homemade appearance: spiral bound, hand typed, partly hand lettered, rough drawings.

Larry, an educator, had re-connected with his Cajun heritage at a relatively late age, in his thirties. He'd set out to learn to make—and play—accordions, following in the footsteps of a handful of established Louisiana builders, who had begun their craft in the post–World War II years, when the imported German-made accordions were no longer available.

So my accordion's German roots were no accident. As I'd later learn, the very first accordion was patented in 1829 in Vienna. The sturdy instrument spread quickly throughout Europe—and beyond. It was loud, versatile, practically indestructible—a one-man band that found a place in folk cultures all over the world. It eventually showed up in Louisiana in the mid- to late 1800s—imported, some historians suggest, by German Jewish merchants. Although the accordion didn't become popular in southwest Louisiana until the early 1900s, it soon came to have a dominant role, reshaping the traditional Acadian folk music in which fiddle had been the primary instrument.

As Larry explained, the most prized instruments in Louisiana were the "tits noirs"—little black ones—manufactured by the Monarch Company in Germany. The Monarch factory changed hands over the years: to the Sterling family in the 1920s, and then to another family, who changed the Sterling name to Eagle. That caught my attention: the same name printed on my little black accordion. Perhaps it had a distinguished pedigree.

Larry offered a minimum of music theory. He had developed a simple notation system: a number corresponding to each of the ten buttons, along with a symbol indicating whether the bellows were to be pushed or pulled. The book included a handful of Cajun songs, the bare bones of each translated into button notation, along with French lyrics written phonetically.

But Larry offered this as a temporary crutch. Cajun music, he wrote, was supposed to be played "by ear."

> *At first concentrate on one or two tunes to be learned. This is very important if you wish to succeed.* Commit to memory one or two tunes, no more, at first. Be able to whistle or sing musically correct with each note done on key before you attempt to play it on the accordion or any musical instrument. Use the push-pull patterns if you need them so as to find the correct order of buttons for the first

one or two tunes. Then play these two tunes each 100,000 times till your family runs you out of town. But be sure to play the one or two tunes many times over and over in order to get the brain to begin to learn where to send your fingers to find where those sounds are located. THERE ARE NO SHORTCUTS TO THIS NECESSITY! *You simply must take the medicine and spend the time!*

Playing by ear is more complicated than people realize. It means relying on a pattern you have inside you, a cognitive structure—an idea of a melody, internalized after listening to the music as it is played or sung by other people. Trying to play the music of another culture is even more complex, because of the challenge of learning unfamiliar patterns of sound.

If you grew up as an English speaker in the United States, you wouldn't have to think twice about the melody for a children's classic like "Twinkle, Twinkle Little Star." You would have absorbed it naturally, by listening, following along—and probably by matching your voice to the grown-ups.

If you tried to play "Twinkle, Twinkle" by ear on an unfamiliar instrument for the first time, the tune probably wouldn't come right away. You might have to struggle, like someone using the "hunt and peck" approach to typing. But at least you'd already know what you wanted to say.

What I was attempting with the Cajun accordion resembled trying to type, without first knowing the language. Granted, I had spent many hours listening to Cajun music. But I hadn't listened in a way that was truly focused, listening until I could hold the pattern of sound in my head. Then—the critical point—I needed to find a way to check the accuracy of my internal model. In other words, I needed to reproduce the sound with my voice, before I tried to find the matching sound on those ten white buttons.

Larry left no room for doubt about the importance of this last step:

THE MOST IMPORTANT LESSON *in learning to play by ear is that one must thoroughly memorize and be able to sing, whistle or hum musically correct a given tune before attempting to play on the accordion.*

It was the most fundamental piece of advice in the book—but I managed to sidestep it, as quickly as Steve and I might swerve on the dance floor to avoid another couple in our path. It sounded too simple—and deep down, I probably believed it was impossible for me.

Here was the problem: I could not whistle, though I had tried. I rarely hummed, and I certainly didn't sing. Even though no one ever told me to just move my lips, I had absorbed this message in the course of growing up. I had built up layers of inhibition around the possibility of singing aloud, even when I was alone. I didn't even sing in the shower.

So I disregarded this key bit of advice, not realizing how much of a barrier I was creating for myself. Day after day, I pushed and pulled, coaxed and squeezed, guided either by button numbers—the connect-the-dots approach—or by some vague idea of a tune I half-held in my head. Sometimes I tried to play along with recordings. But I quickly discovered I couldn't do that. The ten button accordion is a diatonic instrument—in other words, limited to the notes of a single major scale. G, in the case of my little Eagle Brand. But the instrument of choice in Cajun music is usually a C accordion, with D as the runner-up.

My questions about my accordion kept growing. The sound didn't seem to correspond to anything I was listening to—and not only because of the difference in keys, or even my lack of skill. The tone itself was wrong: thin and high pitched. And I strongly suspected the instrument had spent more than a few years in the back room at Walles Music. Perhaps that old woman had sold me an antique toy.

I found another clue at Christmas, when my parents gave me a book that was high on my wish list, Ann Savoy's *Cajun Music: A Reflection of a People*. The book painted a loving portrait of the music and culture that Ann, a Virginia native, had embraced when she married Marc. It had everything: serious scholarship, oral history, profiles of musicians, interviews in French, photos, song lyrics, and discographies. As I pored over it, I came across an old photo of a young Cajun boy, barefoot and in overalls, playing an accordion that looked just like mine. So it seemed my little black Eagle, or something very close to it, had once been played in Louisiana.

I decided to write to Marc Savoy, who was a true Cajun Renaissance man: cultural preservationist, master musician, and the most respected of the Louisiana accordion builders. I introduced myself, described my accordion, and included a few photos. It was a bold step, not something I would normally do. But I was on a quest, and I figured Marc would solve the mystery, if anyone could.

Marc wrote back immediately. He explained that I did indeed have an old instrument, predating the famed Monarch accordions by ten or fifteen years. If I opened it up, I would discover something similar to a harmonica: just two sets of reeds instead of the usual four, with each set mounted on a single plate, rather than individual ones. My accordion was a curiosity, perhaps a collector's item—but it simply wasn't a playable instrument. I was disappointed, though not really surprised to have my suspicions confirmed.

Marc had written the letter on the back of a glossy flier for the new Hohner Cajun accordion, a variant of the first model I had seen described in the music catalog, but customized to resemble the "tits noirs." The new Hohner was available through his shop, at a somewhat reduced price, considerably less than one of his hand-built Acadian accordions.

But my resourceful husband was a step ahead. I had another birthday coming up, and Steve had been doing his own research. Somebody referred him to a mail-order music store with a fitting name: "Elderly Instruments."

"I've found you an accordion," Steve told me. "It's on order, but it might get here a little late, not quite in time for your birthday." I was thrilled—and the wait only added to my feeling of anticipation.

A few weeks later, just after my forty-first birthday, it arrived. Steve arranged to have the new accordion delivered to me at work, at the upscale suite of offices in the university hospital where I'd taken the new position a few months earlier.

"Blair, a package just arrived for you," our department secretary said. A few of the other therapists happened to be standing around her desk.

"Oh! That's great! I've been waiting for it. It's a birthday present from my husband." I paused, considered a moment, before I decided to let my staff in on my secret life.

"It's my new Cajun accordion."

If they were surprised, they managed to keep it to themselves.

"Well, open it!"

So I did. I cut open the box, pulled out the packing, then gently lifted it out: a shiny black Hohner accordion, Cajun-style, in the key of C.

The Hohner was bigger than my Eagle Brand accordion and heavier than I expected. It felt unfamiliar in my hands. But I knew that would change, once I got it home after work and started playing. Unfortunately, evening was hours away—and I couldn't wait that long.

I didn't even retreat to my office. Discreetly, since everyone was watching, I moved the bellows just a little, my finger depressing a single white button, one of the low notes on the treble side. I bent my ear close. There—I heard it! A throaty whisper that promised to turn into the real thing once I really let go. I could already picture it, and I could practically feel it: bellows pumping, air rushing, all four reeds vibrating in the thrilling growl and wail of a Cajun accordion in full voice. The accordion of my dreams.

Four Allons à Lafayette

Let's go to Lafayette. That was the proposition of a young man to his sweetheart in "Allons à Lafayette"—the first Cajun song ever recorded, back in 1928. I'd made exactly the same pitch to Steve and he was happy to follow along. So now we found ourselves driving west on Interstate 10 toward the largest city in Acadiana, the capital of Cajun country.

Much as I loved the color and excitement of New Orleans, I wanted a more authentic experience of Cajun music and culture. I hoped to find it in Lafayette, a setting I dreamed would look as exotic as the French Quarter—but with everyone speaking French, restaurants serving nothing but gumbo and jambalaya, and Cajun musicians at every turn.

The closer we got to Lafayette, the more I wondered why I had pulled Steve and the boys into this excursion. Signs and billboards lined the four-lane highway, passing in a blur on either side. Fast-food restaurants and chain motels. Video stores and lottery tickets. Discount stores and insurance brokers. Clear signs of civilization, and I could see nothing picturesque—or especially French—about them, unless you counted the Cajun motifs sprinkled liberally in the advertisements.

Steve and I had taken advantage of spring break to make our third visit to New Orleans, the second with the boys—who were starting to regard the city as our family's offbeat version of Disneyland. We spent the first part of the week in an old Creole mansion just off Bourbon Street—the Biscuit Palace, named after the fading old advertisement for Uneeda Biscuits painted high on one of the exterior walls.

Our guesthouse provided a fine base for exploring the French Quarter, along with side trips to the leafy Garden District and the Audubon Zoo. Although we didn't spend much time there, our antique-filled suite looked sunny and charming by day. But at night,

37

we heard strange noises, and then we began to notice lights turning on unexpectedly and cabinet doors swinging open by themselves. "Do you think it might be haunted?" we asked each other, savoring the tantalizing story not even the boys quite believed.

When we set out for the two-hour drive to Lafayette, I had visions in my head, a distillation of all those hours of listening to Cajun music. I thought of Joe and Cléoma Falcon, whose recording of "Allons à Lafayette" on the Columbia label had become a regional hit. I had no trouble picturing the young couple, because their photo adorned the cover of Ann Savoy's book, my indispensable guide to Cajun music.

Joe, serious and unsmiling, is a dapper young man dressed in a suit, with an accordion on his knees. Cléoma, posed with her guitar, has the sultry look of a Cajun Mata Hari. She is a small round woman with wavy dark hair, eyes like two plums, bowed lips—decked out in pearls, high heels, and a filmy sleeveless dress that just covers her knees. She was the only woman who ventured into the rowdy bars and public dance halls to sing and play Cajun music.

"Allons à Lafayette" was one of those tunes everyone knew. Judging from the words, a trip to Lafayette meant freedom and opportunity—a place to get married or perhaps to have other escapades with a sweetheart, depending on how you interpret those playful opening lines: "Allons à Lafayette, c'est pour changer ton nom. On va t'appeller Madame, Madame 'Canaille' Comeaux." *Let's go to Lafayette. We'll call you Missus, Missus "Sly" Comeaux.*

When we reached Lafayette, my first reaction was disappointment, because the place looked so ordinary—and American. One of the city's main motel strips lined a highway named after Evangeline, Longfellow's Acadian heroine. As soon as we checked into our room at one of the big national chains, I began to long for our picturesque guesthouse back in the French Quarter.

Lafayette reminded me of another small southern city—Durham, North Carolina, where Steve and I had lived in the mid-seventies. Both were regional hubs and university towns, and both had depressed economies. Durham was a fading tobacco town, and Lafayette had been a thriving oil center, until the petroleum industry collapsed in the eighties. Downtown Lafayette looked weary, as though it still carried the scars of the "boom and bust" years.

But as we drove through the city, I realized Lafayette also had an inviting small-town feeling—particularly in the outlying neighborhoods, where the streets resembled country roads and the modest wood-framed houses looked to be in a state of gentle decay. When we discovered some all-Cajun music stations on the radio, with announcers speaking nothing but French, my spirits began to pick up.

We soon found an alternative to fast food: the "dine and dance" Cajun-themed restaurant. Randol's and Prejean's were right in Lafayette, while Mulate's, the oldest and best known, was in Breaux Bridge, six miles to the east. They all followed the same formula: decent renditions of Cajun food at reasonable prices, tables surrounding a central dance floor, Cajun bands playing every day, t-shirts and other memorabilia for sale. Busloads of tourists came—but so did locals, especially families, who preferred to avoid the dance hall scene.

The set-up was ideal—the grown-ups could set aside their gumbo or jambalaya and slip out for a quick turn around the dance floor, while the kids kept busy with their food. I was so taken by the whole idea I forgot to be nervous about joining in with homegrown Cajun dancers.

The dance crowd usually numbered eight or ten couples—fewer than I expected. Most people treated the music as backdrop to food and conversation. The musicians sounded good—solid and traditional, if not exactly charged up by playing for a lunch or dinner crowd.

I tried to keep one eye on the accordion and the other on the boys, as Steve and I stepped onto the floor, looking both ways to make sure we had an opening. These dancers all knew what they were doing. One or two couples always drew everyone's attention, doing what I considered "exhibition dancing": elaborate twirling, spinning, passing over and under each other's arms, even looking at each other through a keyhole created by their interlaced arms. Back in Chicago, I always felt as twisted—and as graceful—as a pretzel when a partner tried that with me.

Most of the couples danced more simply—moving smoothly around the floor, taking the turns easily, the body erect, small steps, with no excess motion at all. That was more in line with what Steve and I tried to do. I hoped we were fitting in—especially one night, when I realized some of the other dancers were keeping a close eye on us.

Steve and I straightened to attention, checking to make sure we maintained the squared-off stance we'd learned in those dance lessons he'd taken so reluctantly. My left hand on his shoulder, my right hand held aloft in his. His stance a mirror image of mine, except for his right hand resting on my waist. Enough tension in my arms to give him something to work against. "Pretend you are hugging a tree trunk," the dance teacher in Chicago had suggested.

We locked eyes. Steve stepped forward with his left foot, I stepped back with my right. Good thing this one was a waltz. Less room for error, with the slower pace and more straightforward pattern. ONE-two-three, ONE-two-three. Circling, round and round.

We tried to remember everything we'd been taught about dance-floor etiquette, especially the part about staying in formation, and not getting too close to the other dancers—or to each other. Dancing thigh-to-thigh might be popular in some circles, but not with traditional Cajun dancers. Even the suitor in "Allons à Lafayette" had to admonish his sweetheart: "Le monde parle mal de toi, tu danses mais trop collée. Quoi faire tu fais tout ça, c'est juste pour me faire faché!" *Everyone's talking about you, because you dance too close. Why do you do that—just to make me mad?*

So Steve and I watched our steps, literally. ONE-two-three, ONE-two-three. We tried to glide smoothly across the floor, moved by the alternating call of accordion and fiddle, but anchored by the steady rhythm of guitar, bass, and drums.

One older couple in western dress gave us a nod as they waltzed briefly alongside, then pulled ahead, leaving us in the dust. The next lap around, we received an approving smile. When the song ended, the man in the boots and cowboy hat shook Steve's hand, man to man. He didn't need to say anything. We'd passed. I felt a little silly, but also relieved, standing there by my man. Steve had become my improbable ticket into dance hall society.

These restaurants all specialized in seafood: crab cakes, shrimp salad, crawfish étouffée, oyster po-boys, seafood gumbo. Maybe that's what caused the case of hives that began to blossom on Nate's small body, our second day in Lafayette. We were relieved to find a doctor on short notice. Steve and a nurse had to restrain our wildly protesting son, while the doctor administered—as Alec put it—"a shot in the butt."

The doctor, a middle-aged local man, took it all with good humor and afterward seemed in no hurry to usher us out of his office. He was happy to weigh in when I asked his opinion of a couple of sites we were thinking of visiting—Lafayette's two historical theme parks.

We chose the park our Cajun doctor recommended, a reconstructed nineteenth-century Acadian village on the edge of town. As we wandered in and out of the dozen or so restored buildings, one of the costumed guides caught my attention—a jolly older gentleman with rosy cheeks, a snowy white beard, and an accordion in his hands. We posed for pictures with him, the boys perching on his lap, while I resisted a similar destination. I detected a whiff of alcohol as he tried to pull me closer.

"Would you play something for us?" Maybe that would distract him.

"Of course, chère. You do it like this. You only need to play one side of the accordion."

He depressed one of the two bass buttons and began to pump the bellows back and forth, producing a low two-note honk that did not resemble any kind of tune. How disappointing—the accordion was just a prop. Or perhaps our Acadian Santa liked to play tricks with the tourists.

By the next morning, we'd seen enough of Lafayette, so we decided to head northwest to Eunice, less than an hour away. The small prairie town had become the center of the traditional Cajun music world. For one thing, it was home to the Liberty Theater, known for its weekly radio broadcast of "Rendez-vous des Cajuns," a live music and variety show often compared to "A Prairie Home Companion." The show was hosted—in French—by a well-known folklorist and professor named Barry Ancelet.

But I considered Marc Savoy the biggest attraction in town. I wondered if he'd recall our exchange of letters two months earlier, when he had solved the mystery of my little Eagle Brand accordion. I hoped to pay Marc a visit—unless I lost my nerve.

When we arrived at lunchtime, Eunice appeared shut down. Even the restaurants looked dark. Finally, we spotted one small establishment with a flashing gumbo sign in the window. When we entered, the place resembled a lounge more than a restaurant, with a few men sitting at a long bar. We settled at one of the handful of tables. After we placed our order at the bar, I asked where we could hear some Cajun music.

The man behind the bar shook his head, considering. "Well, I don't know about that. Not too much going on during Lent."

Lent. Now I got it. That accounted for the shut-down feeling. In the traditional Catholic culture of southwest Louisiana, the weeks between Mardi Gras and Easter were taken far more seriously than in New Orleans or even Lafayette. People didn't stop at small private sacrifices, like giving up chocolate or meat. Lent was a time for sobriety and communal restraint. I felt embarrassed at my faux pas. I should have known.

But the men at the bar seemed concerned about our plight. They conferred back and forth. "Y'all think there might be something at the VFW tonight?" A phone appeared from behind the bar, and one of the men made a couple of calls. I felt touched by the flurry of activity—and surprised.

It turned out somebody knew about a new place—actually, an old place that had just reopened, called the Blue Goose. It used to be a rowdy venue, with chicken wire to protect the musicians and card games going on in the back room. When we walked in, the newly renovated club smelled like fresh wood and could have passed for a country-style bed and breakfast. But I could hear a fiddle playing—so we'd come to the right place.

A tall woman in her thirties, dressed casually in slacks, hurried over to greet us. She smiled warmly, if a little awkwardly, in the way you do when last-minute guests show up.

"Welcome. Bienvenue. Comment ça va?"

I felt pleasantly startled to be addressed in French—and relieved to hear the simple, automatic response coming out of my own mouth:

"Ça va bien, merci."

We continued in English. The Blue Goose hadn't officially opened yet, the woman explained. But we'd be welcome to sit and listen to the musicians practice. She pointed out the leader of the band, a white-haired man with a fiddle in his hand. "That's Harry LaFleur," she said. "He's played with everyone." She went on to list some of the names—Iry LeJeune, Nathan Abshire, Dennis McGee—legendary figures of Cajun music, now gone. I knew enough to be impressed.

It really was a band practice. The musicians kept starting and stopping, talking briefly, then starting up again. We listened for just a little while, not wanting to overstay our welcome, then headed off in search of Marc Savoy's legendary music store.

We almost drove by the sign for the Savoy Music Center. The gravel crunched, as we turned into the empty lot and parked in front of a plain green building, constructed simply of wood, or maybe corrugated metal, with a flat roof, a couple of windows, the picture softened by a few trees. From the outside, there was little to distinguish the store from the other houses and buildings set back from this flat country highway, a couple of miles outside the main part of town.

I eased my way through the door, Steve and the boys trailing behind. The store looked dark, and I felt a moment of relief. Maybe they had closed for Lent. And even if the store had stayed open, why should I expect to find Marc Savoy himself here? Or imagine that this famous man would even talk to me? I got ready to back out the door.

Then, from out of the darkness, a deep, resonant voice rang out:
"Come in, come in. How can I help you folks?"

Marc stepped into view, carrying a piece of accordion innards—ten flappers, it looked like. He looked just like his pictures, but bigger than I had expected: tall, raw-boned, a shock of black hair without a filament of gray.

I introduced myself, along with Steve and the boys, and then mentioned our recent correspondence about my little antique accordion.

"My, you have the most beautiful smile. I think you've just made my day."

Oh. Not quite the shop talk I expected.

"Thanks," I mumbled, dropping my eyes for a moment. Then I

went on with my story. "I did get another accordion a few months ago, that Cajun-style Hohner you recommended. It was good advice."

Marc smiled down at me. "Well then, let's see how you're coming along. Why don't you play something for me?" My heart sank, as he selected one of the accordions sitting on the counter and pushed it in my direction.

"Oh, I can't really play much yet." I resisted the urge to push it back at him.

I moved the bellows hesitantly, testing the musical waters, without even lifting the accordion completely off the counter. I tried to pick out what I hoped were the first few notes of "J'ai Passé Devant Ta Porte"—a sad, graceful waltz, the first one I had tried to learn.

Da—Da—Dum, Da—Dum, Da—Dum.

"Did you recognize that? I've been working on it."

Marc looked puzzled—not that I blamed him. Not even I could recognize the few notes that had just issued from the accordion, in more of a stumble than a dance.

Learning the accordion was slow going for me, I confessed, even though I practiced every day and studied the one instruction book I'd managed to find.

"A book?" Marc managed to sound both dubious and amused. "You didn't learn to love your man by reading a book, did you?"

Marc smiled at me, then cast a knowing side-glance in Steve's direction. What was this, more male bonding? I imagined they might even be winking at each other—except that my husband had never been a winking kind of man. I looked over at Alec and Nate, wondering what they must be thinking about this strange exchange.

Marc went on to explain that the key to playing was first to listen, to soak up as much traditional Cajun music as you could, until it filled you up completely. He had spent his own childhood doing just that, listening to the older men, mostly farmers, who gathered at his home to talk with his father and make music.

"By the time I finally picked up an accordion," he intoned, "the music just leaked out of my fingers." Marc himself seemed lost for a moment in the memory—although I figured he must have told this story a few times before.

Marc insisted we come back for his Saturday morning jam session. Impossible, we explained. We'd already arranged to check out of our motel in Lafayette early Saturday morning, and begin the long drive back to Chicago. But in the space of two minutes, an alternative plan fell into place. We'd leave Lafayette on Friday and spend the night in Eunice, so we could get to the jam session early. Marc even knew where to stay: a little place around the corner called the Stone Motel.

On Saturday morning, just after ten, we drove over to the Savoy Music Center. Even at that early hour, we had to park a distance away, since the cars and trucks had already filled the parking lot. Pickup trucks and rental cars, campers and late-model sedans, Volvos and RV's lined the shoulder on either side of the highway. I saw plenty of vehicles from Louisiana, but also license plates from Texas, Connecticut, Quebec, New York, California, Georgia. Once inside, we would meet visitors from even farther away—France, Germany, England, the Netherlands.

Since I'd read that guests at the jam should contribute drinks or boudin, a spicy Cajun sausage, we had picked up some cokes and beer on the way. As we approached the store, six packs in hand, I could already hear the music. First it was faint, with the sharp clink-a-clink of a triangle slicing through the air, against a quieter chorus of crying fiddles. Then the unmistakable chank-a-chank burst of a single accordion came to the foreground.

I saw a hand-lettered sign on the door, with a stern warning that photos were forbidden. This was a place for local musicians to play their music, not some kind of performance or media event.

Marc greeted us at the door. "Ah, the beautiful smile lady. You came back."

Inside, the store looked transformed. The lights were on and people filled every corner of the place—playing music, listening, eating and drinking. There were even a few couples dancing. We added our six packs to the communal collection on the counter, where I spotted square white bakery boxes, tied with string. But this was no coffee and Danish crowd—beer and boudin were the order of the day. The cans of beer had already started to pop open, and the white boxes housed plump links of boudin.

A man passed through the crowd, offering pieces of boudin. I expected a slice of firm sausage, but found myself with something different—a chunk of moist meaty dressing, overflowing from the casing and into my open palm. Following the lead of people around me, I squeezed the warm filling into my mouth. It was rich and spicy. Then I tasted something else, the musky flavor of my Scottish roots. Boudin must be the zesty Cajun cousin of haggis, the much-maligned Scottish delicacy I had tasted only a couple of times in my life. Haggis was a concoction of sheep organ meats and oatmeal, packed into the lining of a sheep's stomach. In Louisiana, they mixed pork and rice, then stuffed it into an elongated sausage casing. I had to admit it—I preferred the boudin.

But I had more interest in the music than the food. I followed the sound to a corner in the back of the store, where a small group of fiddlers and a couple of guitarists huddled around an older man playing accordion. Other people radiated out from that central cluster—less confident musicians, playing quietly on the periphery, along with folks who wanted to get up closer to listen. A few other accordionists had lined up, waiting their turns. At least a dozen musicians, maybe more, made music together.

I wanted to edge into the circle myself, to get even closer to the source of all that energy, but I kept a respectful distance. At least I could stand near enough to hear that sweet music and the raucous French voices filling the air. I would have given anything to be able to join the high-spirited party, to let my voice merge with the others. But I knew it was out of the question, at least for now.

I looked around the room, noticing more of those hand-lettered signs posted almost at random on the walls, ranging from big placards to index cards. Some were long essays on cultural preservation, signed "Marc Savoy." Others were short and pointed, Marc's postcards to the world at large: "Do not replace family traditions with media conventions." "If you don't like my black friends you can just leave."

Marc himself kept circulating around the room, playing the host, greeting people in a hearty mix of French and English. He paused to chat with us briefly, mostly about family. He pointed out a little dark-haired girl of three or four, scampering underfoot. "That's my baby," he said proudly. His three older kids were close in age to our boys. Ann, he explained, had left to visit her mother in Virginia, so I wouldn't get the chance to meet her.

Marc had one more suggestion for us, before he moved on. "Why don't you buy one of those toy accordions for your kids? The reeds are pretty good. It's not a bad way to start learning." I'd already seen those little Cajun accordions. Made in China, for sale in all the local gas stations and souvenir stands. I hadn't realized you could actually play them.

"Maybe we will," I told Marc.

Eventually Marc joined the jam himself, alternating between fiddle and the old upright piano sitting in the corner. Cajun piano— I didn't know what to think. I wondered why he didn't pick up the accordion.

Even though we had to leave by noon, I resisted when the time came. We'd barely arrived, and now I had to pull myself away, with the jam still going strong. I felt completely absorbed by the scene unfolding around me. More musicians kept showing up, shouting out greetings in French and English: "Hey mon nèg, where you been?" "Come on, chère, you can sit right here by me." "Y'all play that tune on the push or the pull?" "Hey man, don't you know the words? Moi, j'connais pas."

It was a fluid scene, with musicians changing places and sometimes instruments. Whenever somebody new took over on accordion, he'd kick off a whole new round of songs—his choice, as the top dog of the moment.

Finally, inside this unassuming green building, I had found the magic I had been looking for when we set out from New Orleans. How could we leave now? We hadn't even said good-bye to Marc.

But he was obviously tied up, completely in the thick of things: pounding away on that old piano, shouting out to the other musicians, pushing them ever onward. Let the good times roll. But also: lâche pas la patate. Don't drop the potato.

I kept my eyes fixed on the jam as I slowly edged toward the door, closing it reluctantly behind me. As I walked along the highway with Steve and the boys, I tried to hold onto the sound as long as I could, but it slowly receded. By the time we reached the car, we were out of range and the music had vanished. We played our Cajun tapes on the car stereo, all the way back to Chicago—but it wasn't the same.

We got home late on Sunday. On Monday morning, back at work, I felt a strange sense of longing. I had just begun to get a taste of something I was seeking, during those last few days of the trip, and now it was gone.

I couldn't find the words for what I'd lost. The music was a big part of it, of course. I had heard the real thing at last—Cajun music played in a natural, down-to-earth way. But it was more than just the music. It was also the people—so warm and earthy, and with that funny directness that kept me a little off balance.

I had to smile when I thought back to that whole series of improbable encounters: the Cajun doctor, the dancing couple who checked us out, the make-believe accordion player, the men in the bar, the woman at the Blue Goose—and then our meeting with Marc Savoy, culminating in the festive scene at his Saturday morning jam session. I wanted to hold onto the feelings, the memories. But I was afraid they would slip away.

Even the boys seemed to feel it. Nate had his eye on the toy accordion we'd picked up for them—for just nineteen dollars at a gas station outside Lafayette.

"Can you play 'Allons à Lafayette' on the new accordion?" he asked.

No, I confessed, I couldn't. I'd never even attempted the song.

"Oh. Do you think Marc Savoy could make Cajun music on that accordion?"

"I think Marc Savoy could make Cajun music on just about anything."

Then Nate considered, and came up with a deal for me. "Do you want to trade? You can have the new accordion, if you give me your old one." It made complete sense, in his eight-year-old mind.

A few days later, I decided to write a letter to Marc Savoy. I closed the door to my office at the hospital, pulled out a pad of paper, and began to write. I thought of it as a message in a bottle, directed to myself as much as to him, since I had no way of knowing whether he would actually read it, much less respond.

I wrote slowly in my careful, labored handwriting, always on the verge of spinning off into illegibility:

Dear Marc,

It seems hard to believe that only two days have passed since that wonderful jam session on Saturday morning. It seems sadly far away as we get swallowed up by the demands of jobs, school, daily life. The several days we spent in and around Eunice (meeting you, in particular) had a kind of magic that's difficult to put into words, exactly, but it seems to go beyond the music alone. A sense of warmth, vitality—perhaps integrity? Whatever it was, it will stay with us for a long time. At least I hope it will. I suppose that there's always the fear that an experience, no matter how special, can become an isolated little island of memory that becomes harder to evoke with the passage of time. I wonder if boudin can work like Proust's Madeleine? Though I suppose now the music will serve to evoke much more than it did before for me—specific memories of those days, plus a fuller appreciation of the people, places, and history it springs from.

For all of this—thank you.

I hope that we'll be able to plan another trip sometime, and we will certainly arrange to be around longer. We all (even the boys) felt sad at leaving, as though we were leaving something behind. It's a little strange—how can you miss something that was never yours in the first place?

In the meantime, we'll look forward to seeing Dewey Balfa again later in the month here in Chicago, try to find a local source for boudin, and—of course—listen to endless tapes in the hope that something will sink in and, as you say, "leak out" onto the accordion through my fingers.

Two weeks later, I had a response. More succinct than my letter, but warm and direct—and very Cajun.

"Hey Bad Blair," Marc began. "Thanks for your very nice letter. Maybe you should give up music and become a writer. No don't do that—do both."

Five Les Femmes d'Enfer

Les Femmes d'Enfer. The women from hell. Not a sorority I ever expected to join, but I signed on gladly, after a meeting in a church
social hall—just after my first Cajun music workshop.
The name didn't really suit a group of beginners who played
with more hesitation than fire. And we certainly didn't qualify as a
bunch of hell raisers: four women in our forties, three of us therapists, with six kids and two husbands among us. But the creation of
our little group, and maybe even the name itself, added a new kind
of boldness to my musical life.

I had approached the music workshop with high hopes, figuring
some face-to-face instruction might get me through the impasse I'd
reached after four months of working on my own. I borrowed an
accordion for the occasion—from the woman who had organized
the workshop—since that fancy new Hohner Steve had ordered for
my birthday wouldn't arrive for a few weeks.

The prospect of finally getting my hands on a legitimate Cajun
accordion—and in C, the proper key—excited me. But as I sat in
the drafty church hall, on a chilly day in January, the borrowed accordion in my hands felt cold and alien—and completely wrong,
like picking up someone else's child by mistake, or dancing with
a stranger. It threw me off, as though I'd slipped on someone else's
shoes, and now I couldn't walk without stumbling.

I studied the people around me, cloaked in the shyness I usually
wore in a group of strangers. Twenty of us sat in a big circle—a
couple of children, but mostly adults in their thirties and forties,
more men than women. Fiddles, accordions, and guitars rested in
stacks on the floor, outnumbering the people. Then I spotted the fiddler and the triangle player from the Chicago Cajun Aces—and my
confidence continued to plummet. How had I ended up in a workshop with real musicians?

I knew just one person in the room—Joan, the workshop organizer. I had met her only recently, and through an unlikely connection: my Friday morning psychoanalytic study group. A few weeks earlier, in an office at the Institute for Psychoanalysis, my thoughts had begun to drift away from the theoretical paper we planned to discuss. I pictured myself at the Cajun Aces dance that evening, already dancing to the sound of Charlie's accordion. I couldn't help myself—in the midst of the casual pre-meeting conversation, I mentioned my new musical passion to the therapist sitting next to me. I expected a blank look or an amused smile.

"Oh—I'm a barn dancer!" she said, with that fast grin of recognition you might flash at a long-lost cousin or fellow member of some secret society.

"No kidding!" I smiled back at her—not letting on that I'd never heard of barn dancing.

My colleague had also done her share of Cajun dancing, she told me. But her friend Joan—a social worker by day and dancer by night—could tell me everything I needed to know about the local Cajun scene. She knew the Cajun Aces personally, had become a polished dancer, attended a Cajun music camp every summer. And—the big selling point—she'd taken up the accordion.

I called Joan just in time for a one-day Cajun music workshop she'd put together, to be taught by a visiting instructor from her music camp. She offered enthusiasm, a flood of information, and one cautionary note: she'd recently dropped the accordion in favor of guitar. Too difficult without a local teacher, she said.

Joan's accordion turned out to be an old-fashioned Hohner, similar to the one I'd first spotted in the catalog. It looked well traveled, with loose bellows and grooves worn into the fingerboard. Compared to my antique Eagle Brand, it felt big and sprawling, like an unruly toddler ready to scramble down off my lap. I missed the comforting familiarity of the homely little accordion I'd left back at the house.

My accordion reverie stopped when our teacher walked into the room. Tracy Schwarz, a rangy bearded man, reminded me of a professor I'd had in college. He'd driven into town late the previous night, and he looked a little weary, as he surveyed the scene. He laid out his plan for the afternoon: to introduce the newcomers among us to the basics of Cajun music, and then to teach the whole group a song.

I recognized the song he'd chosen—one of my Savoy-Doucet favorites, a two-step called "Jongle à Moi." Think of Me, in Cajun French. I felt relieved—at least something felt familiar. A musician named J. B. Fusilier, back in the 1940s, had first recorded "Jongle à Moi" as a fiddle tune. Savoy-Doucet added an accordion and made some changes to the lyrics. I'd learned to recognize it early on, and after a year of constant listening the song still stood out. I liked the contrast between the lively dance rhythm and the sadness of the simple words, the complaint of a jilted lover to his sweetheart: "Quand-même tu m'as quitté, jongle à moi catin, au moins une fois par jour. Oh yé yaille! Quo faire t'es comme ça?" *Even though you've left me, think of me, doll, at least once a day. Oh yé yaille! Why are you like that?*

The song provided a good introduction to Cajun French—an earthy language I had come to love. I relished all those colorful idioms, and the words that either meant something entirely different in standard French or simply didn't translate at all. Like the verb *jongler*—to think about, reflect, or worry. In standard French, it meant "to juggle." Or *catin*—literally, a toy doll in Cajun French, the same as *poupée*. It also served as a common—and perfectly proper—term of endearment for a sweetheart. But in France, *catin* would get you into big trouble, since it was a coarse label for a prostitute, just like *putain*. As for *yé yaille*, the expression seemed to defy translation. Sometimes it came out as an exuberant yell, a sort of French *yee-haw!* you might hear shouted out from a bandstand. Other times, as in this song, it conveyed a mixture of surprise, reproach, and resignation, like a Cajun-style *oy veh*.

Much as I liked the tune, I had never actually tried to play it. I wondered how Tracy planned to teach us—such a big group, ranging from beginners to performing musicians. I hoped maybe he'd give us button patterns, at least to start us out. But Tracy taught strictly by ear, following the oral tradition recommended in Larry Miller's book. We would watch, listen, and then try to play back what we heard. "By ear" hadn't been working for me so far, but perhaps I'd have better luck after seeing a song demonstrated.

Everyone listened, as Tracy played "Jongle à Moi" at full speed, with all the embellishments, first on the fiddle, and then on the accordion, with one of the more seasoned musicians backing him on guitar. Then Tracy played the guitar accompaniment himself— simple and straightforward, in terms of the chord pattern. But the rhythm was tricky, he explained—different in important but subtle ways from other kinds of American folk music.

Tracy also sang, in a lonesome tenor voice that sounded sharp and clear, with that faintly nasal quality of traditional Cajun singers. It was easy to forget that Tracy's roots were in southern mountain music, and not Louisiana. I was impressed by the handful of others who jumped right in and sang along with him.

After that, Tracy focused on one instrument at a time, starting with the fiddles. First, he played a slower, simpler version of the tune, all the way through. Then, he broke it down, phrase by phrase, so the fiddlers could follow along, call-and-response style.

I listened. Not bad. You could tell most of the fiddlers felt at ease with their instruments, even if Cajun music might be new to them. As a group, they blended easily, with the stronger, more assured players taking the lead, the more tentative playing behind them, a little bit underneath.

Time for the accordions. Tracy played a phrase: da-da-DUM, da-da-DUM, da-da-DUM, da-da-DUM. and a-ONE and-a-TWO, and-a-ONE and-a-TWO.

Then we tried to play the phrase back. Hmm. Not quite there. Perhaps he needed to simplify it even more for us. Slowly, single notes, one finger: Da-DUM da-DUM, da-DUM da-DUM. and ONE and TWO, and ONE and TWO.

Five pairs of ears listened, five sets of fingers tried once again to match the phrase. Tracy played again: DUM. DUM. DUM. DUM.

We gave it another shot. He had called, and we did our best to respond. Through repetition, maybe we'd arrive at a successive approximation of the true sound. The fiddlers had done it, after all.

But the accordions didn't seem to be getting much better. We did have plenty of volume. Unfortunately, our sound had no pattern, either rhythmically or melodically. Even if one of us had been catching on, the general cacophony would have masked it. In a group, new fiddlers can strive for subtlety, or opt for a quiet supporting role. But a beginning accordionist has only two options: loud and bad, or completely submerged in the collective sound.

As we played and repeated, I felt progressively less able to hear the pattern of notes Tracy played, much less match them on my accordion. Now and then, I did manage to find the right button, but by then the tune had already moved on, leaving me behind.

By now, we had repeated the tune multiple times. It was time to put it all together. The accordions took the first lead, with the fiddles seconding. The guitarists strummed along in a more-or-less steady rhythm, with one or two triangles offering a percussive accent. Next, the fiddlers played lead, while the accordions held back. Then back to the accordions. Round and round a few times, until our would-be Cajun orchestra had played itself out.

Tracy had listened thoughtfully to our final collective version of "Jongle à Moi." Now he appeared to be weighing alternatives, juggling the possibilities. He was far too tactful to say aloud what everyone must have recognized: we had just witnessed the slow, inevitable derailment of a twenty-car train. Finally, Tracy spoke.

"Maybe the accordions would like to go off by themselves and woodshed."

I had never heard the term, but I figured "woodshed" must be musicians' lingo for "practice." In this case, it also appeared to mean banishment. My own ears could tell me why. We were the weakest—and loudest—link in this musical chain.

The five of us slipped off to a small side room. The group included one other woman, who looked like one of the Cajun dance regulars. I recognized the triangle player from the Aces. But he seemed just like the rest of us—engaged in a wrestling match with our unwieldy little boxes. That was some comfort—at least we were all in the same boat. Maybe the accordion really was an impossible instrument.

Then I noticed a dark-haired man with a beard, sitting a little apart from the rest of us. He kept practicing the same sequence of notes, a look of concentration on his face. He was working on the hardest part of the tune—the chorus, also called the "bridge" or "B part"—a fast series of notes, with rapid in-and-out bellows action.

Da-da-DA-da, da-da-DA-da, da-da-Da-da, da-da-DUM,
Da-da-DA-da, da-da-DA da, da-da-DA-da, da-da-DUM

As he played, I could detect the beginnings of a tune—a tune
that bore an uncanny resemblance to "Jongle à Moi."

"How long have you been playing the accordion?" I hoped I
didn't sound as jealous as I felt. After four months, I still couldn't
play a complete song anyone would recognize.

"Oh, about six weeks," he replied, with a show of modesty. "But
I've been a musician for over thirty years."

Well, I couldn't match that. I had a checkered musical past—a
whole string of encounters that never really lasted. In grade school, I
started out like everyone else—with one of those little plastic fluto-
phones. I graduated to six tortured weeks with the violin, and then
two years of piano lessons with the motherly woman who lived next
door. In high school, I had a brief and unsuccessful flirtation with
my younger sister's guitar. During our years in North Carolina, Steve
bought me a guitar and then a mountain dulcimer.

But I never stayed with an instrument long enough to master it.
Not enough interest, competing claims on my time, the suspicion I
didn't have a knack for music—probably they all played a part. But
now, finally, I had discovered a deep desire to make music, and I was
determined to learn to play the strange little black box. But I feared
too much time had passed, and now I might be too old to learn.

I went back to practicing until Tracy invited the accordions to
return from exile. Once again, the whole group played together,
for one final attempt at "Jongle à Moi." Unfortunately, my grasp of
the tune hadn't improved much, even after a whole afternoon of
trying.

But I came out of that workshop with something better than a
new tune: les Femmes d'Enfer, my all-female Cajun music posse.
Joan pulled us together before the afternoon ended. She already
knew Joy, the dancer I had recognized. Then there was Jessie—a social worker like Joan, who had recently picked up the Cajun fiddle.
Joan figured she'd play guitar, leaving the accordion to Joy and me.

So that made four of us—a good number, we thought, for a
jam group. The name we picked—the women from hell—was a

play on words, an allusion to a hard-driving Cajun tune called "Les Flammes d'Enfer"—the flames of hell. Someone—Tracy?—had suggested it to us. Perhaps he was being tongue-in-cheek.

"Les Femmes" began to meet every few weeks, rotating from house to house, instruments in hand, gamely trying to play Cajun music. Our musical development proceeded slowly. "But we do have great camaraderie," someone would always point out, as we soldiered on.

We did spend a fair amount of time talking during our music sessions. Joan and Joy, both single and in demand as dance partners, kept us laughing with pithy observations about some of the male dance regulars—this guy danced too close, that one crushed your hand in his, and watch out for that fellow who preyed on the newcomers. Jessie and I had our own struggles with our husbands—both of them cautious, cerebral guys who'd resisted as we pulled them onto the dance floor.

We had moments of sounding like breathless teenagers, all set to rush out to hear our favorite touring bands. BeauSoleil topped the list. But we had serious conversations, too, about balancing the demands of work and family with music. Sometimes we tried to identify what it was, exactly, that drew us together in this unusual pursuit. We all felt it, the clear pull of Cajun music—but we found it hard to explain, even to ourselves. It seemed deep and completely improbable, all at the same time.

We had been meeting for a year when Joan and Jessie began urging me to join them at Cajun music camp that summer. They referred to it as "Augusta," but they made it sound like a pilgrimage to Mecca. Joan had been attending for years. Jessie had gone for the first time the previous summer, but had already turned into a devotee. They couldn't wait to initiate me.

"It's incredible—the music starts in the morning, and it doesn't stop till you go to bed at night." "And of course you don't actually go to sleep till—oh, like two in the morning." "Hey, some of those people play all night." "Well, yes, but they're fanatics." "And you'll love the guy who teaches beginning accordion. Steve Riley. He's not much more than twenty—and he's the cutest, nicest guy. And an amazing accordion player!"

I had a hard time picturing a summer camp for adults, and

I didn't understand why they went to a college in West Virginia to study music from Louisiana. I also wondered about this cute young accordion teacher. He was not exactly a venerable old master, speaking French, and steeped in tradition. I'd probably feel like his mother.

But the prospect of going alone presented the biggest barrier. Even if the idea of Cajun music camp had appealed to Steve, he couldn't have done it, because of his work schedule that year. Out of the question, I figured.

When I mentioned this music camp business to Steve, I felt certain he'd dismiss it as quickly as I had, when les Femmes first proposed it to me.

"Well, maybe you should think about going along with them. The boys and I could manage on our own for a week."

They could? Steve's response surprised me. I hadn't expected his openness to my doing the unthinkable: going off on my own, away from the family. Steve and I rarely traveled separately, even for work. Now and then, we went away for a weekend by ourselves—easy enough, with my parents nearby and always angling for more time with their grandsons. But we simply didn't do separate vacations.

And it would be for an entire week. A few months earlier, I had attended a three-day professional conference in Washington, D.C.— and that struck me as a big deal. I'd felt lonely and strangely vulnerable on my own, even though I'd gone there with one of my work friends. Of course, I hadn't been at my best then. I hadn't been at my best for months. Perhaps that's why Steve had encouraged me to go to music camp with my new friends. An adventure might raise my spirits.

My spirits did need lifting. Partly, I was facing new pressures at work, since I'd recently accepted—with mixed feelings—a promotion into an even higher-level administrative role that brought a whole new set of demands, along with less direct patient contact. But the change at work followed a personal loss that was far more profound: my father's unexpected death six months earlier. The loss had been shattering for everyone in my family, and I still didn't feel like myself.

My parents—a healthy couple in their late sixties—had been enjoying an active post-retirement life. No one knew what to think when my father started to complain of brief, puzzling episodes of weakness and elevated temperature.

Finally, my father had an episode that lasted long enough for him to be admitted to the hospital, one Sunday night in September. My mother sounded relieved that the doctors were taking his complaints seriously. We visited him in the hospital on Monday evening, bearing gifts, trying to be cheerful. My father even tried to draw Alec and Nate into talk of tennis. The doctors had been running some tests, but still couldn't figure out what was wrong. My parents both tried to be reassuring.

As we were leaving that night, I turned and saw something in my father's face that chilled me. This is how people look when they are about to die, I thought. Then I pushed the thought away.

I got the call from my mother just before dawn. My father had experienced a sudden crisis and was now in intensive care. Call the family, they told her. By the time we got back to the hospital, an hour later, my father had fallen into a coma. Hemolytic anemia, one doctor called it, possibly caused by an autoimmune reaction.

They could name it, but they couldn't reverse it, and they never did determine what caused it. I spent the next three days at the hospital, as my father's body slowly shut down. He died on Thursday. I didn't know what time it was, but when I looked out the window I saw a black sky pierced by slashes of lightning.

A thunderstorm raged that night, but it felt like an earthquake. My family's world had suddenly cracked apart, leaving gaping crevices a person could easily fall through. Time stopped. We moved in slow motion, only half aware, knowing the earth was still shifting in ways we couldn't see.

There is such a sense of aloneness after sudden loss. You struggle with the twin burdens of grief, along with the weight of a new and terrible knowledge the rest of the world doesn't seem to share: nothing is secure, and life can change in an instant.

But you can't go on this way indefinitely. It is not so much that time heals. It just changes the experience. Shock and grief slowly yield to a lingering, pervasive sadness. Life, in its insistent way, calls you back.

I never did stop listening to my music, since it brought me solace from the beginning. Not that it was an escape. If anything, Cajun music seemed to echo the very things I was feeling: sadness, lone-liness, a desire to cry out in frustration and anger. But it was like the paradox of listening to someone sing the blues when you feel sad. You begin to feel lighter because the pain inside you has been drawn out, and now other voices, stronger voices, are helping you speak it.

I listened to my Cajun tapes quietly, through earphones, won-dering what other people might think, if they could hear. My father wouldn't have minded—I was sure of that, because he was never one for following the rules or for shows of piety. "I'd like a jazz fu-neral, the way they do it in New Orleans," I remembered him say-ing once, years earlier.

But my desire to play the accordion had disappeared. I'd been ac-customed to playing every day, and now—nothing. This went on for some weeks, and it might have gone on longer, if my son Alec hadn't stepped in.

I was sitting in the kitchen, doing nothing, when he came over to me.

"Mom, you need to play some music."

"I don't really feel like it."

He went to my accordion case, took out the shiny black Hohner, and set it in my lap.

"Play."

Alec, a blunt-spoken ten-year-old, had made it clear he didn't share my passion for Cajun music. And I wasn't much good on the accordion, after just a year of playing. But Alec needed some sign that I was returning to myself and that we would all get through this.

What choice did I have? The accordion was sitting there in my lap, and my young son was looking at me, waiting.

I played one song, then a second. Even though my heart was somewhere else, I began to feel a little better, just knowing the music hadn't died inside me.

So ten months after my father's death, I found myself preparing to head off for a week of Cajun music camp with Joan and Jessie. I felt excited and apprehensive in equal measure. Steve was suppor-tive, as always. Nate, sweetly shy and not quite eight, kept his own counsel. Alec was skeptical:

"Oh, right. Thelma, Louise—and Blair."

My son had no illusions about the part I would be playing in a cross-country road trip with a couple of other women. They would play the free spirits, the female buddies.

I would be the understudy.

Six   Awakening at Augusta

Of all the enchantments at Augusta, the best was this: drifting off to sleep late at night, with the sound of Cajun music ringing out into the mountain air. And then waking up the next morning, after just a few hours of sleep, to the same sweet wild sound. It felt as though the music had awakened me, and not dawn's first light. But the dance of accordion, fiddle, and guitar had gone on all night, out there on the porch. I was the one who had drifted away, until the music called me back.

Each morning, I slowly came to consciousness, as the distant sounds penetrated the cloak of sleep. The music in my ears told me where I was—before my skin had registered the sensation of the narrow single bed, before my eyes had opened to the spartan dormitory room that had come to feel like a haven. Once again, the music had brought me back to myself.

If I had grown up in a different tradition, I might have had a ritual for greeting the new day. Perhaps I would have said a morning prayer, thanking God for restoring my soul to me. But even without a prayer, I was spirit-filled on those West Virginia mornings—alive to the unknown possibilities of the day before me, but steadied by a link to something timeless and enduring.

The first time I tried to explain this, words didn't come at all. Only tears. I sat on the edge of our familiar double bed, back home on the South Side of Chicago, trying to describe to Steve what it had been like, that first week at music camp.

"Next summer, you have to go back there with me," was all I could manage to choke out. "Of course," he said, as he held me.

I had prepared for my first trip to music camp like an eager schoolgirl, as I checked over the instructions from the Augusta people. I didn't want to forget anything, and I wasn't used to traveling alone.

My friends and I had adopted an unofficial dress code for the trip. When Joan and Jessie pulled up late that Saturday morning in July, I discovered we'd dressed alike, in long flowing cotton skirts and oversized t-shirts. My suitcase contained a whole collection of those shirts, adorned with the names of Louisiana bands and landmarks—BeauSoleil, Café du Monde, Mulate's. The three of us looked like refugees from the sixties, or perhaps a group of Mennonites on holiday. The car overflowed with instruments, suitcases, and a fan in case it got hot. But somehow we found space for my things. I kissed Steve and my sons good-bye, and we took off.

Setting out, we all felt giddy with excitement. Joan and Jessie were determined to broaden my horizons—starting at our first stop, a gas station.

"Okay, Blair—we think you should pump the gas." They knew I didn't drive. They took a picture of me poised at the gas pump, beaming, nozzle in hand.

As we headed out of the city, we cranked up the music on the van's stereo. We'd each brought a selection of tapes—more than enough to provide a constant backdrop for the twelve-hour drive. Nearly all of it was Louisiana music.

Our tastes were similar. We all loved BeauSoleil, although I had come to prefer the more traditional sound of the Savoy-Doucet Cajun Band. One of us had a copy of the first recording by Steve Riley and the Mamou Playboys. I'd brought a tape by Nathan Abshire, a raw-sounding Cajun accordionist who'd died a few years back. Jessie had some all-fiddle recordings. Joan contributed some zydeco—the more syncopated, blues-influenced dance music developed by the Creoles, the French-speaking people of color in southwest Louisiana.

Gradually, the flat plains of Illinois and Indiana gave way to the more rolling terrain of Ohio, where I'd spent the first fifteen years of my life. I started out in Cleveland, then on to grade school in Lakewood, a leafy suburb adjacent to the city. We moved again when I started junior high, to a more distant suburb, with a bigger house and more land—the closest my family ever got to "out in the country." Strange, the way I had forgotten how different Ohio looked, not even approaching the flatness of Chicago.

We stopped for the night at a motel well south of Cleveland, in one of those bleak, middle-of-nowhere spots just off the highway.

I felt far from home until I made my nightly call to Chicago, and I heard the sweet, familiar voices of Steve and my sons. At bedtime, my friends and I drew straws, and I got a bed to myself—a rare and guilty pleasure.

On Sunday morning, we had a leisurely breakfast. No need to rush, with less than a half day of driving ahead of us, and check-in not until midafternoon. We were heading to Elkins, West Virginia, in the Appalachian foothills. The small town was home to Davis and Elkins College, sponsor of the Augusta Heritage Arts Center.

As we drove, we watched the southern Ohio landscape turn even more hilly. Before long, we saw the sign: "Welcome to West Virginia." By now, the hills were more than rolling. The highway cut sharply through them, exposing jagged layers of rock on either side. Neat little houses nestled in hollows, along with an occasional shack, surrounded by rusted-out appliances and old cars on cinder blocks. Flowers dotted the green hillsides. We were getting closer to our destination.

We pulled over for lunch at a little roadside café, less than two hours from Elkins. As we sat drinking sweet iced tea and eating white bread sandwiches, we talked of one thing and another, drifting naturally into talk of our families, our pasts, peeling back the layers, in the way people do when they travel together.

I don't recall who first spoke of it. But I remember how our stories spilled out, one by one. And then the bittersweet shock of discovering a hidden bond we all shared: the sudden death of a brother or sister when we were young.

When I was eight, my two-year-old sister got sick and died. I went to school one morning, knowing my parents planned to take her to the hospital, and expecting that my aunt would come to stay with the rest of the children. I thought my sister must have a cold. When I returned that afternoon, I was surprised to find my mother at home. Then she told me: my baby sister had died that day.

My parents, trying to do what they thought best, had shielded me, along with my younger sister and brother, from the reality of the baby's multiple handicaps. I was too young to realize something was wrong, or to suspect—as my father gently explained to me—she would never have walked and talked like other children. I didn't learn the full story until I was in my twenties. But the sharp truth

I faced on that day broke my heart, and it shattered the protected world of my childhood.

My two friends had been older when each lost a sibling—young adults, who died suddenly. Although the circumstances differed, in some fundamental way our stories were the same. Our families retreated from a loss that seemed too overwhelming to face openly. Feelings fled underground, truths hid in the shadows, and nothing was ever the same afterward.

I had talked of this to so few people in my life—and I had never before spoken to anyone else who had faced the early death of a brother or sister. A part of me had always believed it didn't happen to other families I knew. But now the three of us had talked of that terrible thing, the loss almost beyond contemplation. After a time, we weren't talking anymore—just standing outside the café, on the hilltop in the sunlight, embracing and shedding the tears we had learned to keep hidden.

But we were also laughing, because it wasn't just sadness we felt. In that moment, we also felt relief—and a new understanding. We had found an answer to the questions we had been asking ourselves, in our reflections on this musical journey we had come to share. The mixture of joy and sadness in Cajun music, the pull of the past, the hunger for community—it began to make more sense now. We could feel it in the moment we were sharing on the hillside, in the words and rhythms of this music that reverberated so strongly for us. And it was waiting for us, up ahead, as we drove on down the road to Augusta.

We got back into the van for the last leg of the journey. We didn't put on my Balfa Brothers tape until that final stretch, less than an hour out of Elkins.

"I'm glad you brought that one," Joan said.

We all knew why. We were thinking of Dewey, the last surviving member of the Balfa Brothers, who had died of cancer just three weeks earlier.

As we drove, the sweet harmonies of les Frères Balfa filled the car. I listened to the high penetrating voices, and to Dewey and Will's passionate twin fiddles, accompanied by Rodney's rolling guitar. They usually played with an accordionist, but the three brothers were the heart of the sound—until Will and Rodney died in that car accident. The following year, Dewey lost his wife. But he had carried on with his music.

The Balfa Brothers had joined my music collection early, when I found a copy of one of their most well known collections, "The Balfa Brothers Play Traditional Cajun Music." I never got tired of listening to it. Even their driving tunes were full of feeling, like the protest of a mistreated lover. Their waltzes felt dreamy, suffused with sadness and longing, songs like "Drunkard's Sorrow Waltz," or the family tune they recorded as "Valse de Balfa." I'd first fallen in love with that one on the Savoy-Doucet recording.

More than anyone else, Dewey Balfa had been responsible for introducing Cajun music to the world beyond Louisiana. He grew up in a musical family, the son of sharecroppers, and he made his own living selling insurance, operating a furniture store, and driving a school bus. And he played his music, mostly with his brothers.

In 1964, Dewey Balfa had been part of the first Cajun band to play at the prestigious Newport Folk Festival, as a last-minute replacement for the guitarist. The group drew a standing ovation—to the surprise of at least one local paper back in Louisiana, which had predicted ridicule for the little band playing that old-fashioned French music in front of all those Américains up north.

After Newport, Dewey returned home with a renewed commitment to his culture and a deeper understanding of what his heritage meant. A few years later, he returned to Newport, this time with his fiddle and his brothers. After that, Dewey took his music everywhere—into local schools, to national folk festivals, all over the world. He had received numerous honors over the years, including the very first Heritage Fellowship awarded by the National Endowment for the Arts.

Dewey had established Cajun Week at Augusta seven years earlier. He started with a fiddle class of eight students. From there, the offerings expanded each year, with the addition of accordion and guitar and dance, new instructors, and classes at different levels. The single fiddle class had evolved into a comprehensive weeklong immersion that included sessions devoted to the culture itself—history, cooking, the French language. This summer, over a hundred students would come to West Virginia to explore the music and culture of southwest Louisiana. But this would be the first year without Dewey.

As I listened to his music while we traveled the last miles along those country roads, I felt a sense of loss for never having known Dewey. I had heard him perform twice in the last year when he came to Chicago, to play his fiddle and to visit with his friends in the Cajun Aces. I comforted myself with the thought I had been that close to him, at least.

But I could hear Dewey now, as we drove into Elkins, the sounds of his voice and fiddle ringing in the air. It was Sunday afternoon, and the small college campus buzzed with activity. It felt like being dropped into the middle of freshman orientation week, a family reunion, and a religious revival all at once.

We were met by greetings, shouts, and hugs, as we crossed the parking lot and headed over to the registration area. What building was this? I tried to study the campus map, but it wasn't much help. Even at the best of times, I had a terrible sense of direction. It was a good thing I had someone to tag along with. After registration we were off to the dormitory, where Jessie and I would be roommates.

We'd been assigned to the "overflow" dorm, a down-at-the heels men's residence, next in line for renovation. Our room looked like a monk's cell for two: matching twin beds, two thin lumpy mattresses, two desks, two dressers, two closets without doors. No screens on the windows. We unpacked. Two closets filled up with long cotton skirts, two dressers crammed with neat piles of t-shirts.

From there we went off to dinner, assuming I could find the cafeteria. Davis and Elkins was just a small college, maybe a dozen buildings in all, arranged in a big rolling oval. But I would keep on getting lost there, turned around in the wrong direction, year after year.

I joined my friends in crowding around one of the cafeteria tables. There was a flurry of introductions, followed by the inevitable forgetting of the new names I'd just tried to learn. I had memories of being the new girl who arrived in the middle of ninth grade, when we moved to Chicago—hoping to fit in, wondering how I'd find my place, trying to keep track of everything. Here, at least, everyone wore name tags.

I tried to scan the tags without being obvious, picking up useful information at a glance. You could spot the veterans because they had learned to rewrite their first names in big block letters. An echo of my own college days: the people "in the know" seemed to come from the East Coast. They also tended to be in the intermediate or advanced classes. My name tag clearly proclaimed my status: "Chicago, Illinois. Beginning Cajun Accordion."

I managed to pick up on one story: the couple who had just gotten married, after a long-distance courtship that began at camp. (Who were they again? Did their last names match or not?) More strange names floated around—Escoheag, Ashohkan, other places on the music camp circuit that I soon learned.

I studied the schedule in my thick information packet. In less than an hour, I had a general orientation meeting in the college auditorium—along with the rest of the two hundred-plus students and the dozens of staff members participating in this week's sessions. Not everyone was here for Cajun Week, though we made up a sizable contingent, close to half the total. Blues Week was the other big "theme week" for this session, though there were many other individual classes, not all of them involving music: mountain dulcimer, banjo, African American storytelling, basketry, gospel piano. There were so many choices—and this was just the first week out of six held during the summer. Our name tags hinted at the astonishing breadth of Augusta, a place that had evolved far beyond the Appalachian folk arts in its twenty-year history.

A full evening lay ahead. After the general orientation meeting, there was a smaller meeting just for Cajun Week students, and then the evening dance—old-time music, followed by Cajun. After that, jamming until who knows when. I figured this brief after-dinner lull might be a good time for my daily call home, so I found the nearest pay phone and got in line.

The man ahead of me turned and introduced himself, his soft voice as inviting as warmed honey. He listened intently, deep brown eyes steady, as I told him my name and added that I was studying Cajun accordion. I didn't quite catch what he was here for—perhaps some mention of making new friends during the week. Now it was his turn for the phone, but he motioned me toward the booth. "Why don't you go ahead," he drawled. "I'm not in a hurry."

When I reached Steve, I learned that he and the boys had just returned from an outdoor festival at Navy Pier, where they discovered a Louisiana band playing. This pleased me immensely. More than just a coincidence, it struck me as a good omen.

"You'll never guess," I bubbled, as I turned the phone over to the patient man who was still waiting his turn. "I just spoke to my husband back in Chicago, and it turns out he and the kids were just at a festival listening to Terrance Simien's zydeco band!"

"Oh." A pause. "Well, that's nice." Funny, he sounded less charmed by the news than I was. But I felt too excited by my first night at Augusta to think much more about it. "Thanks again for letting me go ahead," I called to him over my shoulder, as I hurried off.

That heady feeling of excitement permeated the entire week, although it was contained by the reassuring routine of the days. After breakfast, each day began—at least for us beginners—with a big class devoted to the foundation of the music: rhythm. Tracy Schwarz, a familiar figure, led the class. His task: to teach everyone, no matter what instrument they played, that distinctive loping rhythm that set Cajun music apart from other styles of traditional music.

Tracy played recordings, and then demonstrated simple rhythm accompaniments on accordion, fiddle, guitar, and triangle. He suggested a few verbal devices: *clunk-a-ring-a clunk-a-ring-a. Dile crock-a-dile crock-a-diiiile.* He had us recite them, all together.

Finally, he offered up this image:

"Cajun music is like an egg-shaped wheel."

The picture made me smile, but it crystallized Tracy's message in a way that nothing else had. I could picture an egg rolling along, end over end. It fit so well with the feeling I had when I listened to the music or when I danced—surging ahead, then falling back, with a momentary hesitation. Rising and falling, peaks and valleys, rocking on the water.

After the Cajun rhythms class, we moved on to small classes devoted to our instruments of choice, where we would spend the rest of the morning and much of the afternoon. I double-checked the map, then hurried over to my beginning accordion class. Our instructor was Steve Riley, a young Cajun musician who apparently had some Irish ancestry on his father's side.

Twelve of us sat in a circle. I had never seen so many Cajun accordions in one spot. A few other Hohners, but a fair number of hand-built Louisiana accordions—definitely the preferred choice. I wondered how we'd manage, with so many accordions blasting away. It had been difficult enough in Tracy's Chicago workshop, with just five of us.

Steve's approach turned out to be much like Tracy's: the by-ear, call-and-response style of learning. Once again, I experienced frustration, made worse by the nagging sense that everyone but me was catching on. I'd listen and play, repeating phrase by phrase, trying to keep up with the rest of the class. Then I'd find myself lost in the middle of a phrase, my brain too overloaded to even recall the name of the new tune we were learning.

Fortunately, there was more to the class than just endless drill. Steve also showed us helpful techniques, standard ways of ornamenting the simple, bare-bones melody that provided the foundation of a tune. Some of what he explained—like playing two notes together, to make a chord or octave—I already knew, from Larry Miller's instruction book, and from Tracy's workshop. But Steve went beyond this, showing us ways to add embellishments, the extra ornamentation that took a tune to the next level.

I eventually caught on to one important technique: playing "the note before the note," by bringing the third finger down a split second before the first and fourth fingers that made the octave. A grace note, some might call it. It would be quite awhile, though, before I could incorporate this technique comfortably into my own playing.

So much of what Steve tried to teach the class was beyond me. Some of this would have to wait until the next class, the next year at Augusta, and other instructors. It might be years down the road before I would have that "ah-hah" feeling that comes with dawning comprehension. Fortunately, I wasn't so preoccupied with my own playing that I forgot Mark Savoy's advice: first, soak up as much music as you can. The class provided a real opportunity to absorb Steve's music—and his stories.

At twenty-two, Steve was already a rising star in traditional music circles, with one recording to his credit. But the Grammy nominations were still a few years down the road, and sometimes he came across as an affable, good-looking Cajun kid from a small town who couldn't quite believe what was happening to him. He would dazzle the class with his playing and then disarm us with comments like: "Without the music, I'd still be in Mamou, and I wouldn't be sitting here with y'all." Or he'd offer up an unassuming analysis of the pleasure of playing in a band: "Having your toys, and being part of a group of friends, that's what it's about, no matter how old you are."

Dewey Balfa had taken Steve on tour as a teenage accordion prodigy and had introduced him to the larger musical world. Steve talked about Dewey with reverence. Everyone did, that whole week long, with his loss so fresh. Memories of Dewey were everywhere. During lunch, you could even watch uncut video footage from the tribute concert held two months earlier, at the Liberty Theater in Eunice. People had flown in from all over the country to honor Dewey, who had listened from his hospital bed in a nearby town, just weeks away from death.

Each day at lunch, I joined the crowd gathered around the small screen. We sat on the floor, on chairs, wherever we found space, as we watched the videotape of the concert. One after the other, groups of musicians got up, played, and shared their memories of Dewey, English and French intermingled. The camera lingered over Dewey's four grown daughters in the front row, bravely holding hands, trying not to cry.

On screen, couples danced past the camera—and around me, I could recognize some of the same people, watching intently, sometimes smiling as they caught sight of themselves, but more often looking somber, close to tears.

I listened to the music, observed the musicians—on the screen, and then seated in our midst. Many of them were crying openly as they watched and listened and remembered. The young ones especially, who'd been mentored by Dewey, and who felt like his children—my teacher Steve, Tracy's son Peter, Dirk Powell—and Dewey's daughter Christine, his youngest child, who would eventually marry Dirk. They all seemed linked by a web of grief shared by all of us—and at the same time theirs alone.

The feelings of grief and loss seemed to be everywhere I turned, on each face, echoing as strongly as the music. We all felt it, even those of us who had never known Dewey Balfa. For me, it was tied up with the feelings about my own father, who had died exactly ten months earlier. I felt it especially when I looked at Christine, a lovely blonde woman in her early twenties, who had accompanied her father on triangle from the time she was small. She was on staff this week, scheduled to assist with the guitar and Cajun singing classes.

I watched Christine during the week, as she shared her private sorrow with the people around her. She was so young to be facing this, to open herself to the fresh grief of others, at the cost of being plunged farther back into her own. When I finally approached her, later in the week, I spoke to her briefly, just to tell her how sorry I was, and to tell her I had experienced some of what she must be facing. "But you've lost someone too. I'm so sorry," she said, hugging me. She never failed to respond with poise and graciousness to all those people around her, even the ones like me, who were strangers to her.

After lunch, we all gathered for our big class meeting of the day, where we drank strong Community Coffee and learned about the culture of the Cajuns and the Creoles. You couldn't really talk about one group without the other, and in a few years, this close connection would be made even clearer with the adoption of a new name: Cajun-Creole Week. We listened to lectures about cooking, Mardi Gras customs, Louisiana history, the French language. We watched dance demonstrations. And the musicians played. Some let their music speak for itself, while others were more than willing to tell stories, to talk about how they had learned and who had influenced them.

We heard so many tales: kids who had to sneak the accordion out of the box when the grown-ups were working in the fields, risking punishment to play, unable to turn away from the forbidden fruit. Young boys who made fiddles out of cigar boxes, with wires unraveled from the screen door. Old men smiling at the remembered long-ago thrill of a ten-dollar guitar ordered from the Sears catalog.

The older generation recalled getting punished for speaking French in school. In some families, that sense of shame led them to play the old-fashioned music some folks dismissed as "chanky-chank" in secret. Sometimes the children were actively discouraged from playing at all.

In others families, though, they were proud, even defiant, and the kids looked forward to finding a place in the family band. The youngest started out on rubboard or triangle, before moving on to guitar or drums, eventually maybe fiddle or accordion. Sometimes, of course, the younger Cajuns and Creoles resisted the pull. I heard more than one musician confess to starting out in a rock, blues, or country western band, before finding his way back to his own traditions.

There were some wonderful moments when two or three generations of a family played together, showing how the same tune had evolved over time. We could see and hear the legacy of these families, Cajun and Creole, who held on to their traditions and passed them along. The two cultures were both distinctive and intertwined—Balfas and Ardoins, Carrières and LeJeunes, Broussards and Millers and Fontenots. They told us their stories and they played their music.

Now and then, an older musician shook his head a little, listening to the way a young one played the old family tune with a modern edge. He might mutter about rock 'n' roll or say pointedly, "Me, I don't play that zydeco." But you could always hear the pride in his voice and see the smile in the eyes.

Later in the afternoon, we'd move on to more music classes, and then we had an hour of free time before dinner—time to practice alone, find a jam group, or just relax. Accordion students could visit Larry Miller, who had set up shop in one of the classrooms, prepared to sell instruments, do simple repairs, or tell tales. Some afternoons I even found time for a short nap back in my room, before I showered and changed for dinner. It always helped to get a second wind before the evening's activities—and maybe trick my body into believing a whole new day was starting.

The early evening schedule varied: concerts in the big auditorium on three nights, a gumbo party on the porch at midweek. But a dance always followed, with music provided by an ever-changing line-up of the staff musicians. The dances took place in a beautiful setting: an open-air pavilion, set out among the trees and under the stars, with the mountains overlooking us. I had never heard Louisiana French music played so powerfully before and by such a collection of incredible musicians. They were our instructors by day, our inspiration at night.

But it was hard to be at a dance without Steve. I had been part of a couple since I was twenty, and in my teens I had logged more hours reading books than going out on dates. Left on my own, I started to feel like a wallflower, not sure what was worse: to be ignored, or to face the discomfort of having to dance with a whole series of men I didn't know. And some of them were serious dancers, who came to Augusta to perfect their skills and wanted to show off their new moves at night. I felt intimidated and lapsed into my old pattern of apologizing before I took a single step.

Eventually, I ended up apologizing one time too many—to someone who had already heard my disclaimer and had actually come back for a second round. It was the man I'd met the first evening, by the phone. He turned out to be from Louisiana, and one of the music instructors to boot.

"I had to take dance lessons myself, back home," he reassured me. "I was doing it all wrong—moving my feet the same way I do when I play the fiddle on stage." He demonstrated for me, a simple move that did look more like a jig than a two-step. "So stop apologizing. Your dancing is fine."

I did stop apologizing, and I began to relax into the music. I became more comfortable with him and with some of the other men I was getting to know. Sometimes I even managed to lose myself in the rhythms of the music and let my body respond naturally, without counting steps or worrying about which foot belonged where.

But I felt most at ease when I danced with other women—especially Joan, along with a free-spirited woman I'd met in my accordion class. They both tried to teach me to dance zydeco style—standing close instead of apart, doing a slow-quick-quick instead of the Cajun quick-quick-slow. Standing erect and shifting your weight instead of traveling in circles around the room. I had moments where I began to get it—but then it would slip away.

The dance at the pavilion usually went on until midnight, sometimes even later. Afterward, some people went to bed, but most stayed up, a few until dawn. All over campus, big and little clusters of people made music of all kinds—blues, old time, bluegrass, Irish.

Most of the Cajun-Creole jams took place on the big porch at Halliehurst Hall, the stately old mansion at the heart of the campus. I wandered from group to group—listening, dancing, visiting. Everywhere I turned, I heard music and laughter, as instructors and students played together. Their music floated up and out, rising into the warm night air. Fiddles, accordions, and guitars danced together, locked in an embrace that could last till dawn.

How I wished I could be one of those people playing! I had tried sitting on the outskirts of one of the big jams, accordion on my knees, figuring the crowd was so large I wouldn't bother anyone. But it was too difficult to keep up. And if I played loudly enough to hear myself, then other people would have to hear me too, with all my false starts and hesitations. It was enough to listen, to absorb that pulsating music coming at me from all directions.

At some point in the evening, I would finally become overwhelmed with sound and fatigue. Usually it was late—perhaps two or three in the morning—when the feeling came over me. I remember one late night in particular, when I found myself transported into an altered state that made it hard to know where I ended and the music began.

I sank down to the floor, leaned my head against the wall, and let the music wash over me. I watched the people around me on the porch, musicians and dancers and listeners, through a kind of shimmering haze. Everything was part of the same undulating wave—the music, the people, me, the trees, the mountains, all rising and falling together, vibrating in some kind of universal rhythm.

Earlier in the week, I'd heard people talk about rhythm lock, but I wasn't sure what it was supposed to feel like. Now I knew.

"This must be it," I thought. "Rhythm lock. I hope it never stops."

Seven   After Augusta

"Let's swear," Joan said. She extended her pinkies, one to each side.

The arrival of the okra had inspired her.

I ignored trucker stares from the nearby tables and linked one little finger with Joan, the other with Jessie. Over a heaping plate of fried okra, we hammered out a pledge to keep the Augusta spirit, the music—and our connection—going strong.

"We promise to practice every day on our own."

"Well—that might be tough. Six days a week?"

"I'm up for that. Six days a week."

"And we check in by phone once a week?"

"Great! And we keep on having our jams—how often?"

"Let's say at least once a month."

"Done! Here's to les Femmes!"

"Les Femmes d'Enfer!"

It was Saturday night, with Chicago on the horizon, when the three of us decided to stop for one final meal together. We didn't really feel hungry, but we had a shared, unspoken wish to hold onto our music camp experience for a little longer.

That week in West Virginia had been an intense time, the air saturated with too much sound and feeling to fully absorb. But I had come away with a sense of freedom and possibility. I wondered how to hold onto it, once I stepped back into the routine of my life.

I had felt so carefree at Augusta, even though the week involved hard work and some degree of frustration. It was like going back to college, before adult responsibilities started to creep into my life. At music camp, I could navigate the entire day armed with nothing but my name tag and my accordion, along with a room key and meal ticket suspended from a lanyard around my neck. I needed some kind of transitional space—a place to pause, to ease the reentry. We all did. We began scanning the horizon, searching for a place to pull over. Then the Petro Truck Stop came into view.

The Petro would have been hard to miss. First, in the distance, we saw a tall sign proclaiming the name of the place, like those personalized water towers that let you know you are nearing a country town. Then, as we approached the looping cloverleaf of the two freeways, the sprawling complex unfolded.

We pulled off the highway, parked the van in the lot, and made our way past the herds of semi trailers and banks of gas pumps. When we walked through the door, I blinked at the suddenness of stepping into another landscape. I felt like Alice, but my wonderland was a smoke-filled, vaguely southern oasis in Indiana, an hour from Chicago, just off the Interstate.

The Petro had that timeless, airless, too-bright quality shared by places that never close, whether they are casinos, emergency rooms, or twenty-four-hour restaurants. The three of us drifted in, feeling disoriented and a little punchy, not quite sure where to go first. This establishment catered to truckers, no doubt about that. Breakfast buffet at all hours, "country style" food served in individual cast iron skillets, telephones at the tables. A giant stuffed bear behind a glass case reared up on its hind legs, guarding the entrance to the restrooms and showers. Smoke and stares filled the air.

We wandered into the big all-purpose store adjoining the restaurant and began to roam the aisles. They revealed a jumble of treasures: packaged snacks, country music tapes, six packs, lottery tickets, turquoise jewelry, cigarettes, Levi's, assorted hardware, cowboy boots, Harley Davidson gear, Stetson hats. I half-expected to find a guitar propped against the wall, or a beat-up old fiddle on some dusty shelf. Finally, we pulled ourselves out of the maze and headed back to the restaurant.

Pairs of eyes followed us as we made our way, single file, to a table at the very back, in the vain hope of escaping the smoke. We scanned the menu, not sure what we wanted to eat. The truth is, we were more in need of sleep than food. Then we saw it, the perfect choice: deep-fried okra.

Okra. Who would have expected that, at a truck stop in Indiana, so close to home? Not exactly gumbo, but at least it could pass for southern cuisine. We chose to take the okra as a good omen, a sign that we could find a bridge between the musical experience we'd just shared at Augusta and our day-to-day lives.

When the okra arrived, Joan had her moment of inspiration, and we took the musical pledge. When we finally left, the sun was setting, a riot of pink and purple and white that backlit the Petro sign. We asked a passing stranger to take our picture. We threw our arms over each other's shoulders and smiled resolutely into the camera, looking tired but satisfied, our Cajun sisterhood sealed over a plate of okra.

Augusta became a touchstone, a point of reference, for everything else.

The most immediate consequence was a widening of our jam circle—starting with Steve. He'd already been an occasional guest, sitting in on mandolin when the rotation brought "les Femmes" to our house. But now he became a regular member.

Steve's early musical history resembled mine, although he claimed to have had even less natural ability. He recalled failing a music aptitude test when he wanted to switch from sax to drums in grade school, and he insisted a junior high choir teacher really did say, "Steve—just move your lips!"

But Steve finally learned to make music in his early twenties, after he received an old mandolin from the grateful parent of a student he'd tutored. He put it to use the following year, when we moved to North Carolina and ended up living next door to a bunch of Duke students who played in a ragged band. The Foggy-Headed Boys combined traditional bluegrass with Grateful Dead tunes, and they happily welcomed yet another mandolin player to the ranks. Once inside their rowdy circle, Steve learned to play music in a casual, seat-of-the-pants way—while I watched from the sidelines, too consumed with graduate school to recognize how much I would have liked to join in.

Steve had enjoyed the band—and the good times—but once we moved back to Chicago, he drifted away from music as easily as he'd drifted into it. His music making became an occasional solo affair, whenever he pulled out the mandolin for the amusement of his elementary school students or our own kids.

But I always wondered how Steve could let the music slip away. A few years before our trip to New Orleans, I'd even forced the issue: I gave him a gift certificate to Chicago's Old Town School of Folk Music for his birthday, hoping he'd take mandolin lessons. But Steve found something more to his liking, a bluegrass ensemble class that evolved into a jam group. Strangely, with all my pushing I never wondered whether I might be the frustrated musician in the family.

After Augusta, Steve became a full-fledged member of our Cajun jam group. At first, he played either mandolin or guitar, another instrument he'd picked up during his bluegrass days. But then I decided we should buy him a fiddle, figuring it would be a relatively easy jump from the mandolin, since the two instruments shared some basic similarities, with four strings tuned to E-A-D-G.

Steve quickly realized his mandolin skills wouldn't transfer as much as we'd hoped. For one thing, Cajun fiddlers often tuned a step down, completely changing the fingering—and bowing instead of picking presented a whole new challenge. But Steve felt ready to give the fiddle a try. Cajun music appealed to him, even though he didn't share my obsession with it, and his bluegrass experience gave him a confidence I lacked.

Next came Denise and Earl, who had studied fiddle and guitar during Cajun Week at Augusta. They seemed eager to help organize a larger jam group, and they soon pulled in her brother, a professional pianist, who had just bought a Cajun accordion. Joy invited her boyfriend, a guitarist.

"Les Femmes" had changed—and not just because we now had almost as many men as women in the ranks. Our cozy little jam group had more than doubled in size, and most of our new members already had some proficiency in other styles of music. Denise and her brother, both classically trained, had grown up in a family of professional musicians. Earl, a Spanish professor, had been playing guitar since his Peace Corps days, and he'd already learned to sing a handful of songs in Cajun French. Set lists began to appear.

The expansion of our group raised the musical bar and improved the quality of our sound. But it also fed my bad habit of comparing myself to others. My private passion had turned into a more public arena—where I believed I fell short. Still, I managed to enjoy our evolving friendships. Our little group hung out together at the Cajun Aces dances, and we began to go out to other local music events and festivals. Eventually, we would travel to Louisiana together.

Six months later, there was a further development. Some of us attended a weekend Cajun festival in Wisconsin, where members of the Aces were teaching. I took an accordion workshop from Charlie and found him to be a patient, helpful instructor. He, in turn, was sufficiently impressed by our group's enthusiasm that he invited us to start holding some of our sessions at his house.

I was excited to have Charlie as a resource. He and his wife, Lynne, had been immersed in Louisiana music and culture for over twenty years, ever since Dewey Balfa took Charlie under his wing. I couldn't wait to get started, particularly since he'd also offered to give me some individual help with the accordion. I didn't know what to make of one comment he made—that before long we'd be sitting in with his band.

We started holding most of the jams at Charlie and Lynne's house. He played along with us and offered a few suggestions. Mostly, though, he seemed to keep his thoughts to himself. When things went better than usual, he'd offer a wry smile and say, "That almost sounded like music."

Sometimes he struggled with how to work with us as a group. Our differences—in experience level, but also in what motivated us to play—seemed to become more apparent as time went on. Some of the group already had performing experience, and they were eager to start a band of their own. For a couple of others, the intent was more social—to have a relaxed time making music together.

I fell somewhere in the middle. I did feel driven to master the accordion, and I worked hard at it. But I couldn't picture myself playing in a more public way. I had a hard enough time at the jams, particularly now that we had an accomplished Cajun musician at the helm. And despite the time I put into practicing, I was developing more slowly than I had hoped.

I tested the tolerance of old friends by carrying on about my accordion struggles. "Better not invite you two to dinner on Friday night," they'd tease, "it might conflict with a Cajun dance." We tried dragging a few other couples along with us, but no one seemed as taken with the music as we were.

I found myself in a state of growing turmoil—more, it seemed, than the others in the jam group. I made uneasy jokes about belonging in the musical equivalent of the slow readers' group. I'd get a sick feeling in my stomach, along with a vague heavy ache in my arms, when Steve and I drove up Charlie's driveway. During my occasional one-on-one sessions, I hung on every word and every note. But later the new tune would disappear, because my anxiety got in the way of learning. Sometimes I had fantasies of casting my accordion into the fireplace. I knew I had become too consumed with the music—and too frustrated—for my own good.

I had started seeing a therapist after my father died—a sweet, down-to-earth woman in her late forties who didn't fit my stereotype of a training analyst. She allowed me to feel the sadness of losing my father without falling into serious depression, and she helped me cope with the growing stress in my professional life. But she also took my musical struggles seriously.

My therapist listened with interest to a BeauSoleil tape I made her, and she even told me about the ongoing debates she and her analyst husband had about the relative merits of different jazz vocalists—she was an Ella Fitzgerald fan, while he favored Sarah Vaughan. Through her responsiveness to me, and by her own example, she helped me bring together the parts of my self that sometimes felt at odds, and she nurtured the creative impulse that found expression in Cajun music.

I also found some comfort in a less likely place: an alternative bookstore specializing in self-help literature. Professionally, my tastes ran more to the theoretical writings of Mahler, Kohut, and Winnicott. But I had come to respect the self-help world through my work with clients affected by addiction, and I was currently running a chemical dependence treatment program. So I tried to stay up-to-date with the recovery literature.

In the midst of all those books for alcoholics, drug addicts, sex addicts, adult children of alcoholics, gamblers, codependents, and overeaters I came across a book called Making Music for the Joy of It—a guide for adult musicians. It was filled with practical advice, vignettes, testimonials, inspirational quotes—all designed to empower adults who wanted to make a place for music in their lives, whether they were returning to music or just starting out.

The author, Stephanie Judy, wrote squarely about the emotional risks that come from opening yourself to music—especially for adults who are just beginning to play. It is difficult, but essential, she argued, to let go of the need to appear competent and in control. That hit home for me.

I made copies of some of the better quotes, and I pasted them inside the lid of my accordion case: "Music is a path, and not a destination." "Music is everyone's birthright." "Your own music is the child of your heart, and you are entitled to love it, not because it is good, but because it is a part of you."

I was a little embarrassed by my attempts at self-help. I couldn't imagine what my fellow musicians—or my professional colleagues— would think. What would be next—crystals in my accordion case? But I needed all the help I could get, and the book reminded me that others shared my struggles.

It turned out that Charlie had been serious about inviting members of our jam group to sit in with his band. First came Joan, who had been starting to sing. She had been working on "The Ninety-nine Year Waltz." It would become her signature song.

I remember the first time she sang. Joan had been prepared, so when she got the nod from Charlie she was ready. She climbed up on stage, smiled sweetly, and clasped her hands behind her back. After the accordion break, she began: "Oh, moi je m'en vas, condamné pour quatre-vingt-dix-neuf ans." *Oh, I'm going away, condemned for ninety-nine years.*

It was one of those heart-stopping waltzes Joan and I both loved—more dramatic because she wasn't playing her guitar. It was just Joan standing up there on the stage—looking slender and girlish, her hair a curly halo, hands clasped behind her, the light shining on her. Her voice filled the room, quavering only a little. She looked so self-possessed, although I know she was nervous.

The rest of us had stopped dancing when we saw Joan preparing to sing. We hurried up to the stage and stood as close as we could, so we wouldn't be in the way of the circling dancers. Afterward, we gathered around, hugging her. It felt like a breakthrough, as though she had done it for all of us.

Then came Denise and Earl, singing together, the first time in honor of their anniversary. Their voices blended so nicely, as they stood there, Earl's arm over his wife's shoulder. It was an affectionate gesture, of course—but they may also have been propping each other up, since they had been just as nervous as Joan. The next time, Charlie invited them to bring their instruments.

It soon became routine to have at least one guest musician sitting in at the Cajun dance. Whenever it happened, there would be the same scenario—friends and supporters gathered close to the stage, and then afterward hugs and congratulations.

There was another side to all this, the part I could barely admit to myself, much less talk about openly. I felt proud and happy for my friends—but I also suffered the twinge of envy. How did they manage to set aside their fears and put themselves on the line, when I was still captive to my fears?

Finally, Charlie began to suggest that it was about time for me to come up and play a song or two on the accordion. I struggled with competing desires: I desperately wanted to be invited to play, to be included with the rest. But I didn't feel ready, and I couldn't fathom actually getting up on that stage.

I could picture it all so clearly: I would freeze up, or maybe hit the wrong button. Then there would be silence, followed by terrible humiliation and—even worse—the sick recognition that I had managed to derail the rest of the band. The song would crash to a halt. All eyes would be on me, slinking off the stage in disgrace.

I found myself going to dances and then carefully avoiding eye contact with the musicians, whenever Steve and I circled near the stage. I figured if I didn't look at them as I danced by, then perhaps I could sidestep the problem altogether.

Charlie's brother John, an easy-going guy who played guitar and sang with the band, started to add some friendly pressure. He joked that one of these days a couple of them would simply take me by each arm and drag me up on stage. But I remained unmoved—until I heard him tell a story one night, after dinner at a weekend Cajun music festival.

John explained that the Aces had been playing at their monthly dance. During the break, he got off the bandstand and headed over to the bar, where a friendly Cajun dance regular hailed him.

"You must be new around here," the dancer said. "Can I buy you a drink?"

John laughed as he told the story, seeming to enjoy a joke at his own expense. So much for being a "star" in the local Cajun scene.

I laughed along, but then felt something shift inside me. If John, who played regularly with the band, had gone unrecognized, then any brief time I spent on stage would hardly register. The truth, both deflating and liberating, stared me in the face. How well—or poorly—I played the accordion was of consuming importance to no one but me.

"The next time I'm asked to play, I'll do it." I made a quick promise to myself, and I shared my new resolve with John later that weekend. So I wasn't surprised when Charlie gave me the nod at the next monthly dance. The time had arrived, and I had promised. Besides, it was spring, a good time for new beginnings.

Even though my heart was racing, I mounted the stage when they called me up. I couldn't very well change my mind. Someone produced a chair. Charlie handed me his accordion, then picked up the fiddle. John, on guitar, gave me an encouraging smile.

When I took the accordion, it felt loose and unfamiliar in my hands. I felt more at ease with my Hohner, even though I knew Charlie's accordion, hand built by Marc Savoy, was a far better instrument. Years of playing, hours of music, had been worn into the buttons and bellows. But it all felt too big for my hands.

I tried to get comfortable with the unwieldy contraption, but the bellows of the accordion seemed to be fighting me, springing all over. The tension in the springs was different, too, and the buttons felt strange to the touch. I got distracted by the clank of the buckles on the unfamiliar shoulder strap, hanging loosely to the side. The big bulbous microphone attached to the front of the accordion didn't help matters.

I needed another pair of hands to manage all this. Preferably hands that weren't slippery with sweat, sliding off the buttons. And I had only a few moments to get oriented, one song to play. One chance to get it right. At least my ordeal would be over soon.

I had already picked the song: "The Reno Waltz," a tune I first heard through the Savoy-Doucet recordings. I loved hearing it live at the Aces' dances, and I had been working on it with Charlie, trying to get it right.

"Waltz time." My introduction—also a hint from Charlie to get started.

I depressed the first button, then pushed the bellows. The sound of the accordion steadied and startled me, all it once. That throaty call was familiar by now—but why did it sound so loud? And it seemed to be coming from somewhere else, filling the entire room. Of course—the sound was coming from two places at once: the accordion in my hands, and then from the speakers, off to the sides of the stage. Well, I had announced myself. No place to hide now.

I heard the sad waltz come out of the accordion, note by note. A few pick-up notes to lead in, and then the verse. I could hear the other instruments jumping in, following me. The song flowed along—simple, but steady and methodical. This was one of the easier waltzes, with no bridge after the verse. Whew. I got through the first accordion break without any big mistakes, except for dropping one note. Maybe no one had noticed. At least I had maintained the rhythm.

Now I could sit back and listen to Charlie sing. "Ouais la place, que moi, je voudrais mourir, c'est dans les bras de mon 'tit bébé," he began. *Yes, the place I'd like to die, it's in my little baby's arms.*

But I couldn't let myself get lost in the music, because I had to remember to listen closely for the fiddle break, and come in again at the right point, just as it was ending. Now—my turn again. John's guitar throbbed, steady and uncompromising as a drum, anchoring the rhythm. The sharp ring of the triangle, lighter but insistent, also helped keep me on track. I suddenly remembered the dancers and looked out into the gym. People were happily waltzing around the room—to my music!

I played one more time through on the accordion, then I listened to Charlie sing the second verse: "Quand j'vas mourir, j'aimerais tu viens, fermer mes veux, 'tit bébé, pour moi j'm'en vas." *When I'm getting ready to die, I'd like you to come close my eyes, little baby, so I can leave.*

Then came the fiddle break, and my final ride on the accordion. It was easier this time around, after the two earlier tries. The strange accordion had begun to feel almost familiar—not that I wanted to prolong this song. We were nearing the end, and I remembered to stick out my foot, to signal the rest of the band. Incredible—it worked. We all managed to stop at the same time.

"That was Blair Kilpatrick on accordion." I heard John's voice, along with applause—from the dance floor. In less time than it took him to make the announcement, I had set down Charlie's accordion, stood up, marched down the steps at the side of the stage, and hurried over to Steve's side. I had exited in record time.

Steve hugged me. My friends gathered round, offering congratulations. I had survived. I could hear the first notes of the next song beginning to sound, but I didn't feel like dancing just yet. I felt like flying.

Eight   Return to Acadiana

"Do we really have to go to Lafayette—again? It was so boring last time."

Alec's voice mixed the whine of a toddler with the disdain of a worldly thirteen-year-old. Not that he minded another family trip to New Orleans, his fifth in four years. But the thought of a second excursion into southwest Louisiana left him cold.

"We'll have plenty of time in New Orleans at the end of the week," I reminded him. "And Lafayette will be better this time. You'll see."

At least I hoped so. For my city-bred sons, the small towns and countryside couldn't compete with the funky excitement of New Orleans. Even for me, the charms of Acadiana could be subtle, harder to penetrate.

But we did the trip right this time around. We'd picked a good time to go—in June, well past Lent, but before the summer heat became unbearable. We hoped to find more going on—more music in the clubs, maybe even some festivals. And we'd arranged to meet up with four of our friends from the jam group. I felt more confident as part of a group, especially with Joan, the veteran of countless visits to Louisiana. I hoped we'd be able to encounter the music and culture at a deeper level this time, without feeling so much like tourists. Beyond that, I had one important item on my agenda: I wanted to buy a hand-built Cajun accordion.

I found my dazzling new accordion at Larry Miller's place in Iota, a small prairie settlement not far from Eunice. He'd made it out of a piece of driftwood he discovered at Holly Beach, the tattered Gulf Coast resort that Louisiana people, with their self-mocking humor, called the Cajun Riviera.

"The wood in that accordion floated all the way across the Gulf of Mexico," Larry told me. He was completely caught up in the romance of woods—their weight, colors, grains, and origins. You could tell when he showed Steve and me around the workshop behind his house that morning, talking nonstop, moving in double time, as he told us about the dozens of instruments arranged on the shelves. Some he'd collected, including a few rare antiques, but most were his own creation. He'd stained some of his accordions black, to resemble the old Monarchs and Sterlings, and a couple in brighter hues—red, even green, probably meant for some flashy young zydeco musician. But most of Larry's hand built accordions glowed with the soft warmth of natural wood.

Although Larry knew the history behind my accordion, he hadn't been able to identify the species of wood he'd used. I could read the whole story, handwritten by his wife, Jackie, on the big tag attached to the accordion. Larry picked up the piece of driftwood while beachcombing in 1992, struck by the "unusual natural light red color with unique small grain patterns." After two years of air-drying, the wood was ready to be crafted into an accordion.

Larry had just finished the accordion, and he had taken it on a family trip to Holly Beach the previous weekend in order to break it in. He already had his newest instrument in mind for me, mostly because of the light weight. The other woods Larry used tended to be heavier than the mysterious driftwood: maple and walnut, and then some of those exotic South American and African woods, like rosewood and zebra.

Under his watchful eye, I picked up several different accordions in the key of C, trying to judge their feel, their weight. I agreed with him: the driftwood accordion felt the most comfortable in my hands. But I also loved the story behind it—and the way it looked.

That accordion looked almost too beautiful to play. To complement the driftwood, Larry had finished the accordion using two other woods with natural reddish hues. He'd covered the end pieces at the sides with a veneer of padauk, a slightly deeper colored wood with a fine, narrow white grain that reminded me of falling rain drops. On the fingerboard, he added decorative strips of purple heart, a wood with a deep burnished maroon color. The red accents were picked up on the rest of the instrument: red tips on the ten golden flappers, a red-and-black zigzag pattern in the two thin strips of decorative wood inlay running down the front, and black-edged bellows that turned out to be red when extended. The white buttons—ten on the treble side, two on the bass side—felt smooth and cool to my touch, and they had the milky shimmer of pearls from the sea.

Larry and Jackie's country ranch house teemed with life: family and friends coming and going, Larry's customers, constant phone calls, and then the regular stream of visitors from all over the country and the world, especially at festival time, like Mardi Gras and Festivals Acadiens. That week, Joan was staying with them. She'd become a good friend, and I figured it was on her account the Millers decided to host a gumbo party and jam session for our Chicago contingent later that afternoon.

It was a memorable gathering. Alec and Nate, thirteen and ten, became absorbed with surprising ease into a clutch of Miller grandkids—playing with the cats, chattering in French, then going for an exciting ride in somebody's daddy's pickup truck. Meanwhile, the grown-ups ate Jackie's good gumbo, drank beer, listened to Larry's endless stories, and made music. We all got to play: Steve and me, our four friends, along with Larry and a married couple, JB and Pilar, who played in his band.

I tried to balance that now-familiar mix of feelings: the excitement of stepping up to a better accordion, the disconcerting newness of an unfamiliar instrument in my hands, and my ever-present worry about how I'd sound in front of everyone else, whenever Larry gave me the sign that it was my turn to take a lead. My new driftwood accordion was an inch or so taller and several pounds heavier than the factory-made Hohner I'd been playing for the past three years. And it had a fuller, deeper voice, thanks to the premium Binci reeds Larry imported from Italy. Still, it took some getting used to. But there was no doubt about it: I loved my new accordion. I was happy to just gaze at it, never mind trying to play it.

"All right, kid, maybe this accordion will change your personality!" That was Larry's cheerful prediction, as I left his house at the end of a long evening, with my new treasure cradled in my arms.

I didn't question his remark. After all, I knew better than anyone that my musical personality could use some adjusting. I did squirm a little at his ability to peg me so quickly, though. Perhaps he'd noticed me holding back at his jam, in comparison to my bolder friends.

I'd certainly held back two days earlier, when we'd all headed over to Marc Savoy's music store for his Saturday morning jam session. I didn't play my accordion at all. Not even when Marc yelled out an exuberant but pointed invitation: "All right! The lady from Chicago has to play!" I only halfway heard him—and maybe he meant someone else. Meanwhile, Dennis had already taken his place in the accordion queue, while Steve and Denise had found their spots among the fiddlers, and Earl and Joan were happily strumming away on guitar.

I'd felt safer sticking with the triangle—an instrument that is much harder to master than people think. I'd had to take a workshop at music camp, then spend time practicing, to get it right. An old Cajun man in overalls had watched me at Marc's jam, with a curious but critical eye that gave way to acceptance, as I managed to keep the rhythm without throwing anyone off. During a break in the music he asked where I was from, then said in wonder, "Ya'll have French music in Ella-noise?"

I played the accordion freely just once on the trip, the day after Larry's jam session, when Joan took us to visit Canray Fontenot. The level of comfort I felt with him came as a surprise, because he was such a prominent musician, considered the greatest living Creole fiddler.

Canray and his musical partner, the accordionist Alphonse "Bois Sec" Ardoin, had both become near-iconic figures in the world of traditional Louisiana French music. They were the masters of a unique sound: that older style of French music that had developed in the Creole community, alongside Cajun music. Over the years, various labels had been attached to it: La-La, pic-nic, early zydeco— and old-time Creole, the term in widest use.

Although I owned several recordings by Bois Sec and Canray, I'd never heard them play live. It was easy to find zydeco—touring bands appeared regularly in Chicago's blues clubs—but the only old-time Creole musician I'd heard in person had been Delton Broussard, at Augusta. I'd felt drawn to him and had even passed up a class with Steve Riley in order to attend Delton's. I knew his class was intended for advanced students, but I got permission to sit in as a sort of auditor, grateful to be absorbing the music and stories of a gentle, frail older man who seemed more at ease in French than English.

When I heard he died six months later, I knew I'd made the right choice.

The sound of old-time Creole music captivated me. Although it overlapped significantly with Cajun music, the Creole style was more bluesy and syncopated. The accordion, although often simpler melodically, sounded more rhythmic and punchy. The fiddle seemed to moan and cry, as it slid from one note into the other. That older Creole music also had a kind of percussive edginess, especially when rubboard replaced the triangle.

But the old-time Creole style remained a simple folk music. Just like the traditional Cajun sound of the Savoy-Doucet trio, it represented a link to the old days, when everyone—Cajun and Creole alike—played what they called "French music" at picnics and barbecues, at house dances and fais-do-do's, at church socials and tiny dance halls way out in the countryside.

The older Creole style had a stronger appeal for me than the more sophisticated zydeco sound that emerged from it, and in many ways replaced it. The attraction of zydeco did make sense, though—especially for younger people and for audiences outside Louisiana. A modern zydeco band could lay down a powerful, compelling sound: heavy drums and bass, energetic rubboard, flashy electric guitar solos, punchy lyrics, and a definite influence from other popular styles of music. Zydeco had been heavily marked by blues and R&B, along with traces of rap and hip-hop, especially among the youngest musicians.

Although accordion remained the dominant instrument, zydeco players often favored double- or triple-row models, or even piano accordions, which allowed for more musical flexibility than the traditional single-row diatonic. But along with this evolution came the fading away of other components of the music: the fiddle, the French language, and—at least for me—some of the emotional pull.

I'd listened to Bois Sec and Canray's recordings, studied their pictures, and pored over their histories. I desperately wanted to hear them in person, but feared I'd never get the chance. They didn't tour much, and even though they'd come to Augusta in the past, their advancing years and poor health had kept them away in recent years.

When I read they were due back at music camp this year, I'd allowed myself to feel hopeful. "It will be great to pick up some licks from them," one of our jam friends agreed. But this startled me, because I hadn't been thinking about it in such a pragmatic way. I just wanted to be in the presence of these two venerable musicians.

So it felt like an unexpected gift when we discovered a small music festival at Vermilionville, one of Lafayette's living history museums, and we learned Bois Sec and Canray were scheduled to perform. When they finally appeared on stage, looking like all the pictures I'd ever seen of them, something caught in my throat.

Despite their years—Canray was seventy-one, Bois Sec seventy-eight—they radiated a kind of passion and energy that transformed them into younger men. Bois Sec looked erect and dignified, like the respected family patriarch he was, but lightened with a dapper air. Canray seemed mischievous, *canaille* as they'd say in French, with the boyish smile and rascal eyes that jumped out at you in all the photos.

When they started to play—just the two of them, fiddle and accordion together, wailing away, feet stomping, filled up by their own joyous rhythms, the near-audible grin in Canray's voice—I felt tears rolling down my cheeks. I felt unaccountably moved—and embarrassed, sitting among the tourists, alongside my family and friends. I hoped no one would notice me, ambushed by unexpected emotions.

Joan had become friendly with Canray and his wife, Miss Artile, and she invited us to accompany her on a visit. We got lost on the way, but eventually found their house, on a dusty road in a small town not far from Eunice. We'd had to ask directions from a young Creole boy on a bike, who gave Joan a blank look when she spoke Canray's name, unaware that a renowned musician was living in the neighborhood.

When he came to the door, Canray looked tired and drawn, with a grayish cast to his burnished skin. But his expression changed when he recognized Joan, and he welcomed us all inside. He'd been expecting us. The small house was dark and cool, and as my eyes adjusted I found myself in a neat living room, the walls lined with family photos, some of them very old, interspersed with Canray's music awards and pictures of saints.

After the preliminaries—warm greetings, introductions—Canray got down to business. He pulled out his fiddle, and it was as though someone flipped a switch. That smile started to blossom, just as it had in Vermilionville. Almost wider than his narrow face, probably made thinner by the cancer he had been battling. It didn't seem to matter that he didn't have Bois Sec at his side, or a big audience. "Why don't y'all get out your instruments?" he said. It was a command as much as an invitation.

"I'll make us some coffee," Miss Artile announced.

Steve pulled out his fiddle and Joan started to tune up her guitar. I hesitated, then decided I'd best follow Miss Artile out to the kitchen. The idea of her waiting on all of us just hit me wrong. Age, race, the invisible sideline role so many musicians' wives assumed—they all factored in to my discomfort. I figured I should offer to help her, or at least make conversation.

Miss Artile was a gracious and dignified woman, a little younger than Canray, with smooth skin and gray hair pulled back in a bun. She had the look of a sweet but no-nonsense Sunday school teacher— but I could imagine her as a comely young woman, who caught the eye of a dashing fiddle player with the look of the devil in his eyes. When I admired the photos lining the walls, she seemed happy to tell me a little about their family, especially the daughter who was a lawyer in Houston. But she shooed me back into the living room when I offered to help with the coffee. "No, baby, you go sit by Canray and play," she insisted.

So I did. I sat down right beside him and pulled out my new driftwood accordion. They had already started to play—Canray's bow flying, fiddle crying, his keening voice, the flashing teeth, a smile that never dimmed. Steve played second fiddle, simple chords and a little embellishment, underneath and around the edges of Canray's dominant sound, while Joan provided a rhythmic accompaniment on her guitar. Accordion seemed beside the point. But when Canray nodded at me, I played a lead, for once not even hesitating. His radiance had melted away my reserve, just as it illuminated every corner of that neat little house, darkened to keep the Louisiana heat at bay.

Our music filled the air, rose to heaven. What an honor, I thought, to be playing with this man. Canray had performed everywhere, and he'd been one of Michael Doucet's mentors. But he acted delighted to be playing with the likes of us—beginners, outsiders, *Américains* from up North. Perhaps he didn't really hear us, lost as he was in the joy of his own music.

In between tunes, Canray told tales of his life as a musician—some good times, but also stories of a hard life working in the fields, and later on in a feed store. He spoke of those in the music world who had treated him fairly, others who had been underhanded, the famous Cajun musician who said nasty things about Jewish visitors, the people he suspected of racism. That beatific smile didn't mean Canray had his eyes closed or that he minced words.

Meanwhile, our audience—Alec and Nate—sat solemnly on the couch, hardly stirring. Respectful in a way I hadn't seen before, when they were around the music. I'd told them in advance this was a special experience, one they shouldn't forget, so I wanted to believe they'd been awed by Canray. But they might have been equally impressed by Miss Artile, as she offered them her strong Louisiana coffee, just like the grown-ups, as though it was the most natural thing in the world. And so they shared it with us, a dark brew served in style: against the contrasting whiteness of delicate china cups, laid out on a tray, along with cream and sugar to soften and lighten the bitter taste.

The next day, the four of us drove to New Orleans. We had four days to wander the colorful streets of the French Quarter, eat our fill of muffalettas and beignets and po-boys, visit old haunts and maybe have some new family adventures, before returning home.

After three previous visits, the boys had come to know and love New Orleans, especially after the revelry of the last time, when we'd met up with my brother and his girlfriend for Mardi Gras. We'd all watched the torch-lit nighttime parades, trying to overlook the drunken college kids and bare-breasted women on balconies, while the boys joined in the mad scramble for beads, plastic cups, and other "throws" that dropped out of the sky like gaudy rain.

But now, walking the familiar streets, something felt different.

"Mom," Alec said in a small voice, "Do you miss Larry and Jackie and everyone?"

"I do. How about you?"

"Umm hmm. You know, Larry is—well, he's kinda cool."

"Yes, he is pretty cool."

"Mom, I think maybe I'd like to get a pickup truck someday."

"Well, I guess we'll have to see about that."

Nate, with less need to maintain a veneer of adolescent detachment, was even more direct.

"I wish I were Cajun," he said. "Back there, it's like everyone knows you. Everyone's your friend. It's more—social."

Nate even asked me to dance, when we went out one night to the New Orleans branch of Mulate's. "Remember, Mom—you're the one who follows," he reminded me. As we waltzed to the music of a band called the Swamp Cats, he continued to think about his future as a dancer. "I think I need some shoes that slide better. And where are we going to dance, back in Chicago?"

He also put out the idea that he might want to learn accordion. But who would teach him, in Chicago? The next day he relented, pronouncing accordion "too weird," but allowed as how he might want to try the fiddle.

I was surprised and touched that the boys had expressed what I was also feeling. Walking the streets of New Orleans did feel a little empty. I felt like a tourist—because I was. My head was still filled with the memories of everything we'd seen and heard during those six days in southwest Louisiana.

It was almost too much to absorb—or remember. I'd never forget the time with the Millers, or Bois Sec and Canray, but I was afraid other details might slip away. So I wrote out a short diary of each day's events, then I made a list of the accordionists I'd heard.

Just looking over the names on that list left me shaking me head. Bois Sec and Aldus Roger at Vermilionville—plus the elderly man with the Hackberry Ramblers who didn't even start till he was in his eighties. The amazing Marc Savoy, who finally picked up the accordion at his jam. Blackie Forrestier, along with an eight-year-old boy, at the Liberty Theater. Nonc Allie, when we went out to DI's with Larry and Jackie, to celebrate their anniversary.

The boys were right. Something was missing in New Orleans. But something was also missing in Chicago, at least in my musical life, although it was harder to put a name to it. I felt unsettled when we got back home, and I was filled with longing for the vibrant music—and the people—we'd left back in Louisiana. Among them, I felt able to access some part of myself that seemed to recede at home. The part of me that took risks, that operated out of feeling more than intellect. I feared losing it again.

Nine   Finding My Voice

"It's like Purgatory," wrote a friend of mine from music camp. I knew exactly what she meant, even without reading the rest of her letter. I felt it too, that suffering that came with the music. Burning with desire. Doing penance, as I submitted to the regular discipline of practice. Eyes fixed on the elusive goal of mastery. Like my friend, I agonized, wondering whether I'd ever make it across the gulf that separated the music of my imagination from the confining limits of my own experience.

It was a painful kind of limbo—and I knew it had to do with something beyond frustration over my accordion skills. More was at stake: finding my place, gaining access to half-hidden parts of myself, satisfying the hunger for connection—to a larger community, a deeper experience of the music, to something outside myself.

My recent trip to Louisiana had intensified this yearning, along with a sense of not measuring up. I fell into my unfortunate habit of comparing myself to other people. Not to the Cajuns and Creoles, because they were in a class by themselves, but to everyone else. Outsiders. *Américains.* People like me.

Three of our Chicago friends had recently taken the final bold step: they had formed a band. They had even talked to Steve about joining. They needed a triangle player, but figured he was versatile enough to play a little mandolin and second fiddle, too. Steve declined; for one thing, he didn't actually know how to play the triangle. But I felt excluded, like the last kid picked for a team in gym class.

I felt buffeted by strong and conflicting emotions, as insistent as the waves that must have battered that piece of driftwood Larry Miller found on Holly Beach, and then fashioned into an accordion. All washed up, or waiting to be found, depending on how you looked at it. Ready to be shaped into something new, to become a unique instrument with a strong voice.

Maybe that's why I started to sing. It was just after Augusta when it happened, surprising everyone, especially me—because I had spent most of my life convinced I couldn't sing.

I'm not sure when I lost my voice. I used to chime in freely with the other kids, at least during my early childhood years. But toward the end of grade school, I developed an unshakeable belief that I couldn't sing right. That's what my mother always said about herself, that she couldn't "carry a tune." She insisted she'd lost her voice in college, when she had her tonsils out, and had to quit the glee club. So my father took the lead in any family singing we did, while my mom sang along faintly, in a kind of scratchy pantomime.

My grade school music teacher didn't help matters. Miss Sibley was an intimidating figure: tiny, white-haired, desiccated, impossibly elderly, and with an odd way of looking frail and fierce at the same time. She reminded me of a character out of Dickens, dressed in an old-fashioned dark shirtwaist dress with neat white collar and tightly belted skirt almost to the ankles. She presented a picture of precision and containment—except when she flushed bright crimson with anger, her small body flooding with more feeling than she could handle. She would spin around and glare at the class, shaking, trying to figure out who had strayed off key or who had dared to snicker behind her back.

I kept my head down and studied my songbook, in the vain hope of simultaneously following Miss Sibley's waving arms and the notes wandering up and down the staff. I loved books and was used to pleasing my teachers, but this singing business didn't come so easily to me. And the songs she taught us were heavy and joyless— nothing like the gentle folk tunes about *un canadien errant* we learned in French class, or those ribald camp songs we belted out at Girl Scout meetings.

I worried—a lot—about what might happen if my voice strayed into some territory considered out-of-bounds by Miss Sibley. So I found the perfect solution: lip synching, or something close to it. I learned to sing under my breath, hoping my classmates would provide a convenient cover.

Before long, hiding out vocally became second nature. Whenever I encountered group singing—even something as innocuous as a "Happy Birthday" serenade—I took care to keep my voice submerged beneath the sounds of the others, murmuring so quietly I couldn't even hear myself. Since I never heard the sound of my own voice, I had no reason to question my growing belief that singing was off-limits.

Eventually, singing became so anxiety-laden that it drifted outside the boundaries of anything I recognized as a part of my self, whether good or bad. It wasn't just something I didn't do well, like my cock-eyed aim when I threw a baseball or my messy handwriting. The thought of singing took me into the realm of the not-me, an alien territory filled with unnamed dangers and an uncanny feeling of dread.

So I never considered trying to sing any of those Cajun song lyrics I found so compelling. Not that I was alone in shying away from singing. Most of the aspiring musicians I knew—in our jam group, at Augusta—did the same. Even performing bands often struggled with the French vocals—relying on set lists that were heavy on instrumentals, then turning to "cheat sheets" when it came time to sing.

But I did feel a pang when I watched otherwise confident singers trying to tackle Cajun French songs: stumbling over transliterations, trying to recreate the sounds of an unfamiliar language, or forgetting lines they'd tried to memorize. I knew their biggest hurdle was the one thing that might have come to me without too much struggle. I'd studied French all through school, and already the language had started to come back to me. And I wasn't worried about committing words to memory, because I'd done some acting when I was younger, and learning my lines never presented a problem.

If only I could sing.

But late in the summer, not long after Steve and I returned from music camp, I began to recover my voice. The singing seemed to arrive on its own, without any choice or decision on my part—and just like that, a silence of thirty years ended. At the time, I couldn't explain it, how all those layers of inhibition began to melt away. But the French language had been working on me for the past four years, ever since my first trip to New Orleans. And I think that may have opened the door to singing.

French had always represented a liberating force in my life. I considered it a high-minded intellectual discipline, to study that formal language often dismissed as "Parisian French" by the more down-to-earth Cajuns. But French class also provided a path into the realm of the imagination and the senses. The language became a gateway to a world of light and shadow, to unknown realms that took me outside myself.

At eleven, I played Joan of Arc. I faced down the Inquisitors, then marched off to the stake with a brave "*Le bûcher? Allons-y.*" I learned most of what I know about art history from the high school French teacher who introduced us to *les impressionistes*. I liked the limpid paintings of water lilies and the light-saturated landscapes well enough. But I wrote my term paper on Toulouse-Lautrec, drawn to the shady *demimonde* of the Montmartre dance halls that came alive in his vibrant posters.

In high school I read the *les poètes symbolistes*—Verlaine and Rimbaud and Baudelaire, my favorite. From a safe distance, I contemplated the voluptuous world of *l'absinthe* and *l'opium*, and I wondered—longingly—what it might be like to make love with abandon. I pictured gardens filled with evil flowers, journeys taken on drunken boats. In college, I studied *l'existentialisme* in French, through the words of Sartre and Camus.

Even my French teachers seemed exotic to me—though they were as American as I was. Like Mme. Ball in grade school, with crimson lips and dark hair drawn into a bun, her clothing a little more vivid than what you'd expect from a schoolteacher in Ohio. I always felt shocked when she'd drop off her daughter at Girl Scouts—speaking English, like someone's ordinary mother. In junior high, I studied the dark craggy *visage* of M. Snyder, a face I imagined to be full of suffering. He walked with a limp, and I wondered if he'd lost his leg in The War—though exactly what war it could have been remained hazy to me.

In high school, I fell under the spell of Mme. Hoffmann. She was a tall elegant woman in her early thirties, with long auburn hair arranged above her pale beautiful oval of a face. Sometimes she'd talk to our small Advanced Placement French class as though we were her girlish confidantes—laughing about what she considered her too-generous *cuisses* as she smoothed her skirt over her thighs. In a more serious vein, she'd tell us about the nightly walks she and her businessman husband took around the lake in their suburban Chicago subdivision. It was the one thing, she said, that preserved their *mariage*.

Once she stopped in the middle of a poem, a dreamy look on her face. Then she spoke of a poet she'd loved in France, when she was very young and studying abroad. "*Il m'a presque détruit.*" He nearly destroyed me. We all sighed together. I'd never known a teacher to talk of such intimate matters. But we spoke only in French, so perhaps the rules were different. We felt free and protected at the same time, in that world apart created by the beautiful language that wasn't really our own.

If I'd ever spent a significant period among native French speakers, perhaps my feelings about the language would have evolved in a more realistic direction. But the experiences I had outside the classroom were limited: a French exchange student in his twenties who stayed with my family one summer; a few weeks I spent in Paris when I was nineteen. Later trips to Quebec with Steve, when I discovered my cautious French was still understandable. These scattered experiences offered me a taste of French as a living language, without ever tarnishing the romantic visions I still held in my head.

Along with the French language, another force began to work on me in the year before I started to sing. Steve had finally found a synagogue for us to join a few years earlier, just after my father's death. In the past year we'd started to attend regularly, because Alec was preparing for his bar mitzvah.

Although we belonged to a liberal Reform temple, the weekly Shabbat service still felt heavy with unfamiliar ritual. The Byzantine-inspired building with its high dome, the reverent lifting of the ornate Torah scrolls, the fixed order of the service, the mix of English and Hebrew, the singing—at first everything but the rabbi's sermon seemed otherworldly and impenetrable.

I tried to follow along, grateful to find transliterations in the back-to-front prayer book. Little by little, the Saturday morning service became more familiar, and I looked forward to the reassuring sameness. I felt lifted up somehow, in a way I had never experienced in the mainstream Protestant churches my family visited, with decreasing frequency, during my childhood.

The music was spare, usually just unaccompanied singing, led by the Israeli cantor. The melodies sounded Middle Eastern, in a minor mode that seemed far more beautiful than the conventional hymns and organ music I remembered from church. I found the music haunting, stirring.

Sometimes the sounds of Saturday morning brought me back to the night before, when I'd experienced a similar out-of-body feeling—at the Cajun dance. Then I'd catch myself, alarmed at how readily the secular and the sacred had flowed together, the boundary dissolved by music. I felt foolish to imagine I'd found transcendence in the wild French music of bars and dance halls—and guilty to be imagining such earthy pleasures in a place of worship.

The distinction between word and chant, prayer and song, all began to blur. And the unfamiliarity of Hebrew felt freeing, a series of pure sounds more than individual words. Melodies began to creep into my consciousness, along with fragments of the ritual language that I was starting to recognize. Finally I allowed my voice to merge with the rest of the congregation, rising up, as though we were a single powerful voice, one rather than many.

The day after Alec's bar mitzvah, back at the house, Steve's mother overheard me humming—and she recognized a familiar melody. "Somebody's *davening*," she said with a little smile, using the Hebrew word for praying.

That's how the Cajun singing started, too, except that I was the one who caught myself starting to almost-sing, during unguarded moments. And I was a congregation of one. Strange, the way the music playing inside my head began to slip out through my lips. First a hum, then a few French words, barely audible, when I was alone. I listened, and then I had to face it: I was edging closer and closer to singing. So I decided to sing a few lines out loud—just as a private experiment. I started out with the opening line from "Lovebridge Waltz," one of my first accordion tunes.

"Hey, 'tit fille, moi j'me vois . . ."

Whose voice was that? Surely not mine. It didn't sound ugly or grating, as I'd feared it might. I felt strangely detached as I listened.

I tried again, and my voice sounded nearly the same, this second time around. It was hard for me to believe. So it wasn't just a random event, like a rainbow or a flash of lightning. I actually had some control over this mysterious force.

I tried another line, this time from a two-step:

"Oh, Madeleline, t'as couché dehors . . ."

Same thing. It sounded like someone singing an actual Cajun song—or a little bit of one, at least.

Then, the next big step: I tried out my newfound voice on Steve, one night when we'd pulled out our instruments to play. I sang a couple of lines, waited.

Steve smiled. "Hey! Sounds great! But you know I've always loved the sound of your voice. Haven't I always said you should be singing?"

Well, yes. He had. But I figured that was love, not objectivity. And why should there be a connection between speaking and singing? True, other people had told me the same thing—and even assumed I must be a singer. But I'd always given them a look as though they'd suggested something outlandish, like taking up skydiving or bull-fighting.

But now the unthinkable had turned possible. I had received an unexpected gift, one that gave me an even deeper thrill than a new accordion. Because I wasn't just discovering something new. I'd recovered something I believed to be out of reach. A voice, a missing part of myself.

I made a decision: to learn some Cajun songs, all the way through, by heart. I had an ideal resource in Ann Savoy's book. She'd organized it into chapters devoted to the most influential Cajun and Creole musicians, with lyrics corresponding to the versions of songs they'd recorded. So I could put on Iry LeJeune's original recording of "Lovebridge Waltz" and then follow along as he sang the lyrics on the page in front of me.

Lining up the words with the rhythm of a tune turned out to be a challenge. I listened, over and over, trying to match my voice to Iry's. I also copied the lyrics down on note cards, then tapped my foot and made little marks to indicate the stressed syllables. At odd moments, like on the train to work, I could pull out the cards and study them, trying to commit words to memory.

Memorizing the words wasn't difficult, and I enjoyed the challenge of learning the subtle differences between the standard French I'd studied and the earthy language that evolved in Louisiana. But the act of singing itself—sending my voice in the right direction, approximating the correct melody, hitting the high notes, singing loudly enough to be heard—that was more intimidating. But I tried to convince myself this was mostly about the French language, and the singing was just a vehicle, so perhaps no one would notice too much.

I contemplated the next step: singing in front of other people—besides Steve, that is. I figured our next jam session might be a good way to ease in. I pictured our familiar group of beginners, where it would be natural to slip into singing when I took my turn on the accordion.

But the next opportunity turned out to be a step beyond what I'd imagined. Vicki, the local Cajun dance teacher, decided to host a party. It would be a reunion for the dozen of us who'd gone to Cajun music camp that summer, plus a few others: the rest of our jam group, the Chicago Cajun Aces, assorted friends and neighbors. It promised to be bigger and more daunting than the usual jam session. But I refused to let myself back down. I was ready to make my singing debut.

The party fell on one of those hot September afternoons that still seemed like summer in Chicago. We visited, told stories about camp, ate gumbo. Then somebody decided it was time to bring out the instruments, and the circle began to form in the backyard. The music began.

I had already decided what to sing when my time came. Not an Iry LeJeune classic, but an old-time Creole tune, simple and percussive, called "Chère Ici, Chère Là-Bas." I'd first heard it on a recording by Bois Sec and Canray, and I'd just begun to learn it on the accordion. I'd heard Bois Sec play the tune throughout the week at Augusta, and the words had stayed with me.

I felt anxious, as always, as I waited to take my turn on the accordion. But this time, with an even more perilous step looming, the stakes were higher. I sat quietly, barely hearing the music, poised for a fate I could hardly imagine. I felt alone and vulnerable, like someone getting set to jump off the high diving board for the first time or run down the street naked. My uneasiness began to spread throughout my body: dry mouth, prickly arms, queasy stomach. I tried to push down my rising panic.

"Hey, Blair, why don't you take a turn on the accordion?"

Finally, the inevitable moment.

I took a breath to steady myself, then said in a voice I hoped might pass for casual: "Okay. How about about 'Chère Ici, Chère Là-Bas.' And maybe I'll sing this one."

I said it matter-of-factly, like the way you'd remind everyone of the key, but I wasn't fooling anyone. I felt the group coming to attention and saw the looks of surprise passing around the circle.

First, I played a simple version of the tune on my accordion. I reached the end of the first verse, lifted my fingers from the buttons, and heard the echo of that last note. I fell into the sudden deep silence an accordion creates, when the bellows stop pumping and the air stops passing through the reeds. A pause. Time for the vocal break. Time for me to become my own instrument.

I summoned up my nerve, my desire, my breath—along with memories of all those other voices, past and present, I carried around with me. I could almost hear them. The piercing, urgent sounds of the men: Amédé Ardoin and Iry LeJeune, hardly dimmed by the old recordings, and all those who had followed them. The contrast of Ann Savoy's pure, assured tones. The bluesy joy of Canray and Bois Sec. They were all there, in my ears and heart.

I braced myself, as I prepared to step off a precipice into some looming empty space. Then I sang the first verse, as simple as a child's singsong nursery rhyme:

"Chère ici, et chère là-bas, mais oui, que moi je m'en vas. Moi je m'en vas, chère, d'ici, mais oui, mon coeur fait mal." *Sweetie over here, and sweetie over there. Yeah, I'm gonna leave. I'm gonna leave here, sweetie. But my heart's hurting.*

I listened to the sound of my own voice. It was audible only because everyone had become so quiet. That voice sounded tentative—girlish and a little thin, so much quieter than the booming call of my accordion and not much like the chorus of voices I carried in my head. But at that moment, it didn't really matter. It was mine—and even though it might lack conviction, my voice sounded just fine, perhaps even pleasing to the ear.

I wasn't falling after all. I had stepped through a window and now I floated gently in the air, like one of those smiling women in a Chagall painting: barely anchored to the earth, rising upward with a lightness that comes with revelation.

Ten   Going Deeper

"Hey. It's me. Harton. I just had an idea." To me it sounded more like a brainstorm, judging from the urgency I could detect beneath the low drawl at the other end of the line.

"Why don't you get really drunk some time and then try to sing?"

"Well, I don't know . . ." I hesitated, trying to digest this latest bit of wisdom from my new Cajun friend. So he quickly amended his suggestion:

"You'd only have to do it once. Think about it."

Harton was my first Louisiana-born friend, the first of many, as it would turn out. He had arrived in Chicago at just the right time—in the fall, at an unsettled point in my musical life. Our friendship marked the beginning of the deeper personal connection to the music and culture I'd been missing.

We met at the monthly Cajun Aces dance, in their newest spot, the cavernous gym of a Presbyterian church. That night, I noticed someone new. A well-built man, around my age, with angular features, slightly hooked nose above a small mustache, black beret on top of curly dark hair with silver glints.

I watched him dance, in an unusual style that resembled a jig in slow motion, or maybe a two-step cut in half. But he moved with certainty and appeared to feel the rhythm at a completely different level. Eyes fixed on something only he could see, lips moving slightly, transported by the music into some private world of his own.

I wondered if he might be that friend Charlie had mentioned, a Cajun guy preparing to move to Chicago from Minnesota. I'd heard he was a piano tuner, like Charlie, and that he sang and played the accordion.

When the song ended I approached this man, with the uncharacteristic social confidence Cajun music seemed to bring out in me.

After introducing myself, I asked if he might be Charlie's friend who had just arrived from Minnesota.

"I am," he said. "My name's Harton."

"I thought you might be. Then after I watched you dance, I knew you had to be Cajun."

"Well, actually, I'm Creole."

"Oh."

I looked at him more closely, embarrassed that I had made an assumption. I had thought "Creole" referred to French-speaking people from Louisiana of mixed heritage—black and Native American, along with French European. People of color. But Harton appeared white, with a suggestion of Mediterranean ancestry.

Harton looked faintly amused, as though he might be savoring my confusion, before he offered an explanation: He had always considered himself Cajun, a broadly inclusive term for anyone belonging to the white, French-speaking communities of rural southwest Louisiana. Then his grandmother told him the proper term for their family was "Creole," since their ancestors had come directly from France, and not by way of the Acadian settlements in Nova Scotia.

To Harton's grandmother, this amounted to an important distinction, one that set them apart from their Cajun neighbors, and perhaps a little above. They were Creole—a purely French family with roots in the old world but transplanted to the new. It was an older, broader meaning of the term, unrelated to race.

For Harton himself, the distinction had nothing to do with superiority. The particularities of peoples' stories—his own, and everyone else's—fascinated him, and he considered it important to get the story right. He also liked to keep people off balance, and he felt compelled to educate them about all sorts of things—including his Louisiana heritage.

At that time, my notions about Louisiana remained hazy and romanticized, despite our recent trip in the spring. My experiences of people, whether Cajun or Creole, continued to be filtered through the books I'd read, song lyrics, and my own dreamy fantasies. Most of the people I'd encountered were men connected to the music world—idealized, larger-than-life figures. Added to this complicated mix were my lingering negative stereotypes of southern white men, who might turn out to be rednecks and good old boys, tainted by machismo and racism. I needed to temper all this with an infusion of reality—like getting to know someone from Louisiana as a friend, plain and simple.

Harton defied easy categorization. He'd grown up speaking French in a small rural community in Avoyelles Parish, on the northeast edge of Cajun country, more steeped in the old ways than I ever imagined someone of my generation could be. After college and a short stint in graduate school, he'd left Louisiana in the early seventies and headed to California, where he'd remained for twenty years.

With a few deft phrases, Harton painted a picture of the cosmopolitan, freewheeling life he'd enjoyed in San Francisco: a fast-paced job in advertising, dance clubs with gay friends from work, blues clubs with a black girlfriend, singing with a blues band. Then he attended a Cajun festival in the Bay Area and something stirred. He had reached his thirties and—just like me—he had never mastered a musical instrument, although he had been a singer all his life. But at that moment he knew: he had to play the accordion.

Harton's San Francisco history intrigued me, because I'd learned only recently about the thriving Cajun and zydeco music community in California, the largest outside Louisiana itself. In fact, I had a connection of my own.

"Have you heard of Danny Poullard?" I asked him, during our first conversation. "I took an accordion class with him at Cajun music camp last month."

"Ahh, Poullard—of course! I studied accordion with him. He got to be one of my best friends."

So Harton knew Danny Poullard—not really a surprise, if he'd lived in San Francisco. Danny was a prominent musician and teacher, at the very center of the West Coast scene—and Creole in the way I had originally understood it: a French-speaking person of color from south Louisiana. I was impressed to hear about Harton's close relationship with him.

I had failed to connect with Danny in a personal way during the recent week at Augusta. The class had been large, and he had seemed tentative, deferring to the veteran staff member who assisted him. And then he'd been forced to leave suddenly, because his father died before the week ended.

Steve and I had glimpsed the California music scene firsthand the previous January, when we traveled to San Francisco for my brother's wedding. Just before the trip, I had been studying the course offerings in the latest Augusta catalog—and I came across the profile of Danny and two of his band mates from the California Cajun Orchestra, Suzy and Eric Thompson. All three would be teaching for the first time that summer. I was intrigued by the possibility of Cajun music on the West Coast, and I was determined to sample some of it.

But I found more than just a Cajun dance, when I checked the local alternative paper. A Berkeley folk club was hosting a fundraiser for D. L. Menard, a well-known Louisiana musician whose chair-making factory had just burned down.

Ashkenaz turned out to be an old warehouse on a gritty stretch of San Pablo Avenue in Berkeley, remodeled to resemble an old wooden synagogue from Eastern Europe. Once inside, Steve and I discovered a comfortable sixties-style ambience—and a dazzling dance scene. Political posters and musicians' photos lined the walls. People of every size, shape, age, and color packed the wooden floor. The simple categories I had at my disposal simply fell away. Folk dancers, professors, Deadheads, aging hippies, Creole cowboys, college students, Rastafarians, and regular working people all mingled together: dancing, swaying, sweating, talking, and checking one another out.

The music sounded like the real thing, though I did notice these California people had their own way of dancing. The orderly circling we'd learned in Chicago didn't appear to be in vogue. Couples carved out their own spots on the dance floor, while single dancers floated through the crowd in free-form improvisations. Some people formed little dance circles. Ashkenaz bore scant resemblance to the sedate Cajun dance scene back home.

Alec and Nate were less than enthralled. They parked themselves somewhere to the side of the stage, jet-lagged, and grumbled about my penchant for finding Cajun music wherever I went. So I knew we'd never manage to see all four of the bands scheduled to play.

We stayed just long enough to hear the California Cajun Orchestra begin their set, featuring Danny Poullard on accordion.

I found it difficult to focus much on Danny's playing, with so much going on around me. I watched him as he stood there on stage, unsmiling, surveying the scene unfolding below him as though he owned the place. He looked to be somewhere in his middle years, with powerful arms and shoulders, and a thin mustache that gave him a vaguely Latin look. I felt curious—and impatient for my next summer session at Augusta.

So when Harton talked about his musical life in California, I could already picture the wild carnival at Ashkenaz—and I wondered why he'd ever left such a rich music scene. We talked for a long time, that first night at the dance. I learned that he'd begun to feel restless in San Francisco. Harton never wanted life to be too easy or settled, he explained. So he moved to the Midwest—first to study accordion repair, and then to get training as a piano technician.

I invited Harton to our next jam session. He enjoyed it, but mentioned he wouldn't mind getting together with just Steve and me. I took him up on that—and before long, he started coming by our house regularly.

Harton usually came to visit on Sunday. Dimanche après-midi, we called it, Sunday afternoon, after a Cajun waltz by the same name. He would show up around one o'clock, after making the hour drive from Elgin, where he lived alone in a spartan studio apartment. We'd make music, tell stories, play with the cats, eventually have dinner. Harton, we discovered, was indifferent to food. Another Louisiana stereotype shattered.

Harton had a generous spirit, along with a zeal to get people to see things from his point of view. He also had a quirky, self-deprecating sense of humor, and we became accustomed to his one-liners, since he liked to repeat them. Like that exclamation of his father's: *Tonerre mes chiens!* Thunder my dogs. He never did manage to explain that one. Or one of Harton's personal quips: "It's great to be from Louisiana—you get to be illiterate in two languages." He could afford to joke about literacy, because he read constantly, and he was more aware of serious contemporary fiction than most people I knew. We traded books back and forth, and we sometimes wandered into the used bookstores in our South Side neighborhood.

He'd often arrive with improbable gifts: novels by Paul Auster, a small anvil, homemade blues mix tapes for Alec; a free organ from the music store where he worked; supplies for "egg Paque-ing," a Cajun Easter custom where you duel with hard-boiled eggs. He also had plenty of advice, especially about the music.

Once he learned I had just started to sing, Harton became a man with a mission. Within a few weeks of our meeting, he presented me with a custom-made vocal tape, called "Blair's Vocal Thang," with selections from his extensive collection of recordings. The tracks covered an improbable range, from Cajun to blues to Elvis. In between, Harton had inserted commentary on subtle matters of vocal technique—most of it over my head. He quickly identified inhibition as my biggest musical handicap. "The problem," he once explained, "is that you didn't grow up on a farm, calling the animals, the way I did."

Inhibition was not a problem for Harton, at least when he joined the Cajun Aces on stage to sing a few tunes. He'd slip into a soft-shoe shimmy that sometimes veered dangerously close to bump-and-grind. "It's supposed to be entertainment," he'd say with a shrug. He figured the band could use a little more animation.

Whenever I sang, he would pay close attention, consider, then demonstrate the right way, putting my pallid attempts to shame with a voice that blasted out of him, like someone accelerating from a dead stop to fifty miles an hour. He'd also linger over the words, playing with the sounds, holding on to them. "Don't chop off the phrases at the end," he'd often tell me. "Extend them more."

He also tried to fine-tune my French. Once, as we waltzed to the strains of the Cajun Aces, he suddenly leaned forward and murmered softly into my ear, "Repeat this: m'en aller donc te revoir. M'en aller." Startled, I did as instructed, trying hard to avoid stumbling.

"No," he corrected me. "You're making it sound like mon. It's m'en. And it's more like all-eh than all-ayyy." He shook his head. "Umm, we do need to work a little on your French."

Harton also tried to help me with the accordion, even though he was still learning himself. When all three of us played together, we'd generally end up with Harton on accordion, Steve on fiddle or guitar, and me on triangle. Harton and I took turns singing.

Eventually, we started to venture into public playing. At Steve's school, we visited a couple of French classes, alternating our music with Harton's Louisiana stories. At a New Year's party, the three of us wandered off into a quiet corner and started to play, as much for ourselves as anyone who might listen. To our surprise, a small group of people gathered round and began to dance.

Harton left Chicago for the summer, to work as a piano tuner at the Aspen Music Festival. But he remained a presence through his regular flow of witty letters and postcards and through the wide-ranging music collection he left with us, for safekeeping and listening. Thanks to Harton, I listened for the first time to Astor Piazzolla, Little Feat, Django Reinhardt, and to rare Cajun recordings you couldn't find anymore.

Harton even managed to shape, from a distance, the beginning of my personal connection to Danny Poullard. He'd set me up for the encounter when he mailed me a parody of a Cajun song he'd written. Just one problem: I couldn't find one of the words in the verse when I searched my French dictionary.

"Why don't you ask Danny Poullard what that word means when you see him at Augusta this summer," he wrote back to me, when I asked him to translate.

My opportunity came at the start of the week, when Danny approached me at the end of the first session.

"So, weren't you in my class last year?" Friendly but cautious, like he wasn't quite sure.

Yes, I replied. I added that we had a friend in common: Harton, who had moved to Chicago in the past year.

"Ah, Harton." Danny smiled. "How is he?"

"He's fine—working in Aspen for the summer. And also writing songs. Actually, he just sent me some lyrics, and he thought you could translate this one word I can't seem to make out." I handed him the postcard. "It's in that line about the cow jumping the fence and destroying her—something or other."

Danny pulled out his reading glasses, studied the card, and frowned. Then he stepped closer to me and lowered his voice.

"It means, uhh, titty."

Tit-ton, as Harton had written it. Usually spelled "teton." As in the Grand Tetons. It was not quite the icebreaker Danny or I would have chosen, but it was a start.

Harton's absence over the summer made me realize how much I counted on those Sunday afternoon sessions. Everything else in the local Cajun scene seemed to be in flux. In the spring, Charlie had stopped holding the regular monthly jam sessions. Although his band continued to perform, their line-up kept changing—with a few different fiddlers rotating through. Finally, Denise joined the Chicago Cajun Aces that summer, followed eventually by her husband, Earl. They also had an increasingly active schedule with their own group, the Midway Ramblers. Meanwhile, Joan had decided to pursue a Ph.D. and had less time for music.

I had another big change looming: moving, maybe even leaving Chicago. I tried to avoid thinking about it much. But Steve's growing restlessness at work had forced me to face the possibility.

I had been shocked when Steve first brought up the idea of relocating, not long after my father died. He was disappointed at the more conservative direction his once-progressive school had taken, and he had been frustrated in his attempts to assume a position of greater leadership. But I insisted it was too soon to face another upheaval. A couple of years later, Steve brought up moving again, with greater force, after he had failed to find a new position locally and wanted to widen his search. Finally, I gave in, worn down by his uncharacteristic persistence and by a new kind of professional ambition I had to respect, even if I worried about where it might lead.

I began to feel that all of us in the jam group were heading off in different directions, even though we remained friends and continued to get together periodically. We did enjoy some memorable times—like the party Steve and I hosted for Bois Sec Ardoin and his family, when they performed at the University of Chicago Folk Festival. At least I had one point of musical stability: the sessions with Steve and Harton. There, I found friendship, a chance to grow musically, and a continuing pathway into Louisiana culture.

When Harton came back in the fall, our regular sessions resumed—and I was encouraged to see that we all seemed to be getting better. I attributed my own improvement to the two teachers I'd had at Augusta that summer, Danny Poullard and Eddie LeJeune.

I had spent mornings with Eddie—son of the legendary Iry LeJeune, the nearly blind accordionist widely considered the father of modern Cajun music. Eddie had run his class like a warm-hearted

Danny Poullard and Eddie LeJeune at the Augusta Heritage Center, 1995. Photo courtesy of Susan Pilch.

Cajun drill sergeant. He forced each student to play alone, in front of the class, at the beginning of each session. This was an unusual step at Augusta, and I discovered everyone felt anxious about it. When I listened to my classmates play, I realized I'd been wrong to assume that everyone else was catching on fast. But I still felt out of my depth, and I tried to switch to the less advanced class Eddie taught. He flatly refused. "You belong right here," he said. "With me in the morning, and Danny in the afternoon."

Danny had been much more low-key with his afternoon class. He never singled people out or pushed them. But if a student accepted his offer of a one-on-one session, he didn't hold back. In my case, Danny felt I had to return to the basics, starting with the rhythm. "You have to make your own self want to dance," he said.

So I came back from Augusta with a mix of feelings. For the first time, I had established warm personal connections with two of my teachers, and I'd made major strides in overcoming the fear of being evaluated. But I knew I still had a long road to travel musically.

I also found myself jobless that fall, one of the casualties of a yearlong reorganization at the university hospital where I'd spent the past five years. The elimination of my position wasn't a complete surprise, although it left me feeling disenchanted with institutional politics. I decided to strike out on my own. I found office space not far from the hospital, where I began the slow process of establishing a private practice.

Faced with uncertainty and too much free time, I turned to music and decided to try something new: rhythm guitar. I quickly discovered the truth of something Joan had said. It was liberating to have another choice at jam sessions, instead of simply waiting for a turn on the accordion. And now Steve, Harton, and I could play as a proper trio.

Guitar allowed me to step into the background, and it was easier, on the face of it, than playing accordion or fiddle. But I quickly discovered the simplicity of Cajun-style guitar was deceptive, because it played such a crucial role in the unique rhythm that defined the music. On guitar, I began to understand the structure of the music in a more complete way: hearing the chord changes, counting the beats, and feeling the rhythm more deeply.

With this new musical interest, I welcomed the news that a Louisiana guitarist-singer named Bobby Michot would be involved in the upcoming weekend Cajun festival at Folklore Village in Wisconsin. Along with teaching guitar, he would lead a singing class—something I'd never seen offered at Augusta.

Harton, sure enough, had a personal connection to Bobby Michot. Bobby had been collecting recordings by two little-known Avoyelles Parish musicians from the twenties and thirties, Blind Uncle Gaspard and Delma Lachney, who played an older style of French music. Bobby's field research led him to Harton, because Gaspard had played at his parents' wedding. Then it turned out Bobby's family, a prominent Louisiana clan, also had roots in Avoyelles Parish.

"I think we're supposed to be distant cousins," Harton told me. "Bobby's a really nice guy. You'll like him."

Harton was right. I liked Bobby immediately. He looked like an affable Cajun mountain man: a tall and slightly heavy-set guy in his thirties, dressed in overalls, a round face framed by a wild beard and long hair—and with twinkling eyes. But in class, he turned into a passionate folklorist, jumping up to show us on a map the route a song might follow: from the western coast of France to Canada's Maritime provinces, and then south to Louisiana. He demonstrated the different forms the same song might take. And he led us in singing, in a high piercing voice, just nasal enough—where you could hear the catch in the voice, almost a sob. Bobby was like the best of the old recordings come to life.

After class, I told Bobby about our mutual friend Harton, who would be showing up for the evening dance. Bobby looked pleased. And when I mentioned the trip Steve and I had planned to Louisiana the next month, followed by a trip to France in the summer, he lit up. Bobby and his band would be in France at the same time, headlining a big Cajun festival. He promised to get us information about the festival. And of course we'd have to look him up in Louisiana.

We did our best to connect with Bobby in Louisiana the following month. He told us to meet him at a jam session, at what he called a "camp" just off the levee road in Henderson. When we finally found the dark little shack, we walked in on a handful of young Cajun musicians, most of them under twenty. Among them was a rising young accordionist named Horace Trahan, whom we'd met at Augusta. But no Bobby. We felt awkward, but the young folks welcomed us in. They laughed about Bobby's absence. "Oh, Bobby, well he sometimes gets a little—uh, lost!"

When we finally did catch up with Bobby, he was playing with his family band, les Frères Michot: his three brothers, along with a couple of young nephews. I'd recently got hold of the band's hard-to-find album. The Michot Brothers had a gentle and engaging sound, notable for sweet harmonies and an acoustic "bal de maison" feeling.

Bobby's parents sat on a blanket nearby, eating and listening. He pointed them out to us, during the break. The Michots were an accomplished family, including a judge, a state senator, a wetlands biologist, and a former head of the state department of education. Bobby was one of the free spirits.

The group was playing for the "Bach Lunch," a Friday concert series held on the grounds of the Natural History Museum in Lafayette. Such a refined scene, different from the Cajun festival I'd expected. Grassy lawn, well turned-out women and children, blankets, box lunches, wine. Everyone looked clean-cut, professional. It could have been a lawn concert in an upper-class Chicago suburb.

Even Bobby fit in, more or less, since he had shaved and cut his hair. But I noticed he seemed more subdued in this setting. Or maybe it was the cast on his arm. A fall from a horse, he explained, looking a little sheepish. But it didn't keep him from playing guitar.

Later, when I described the whole scene to the Millers, our hosts during the trip, Larry laughed at my surprise at discovering there was a "wine and cheese" crowd even among the Cajuns.

Before the trip, Larry had asked me what I was most interested in seeing during the visit. I was touched by his offer to set something up, and I did have one wish.

"Well," I admitted, "I'd love to meet a woman who plays accordion."

Women were still a minority among Cajun musicians, especially accordionists. I knew of only two. I'd seen Kristy Guillory, a gifted teenager, at the University of Chicago Folk Festival the previous winter. But for years, just about the only woman who played accordion in public—and the only one to have recorded—was Sheryl Cormier, dubbed the Queen of Cajun Music.

I'd been able to find one of Sheryl's recordings. It had something of a Nashville feeling, both in the music and in the appearance of the stern-looking woman on the cover, in full country western regalia. I was so impressed by the accordion I didn't pay much attention to her vocals—until Harton put together the vocal tape for me, and opened with Sheryl's singing. She had a deep voice, with a slight country twang. A compelling voice, not pretty or girlish, but full of feeling and authority. It grew on me.

Larry knew Sheryl and thought he could arrange a visit. And he was as good as his word. Not long after we arrived at his house, he took us over to meet her. She and her husband, Russell, lived in Carencro, a smaller town just outside Lafayette.

You could not miss the Cormier house, since Russell had built a three-foot tall model of an accordion in the front yard. I was all set to be intimidated by this famous woman musician, but when Sheryl met us at the door, she was a sweet and welcoming southern hostess.

"I'm so honored that another lady accordion player wants to meet me," she said, extending her hand as she ushered us in.

I didn't know what to say to that disarming greeting.

We sat down. "So," she said, as she slapped me on the knee, "let's hear what you can do on that accordion."

The reserve I usually felt simply didn't exist with her. I played, then she followed me—just to show me her version of the same song. Not to suggest that I was doing anything wrong, of course. When I told her how much I liked her singing, she seemed surprised and a little embarrassed. Russell, who managed the band, was the real singer, she said. She only sang a little, hardly at all since she'd had throat surgery.

We were disappointed to learn Sheryl didn't have any public gigs scheduled during our visit. But she invited us to hear her band play at a private party—a crawfish boil given by a local exterminating company for its employees.

When Steve and I approached the low roadhouse, in the countryside just outside Lafayette, the setting looked foreboding. But inside we found a friendly scene. The band was taking a break, and people of all ages had gathered at long tables, with communal piles of crawfish and boiled potatoes heaped on newspaper. There was plenty of beer on ice in big barrels. Sheryl looked up from her table, hailed us, and insisted we join her. She slid over to make room, introduced us all around, then invited us to dive into the mounds of spicy red crawfish.

Steve obliged, since—unlike me—he'd developed a taste for crawfish. I tried to get into the spirit, gingerly pulling off the tail and trying to extract the tender bit of white flesh. I drew the line at sucking the heads. I knew they were a delicacy, but I couldn't help it—I balked at dismantling spiny little creatures that always reminded me of big insects more than miniature lobsters. So I stuck mostly to potatoes and beer.

Finally, Sheryl got back up on the small makeshift stage. Her whole presence was powerful and no-frills. She was a sturdy woman, with a wide, open face, dressed simply in slacks and a t-shirt. The fanciness was in her accordion playing: loud, punchy, plenty of ornamentation.

She did leave most of the singing to Russell, who periodically played some rubboard, along with working the soundboard. He had one of those old-style Cajun voices I'd come to love, something like Bobby Michot's. But I was thrilled when Sheryl sang a raucous duet with her husband—"Jolie Fille," they called it. Trading verses, and the repeating chorus that ended: "Toi t'es trop canaille, canaille." *You're too sly.*

Steve and I alternated dancing, and then just standing over by Russell, who kept adjusting the soundboard. I felt lost in the music and in the presence of this strong, in-charge woman who commanded everyone's attention. After a couple of beers and not much food, I was also very relaxed—until Sheryl's voice cut through my pleasant haze.

"And now Miss Blair from Chicago is going to play us a song or two."

She looked over in my direction, smiling.

What? We hadn't talked about this.

"I can't do this!" I protested quietly into Steve's ear.

He whispered back. "Blair, there's not much choice. You have to."

He was right, of course. And even though this wasn't as cozy as Sheryl's living room, I realized I could do it.

I approached the stage area, sat down, and accepted Sheryl's accordion. I had about three seconds to figure out what to play. "How about 'The Back Door'?" I suggested. Everyone knew the popular two-step, a modern classic by D. L. Menard, dubbed the Cajun Hank Williams. I'd recently learned a slowed-down version from an instructional video, where the accordionist actually called out the button numbers.

"Sounds good," the fiddler said. "Let's go."

So I kicked off the tune. Carefully, note by note, I followed the road map in my head, wishing I'd had one less beer. I remembered to look over at the fiddler when I finished—not that he needed much guidance. And the steel guitar player managed to figure out on his own when to jump in. No singing on this one, since I hadn't tried to learn the words. One more time through, and then we were done. I heard polite applause. "Good job!" Sheryl said firmly, as she took back her accordion.

I hurried back to join Steve—and Russell, who offered his judicious assessment. "Well," he said, considering. "It was a little slower than we do it. But it was tight, I'll say that."

It was a magical evening. A real immersion in Cajun culture, I told myself, far off the tourist track, and an experience we'd never forget.

Finally, at the end of that long night we headed out with Sheryl and Russell to the nearly deserted parking lot. "You'll have to stay with us next time you visit," she said. "We'd love to," I replied. I knew she meant it. It was hard to say good-bye.

Then, as we approached our car, we all saw it: under the stars, little crystal cubes sparkling on the ground. Shattered glass sprayed across the front seat, and sprinkled across the gravel beside the front wheel. Someone had smashed out a side window.

Sheryl and Russell were deeply chagrined, and they immediately took charge. They got on the phone and found someone who agreed to install a new window the next day, even though it was Sunday.

"We are so sorry about this," Shcryl kept repeating. "It's nothing," we assured her. "It could have happened just as easily back home, in Chicago." But I had to wonder what had triggered this: mindless vandalism, the Illinois license plates—or perhaps it was a commentary on my accordion playing.

A few months later, we followed Bobby Michot to the Cajun festival in France. Steve and I had planned the trip, his first time abroad, as a celebration of our twenty-fifth wedding anniversary. We were taking the boys, of course. We hoped to spend much of the time in Paris—a city I had visited during my one and only trip to Europe, when I was nineteen. But we also wanted to head south to Lyon, where Alec had stayed twice during a school exchange program.

The festival turned out to be ideally located: on the road between Paris and Lyon, in a small town in Burgundy. Saulieu, a famed gastronomic center, in recent years had hosted a Cajun and zydeco festival. For one long weekend each summer, the little town was taken over by European fans of Louisiana French music.

We were the only Americans at the Saulieu festival, besides the Louisiana band, and practically the only English speakers. The rest of the musicians came from France, Britain, Germany, and the Netherlands. Alec, who looked like a longhaired teenage rock guitarist, skulked around town with Nate in tow, searching for pizza and pannini. Steve and I danced to a French zydeco band in the shadow of an eleventh-century cathedral, struggled through music workshops taught in French, caught up with our new friend Bobby—once again shaggy and clearly in his element—and drank red wine while the French fans savored the imported Budweiser. "I can't believe we're at a Cajun music festival in France," Alec had said, rolling his eyes. I could hardly believe it myself.

Back in Chicago, we reported our adventures to Harton. We finally had one official gig with him, when a whole collection of us from the jam group volunteered to play at a suburban political fundraiser sponsored by the League of Women Voters. Steve and I appeared as a trio with Harton, then we played with Joan, and finally our friends the Midway Ramblers performed.

For those few hours, I savored the feeling of being an almost-real musician. I felt set apart, as I strolled around with my friends, in between sets. I liked being on the other side: providing the entertainment, instead of just listening in the audience, then writing checks to support our candidates. Never mind that we were just volunteers; I thought we had arrived as musicians.

Our first public appearance with Harton turned out to be our last. When summer arrived, a few months later, he left for Aspen again. But this time, he planned to return to Chicago in the fall just long enough to pack up his belongings. He had decided to move back home to Louisiana.

Harton's departure would leave a big gap in our lives, musically and personally. But I understood. His elderly widowed father lived alone, and Harton was the only one of the children who had moved so far away. He'd felt the need to escape his Louisiana culture when he was younger. But now it was calling him back.

Steve and I saw Harton three months after his return to Louisiana. It was just after Christmas, and the boys had gone to spend a week in Florida with their grandparents. So we decided to make our first trip to southwest Louisiana on our own.

We stayed with Harton for the first part of the week, in the white clapboard house his father, a carpenter, had built when Harton was a boy. He showed us the sites around Bayou Jacques, their small settlement on the edge of Cajun country. Harton even tried to demonstrate the linguistic boundaries for us, by driving just a few miles north and east into nearby towns so we could sample the accents of "les coups rouges"—the rednecks. But the convenience stores all turned out to be closed on Sunday.

Harton also accompanied us on our first trip to two venerable dance halls, La Poussière and Hamilton's. Unlike the wholesome "dine-and-dance" places we always frequented with our kids, these were adults-only establishments, so we'd never been able to visit on past trips.

La Poussière, in Breaux Bridge, was an old-style Cajun club famous for the house accordionist Walter Mouton—a Saturday night fixture for more than thirty years—and for its no-nonsense Cajun dancers who circled so fast and methodically they might mow you down. The place had just settled a highly publicized civil rights lawsuit, after refusing admission to an African American woman who turned out to be a federal prosecutor from Chicago.

Steve and I arrived at La Poussière a little ahead of Harton. We got a cold stare from the grim-faced woman taking money at the door, underneath the sign proclaiming their "no discrimination" policy. Inside, it still felt like a private party for the Cajun couples, middle-aged and up, who all seemed to know one another. Even Harton, with his impeccable French roots, felt the chill when he arrived. "Let's get out of here," he said, after a half hour. "We'll go to Hamilton's to hear some zydeco."

Hamilton's Club, on the outskirts of Lafayette, had the look of an old roadhouse—with a packed parking lot. Not a surprise, because Keith Frank, a rising young zydeco star, was playing. The smiling Creole man at the door welcomed us in, but once inside we found it impossible to penetrate the tightly wedged crowd, crammed around the bandstand in front, swaying more than dancing, because there was so little space. The sweaty crowd was mostly young, Creole, and stylishly hip in snug denim jeans and cowboy boots. I couldn't even see over their heads to catch a glimpse of the band, and the music was so loud I could feel my chest vibrating and the beginning of an ache in my ears.

The three of us tried to ease our way around the edges of the crowd, single file, alongside the bar, acknowledging the smiles and "hey's" some folks cast our way. Finally, we made our way slowly to the back, with some friendly encouragement from the staff, who seemed to be keeping a watchful eye on us.

In back, the room finally opened up, and we discovered a more relaxed scene, with some patrons actually sitting at tables, trying to converse. This section of the crowd looked to be more middle-aged, and a little more racially mixed, with a handful of white people. Overall, it was a far more welcoming atmosphere than La Poussière, but we'd picked a night when it was simply too crowded to dance, too loud to talk, and too hard to even listen comfortably. So we left before much time had passed. "Y'all should come back again, when it's a little less crowded—and quieter," the man at the door apologized.

We spent the second part of the week with Sheryl and Russell Cormier, at their comfortable ranch house in Carencro, where people came and went constantly: band mates, friends, family. We even met Sheryl's mother, a trim spunky woman of seventy or so who used to play drums in the family band.

We heard all kinds of talk swirling around us at the Cormier house: lively banter, gossip, stories about hard times in the old days, music lore. And now and then, some racist remarks emerged. Sheryl seemed to feel personally responsible when the conversation took a wrong turn. "I hate it when they talk like that," she'd say, when she could tell by a shift in my expression how I felt about some passing comment. Quick and offhand, maybe, but to me it felt as sharp as a nasty burr you couldn't shake loose. "But you have to understand how a lot of people around here were raised," she'd explain. Poor. Not knowing any better. Looked down on.

But Sheryl herself wasn't anything like that. She proudly asserted her right to do as she pleased. She'd put together the very first "all girl Cajun band," dismissing speculations about the sexual orientation of some of her musicians. "Hey, it's my business what somebody does on the bandstand, but off the bandstand, it's their business." She invited her Creole musician friends over to the house, no matter what anyone said. When a relative worried that "the wrong kind" might move in to the house next door, she countered: "So who would you rather have for your neighbors, good-quality Creole people or white trash?"

She and Danny Poullard had become friends over the years. In fact, when we arrived at their house she and Russell had been all set to take us on a two-hour drive to Texas, to attend a birthday dance the family was putting on for Danny's mother that afternoon.

We spent New Year's Eve with Sheryl and Russell at La Poussière—sitting at a big group of tables up front, reserved for the Cormiers and two dozen of their closest friends. It made such a difference, to qualify as insiders this time. They had created an impromptu pot-luck, with set-ups purchased from the bar, supplemented by plates of homemade sandwiches and bags of chips brought from home. Walter Mouton presided over the stage, graciously calling up the other musicians in the house: Blackie Forrestier, who'd been Sheryl's mentor, and then Sheryl herself.

New Year's Day we visited Harton in the morning, then we joined the Cormiers at a friend's party in Lafayette. We ate gumbo and watched a few old-time Cajun musicians in a hot game of bourée, the famous high stakes card game I'd heard about but never observed.

Gambling seemed a fitting way to welcome a new year filled with so much uncertainty, with Steve's job search in high gear. The odds were clear: we would probably be leaving Chicago. But I'd never been one for taking chances—and where we'd end up was anyone's guess.

I held up the blue leather miniskirt, considering. I'd squeezed myself into it exactly once, on that first trip to New Orleans. No amount of nostalgia could justify keeping it—and besides, I hadn't grown any thinner in the past seven years. Maybe one of my skinny friends or neighbors would appreciate it. No telling who would show up for our moving sale.

I moved on to the kids' stuff. I gently smoothed out the white and navy sailor suit, size 2T. Both boys had worn it, though I could picture Nate more clearly, from the big-eyed photo of him taken when Steve's mother remarried. I set the little sailor suit aside, imagining I might pass it on to a grandchild someday. And all those miniature sweaters, hand knit by both my mother and Steve's, with the lumps and mismatched arms that always made us laugh—I couldn't let those go, either. The pile of worn out t-shirts, on the other hand, I tossed into the sale box. Then I pulled one back out.

I gazed at the boys' Little League uniforms, white fading to yellow, with grass stains on the knees. Then I picked up my father's baseball bat, dark with age, from his freshman year in college. My mother had passed it along to me after he died. Even though I was less sports-minded than anyone else in the family, I'd become the wistful keeper of these remnants of the past.

I'd been even younger when my mother gave me the six-inch standing brass crucifix that had belonged to her own mother, just after she died. My Slovenian grandma considered me the most religious of the grandchildren, my mother told me. I had my doubts about that, though I probably did qualify as the most serious. I'd never known what to do with that crucifix, a primitive symbol in the eyes of my parents—who'd evolved into casual Unitarians, rather proud to have acquired a Jewish son-in-law. So I'd kept it in a special wicker box, along with a few other treasures, including a tiny silver baby rattle, marked with my own deep teeth marks. I'd been a restless, colicky baby who cried more than slept, my mother reminded me, when Alec turned out to be exactly the same way.

I moved on to the stuffed animals—a more cheerful business, but with their own kind of emotional weight. The boys might laugh at my attachment to their baby clothes, but they shared my affection for their plush army of cats—along with bears, dogs, lambs, bunnies, chicks, a big vulture, and little dancing men on a string. The collection even included a limp-limbed pink bear from my own childhood, grown pale and anorexic after one too many passes through the wash.

The entire stuffed menagerie, just like our two live cats, would be accompanying us to California. Along with whatever else we decided to pack up for the movers. Steve had finally found a new position—in the San Francisco Bay Area.

We never expected to end up on the West Coast. But then Steve's former principal at the Lab School invited him to apply for an administrative position she'd just created at the small private school she now ran—in California, near Berkeley.

I had two reactions. Mostly this: It was too far away, beyond the boundaries we'd set up for Steve's job search, and as far from Chicago as you could get. We barely knew a soul out there.

But then I had another thought: Short of moving to Louisiana, I couldn't imagine a better Cajun-zydeco music community. And my teacher Danny Poullard was at the very center of the Bay Area scene.

Not long after we learned about the California possibility, Danny and his brother Edward came to Chicago, to play at the annual weekend festival at Folkore Village in Wisconsin. We had arranged for them to perform for an assembly at Steve's school—along with Sheryl and Russell Cormier, who had ended up in town at the same time.

I was struggling emotionally, distressed at the thought of uprooting our family and starting over in a new place—but I felt this crazy little pocket of hope, when I imagined living near Danny. As soon as I saw him, I told him about Steve's upcoming job interview in California.

Danny brightened up. "You guys would love it in Berkeley," he said. As though we'd already decided.

Later on, Steve and I were sitting with Danny and Ed at a club called Crawdaddy Bayou, watching Sheryl and her band perform.

"So, Danny, if we move to California, can I be one of your accordion students? Can I come to those jam sessions?"

"Of course." He smiled. "You'd be one of my protégés." Such a funny word, old-fashioned and formal. But that's what he called them.

Danny pulled out a folded-up sheet of pink paper—the Bay Area Cajun-zydeco calendar. He reached for his glasses and started ticking off the names of all the bands he'd had a hand in shaping. It was like someone pulling out photos of the grandkids, though these musical offspring had some unusual names: Tete Rouge and Frog Legs, Motordude and Tee Fee, the Creole Belles.

My eyes widened as I scanned the page: twenty different bands listed in the directory at the top, and then the monthly calendar crowded with events. It appeared you could go out dancing to live Cajun or zydeco music every night of the week in the Bay Area.

But I couldn't sort out my feelings about moving to California, any more than I could sort through all the piles of books, clothing, toys, and old furniture in the basement. I had no way of knowing what we'd need in California or what life would be like there. Would we need our winter coats, our sweaters, our boots? I wasn't even certain the seasons changed.

Steve had remarked on the unfamiliar climate in the Bay Area, when he flew out to interview for the job. He'd called me just after an early morning jog around Berkeley, trying to describe how everything looked and smelled. Even though he wanted to put a positive spin on things, he couldn't disguise his surprise at the alien landscape. Unexpectedly hilly; blooming flowers, even in winter; sweet unfamiliar scents in the air. The houses, clinging to the sides of hills that rose sharply from the bay, struck him as charming and idiosyncratic, but small and insubstantial, especially since they were so expensive by Chicago standards. Perhaps California people didn't spend much time at home, Steve suggested.

So where do they go then, I wanted to ask. I had an image of people drifting through some never-ending party, like unmoored ships, not sure they'd find their way home at the end of the night. Or living in a Japanese teahouse, with sliding doors and panels that allowed a home to shape-shift, with boundaries constantly changing. I was accustomed to sturdy houses and apartment buildings, brick and stone and wood, heavily insulated, built to withstand the northern winters and designed to keep people safe inside.

I hadn't even seen our new house in Berkeley. We'd had no luck on our one family house-hunting trip, so Steve had gone back on his own. He'd found a 1920s stucco bungalow, in a neighborhood midway between the expensive houses up in the hills and the flatlands down by the bay. Charming, he assured me. But the main part of the house looked so small, when he tried to sketch out the floor plan from memory. Three small bedrooms and just one shower—for four people. And no back door, because of the attached studio apartment someone had added. The current owners used it as an artist's studio, but we'd probably need to rent it out. At least that's what we told the mortgage people.

That extra income would certainly help, since I hadn't found a job yet. I'd started buying the *San Francisco Chronicle* as soon as Steve accepted his new position, and I had applied for anything in the classifieds that sounded remotely possible. In my darker moments, I wondered whether I'd find work as a psychologist. I'd heard the Bay Area was swarming with therapists of every stripe, so I expected to face plenty of competition.

So far, I had just one interview lined up. And to get licensed I'd have to jump through all sorts of hoops: special courses in human sexuality and child abuse, then some oral exam on California laws and ethics. It was as though my fifteen years as a psychologist in Illinois didn't count for a thing.

So it appeared we would be arriving in California with one job between us and—at least for the moment—two houses. I felt surprised and a little hurt that no one had bought our graystone row house, built as workingman's housing around the time of the 1892 Columbian Exposition. I loved its history, the look of old-fashioned elegance. I couldn't believe another family didn't want to live there.

Our accordion-playing friend Dennis suggested we bury a statue of St. Joseph—head down—in the backyard. It always worked in his Polish-Italian family, he said, when somebody needed to sell a house. So I'd slipped into a small Catholic religious goods store in downtown Chicago, feeling like an imposter, as I furtively picked out the smallest statue of St. Joseph I could find. "I can't believe I'm doing this," I thought, as I paid the clerk and slipped the plastic figure into my purse. I buried the four-inch statue of St. Joseph, head down in the back yard, hoping no one could see me.

The best thing to come out of our unsuccessful house-hunting trip had been meeting up with Danny Poullard. He'd come by our hotel in Berkeley to say hello and to assure us—once again—how much we'd love living in California.

Maybe. The Cajun-zydeco music scene in the Bay Area offered the only potential bright spot to this move, as far as I could tell. It was a major compensation, but not enough to banish my blues.

While I was stuck down in the basement, surrounded by boxes and my worries, another drama was unfolding upstairs, where Steve and the boys had started to set up for the yard sale.

Our black cat Trent, the younger and wilder of our feline pair, took advantage of the chaos and tried to slip out the back door. Steve lunged at him, and Trent clamped down hard on his hand. Steve shook him loose, yelping, then inspected the damage: four little puncture marks on the fleshy part of his thumb. Not too bad, he thought. He ignored Alec's advice to go to the emergency room, quickly washed and bandaged the bite, and went back to hauling furniture from the house into the back yard.

The next morning, Steve woke up with a red streak running most of the way up his arm. The belated emergency room visit turned into a two-day hospitalization, with Steve hooked up to IV antibiotics.

The following morning I sat at the kitchen table, gazing out the window into our tattered-looking back yard, trying not to let my worries get the best of me. I had another day of selling off our possessions, before heading over to the hospital for visiting hours. Alec appeared and took stock of the situation.

"You need to play some music, Mom."

"I'm not in the mood."

A moment of hesitation, then: "I'll play with you."

It was a major concession, and we both knew it.

Neither boy had shown much interest in joining the family band. Nate had opted out with his unlikely choice of instruments: bagpipe chanter, baritone horn, electric keyboard. Alec, as a budding rock guitarist, was a slightly better candidate. But he'd always declined firmly when we invited him to play. Until now.

Alec left briefly and then reappeared with an electric guitar. At sixteen, after three years of round-the-clock playing, he'd blossomed into a talented musician. We seldom saw him without an instrument in hand, and most of our conversations took place over the steady backdrop of electric guitar riffs.

At that moment, playing accordion was the last thing on my mind. But I couldn't refuse Alec's touching offer to play with me.

Alec and I played a couple of tunes together—a waltz, to match my spirits, and then a fast two-step, to raise them up. It was just enough to get me on my feet again, without pushing my luck with my reluctant accompanist. It helped to be reminded of the two constants I could count on, my family and my music, as I faced the uncertain future ahead.

In the past year, as possibility had shifted into probability, I felt growing turmoil whenever I thought about leaving the place where I had lived for so long. I had moved from Cleveland to the Chicago suburbs when I was fifteen, and I had spent most of the last thirty years in the city itself. I considered it my home. It's not that life was perfect in Chicago. But there was comfort in its familiarity, in the personal ties we had established, in the history we all had here. And I feared change, especially at this stage in life—Steve and I in our forties, Nate turning thirteen, Alec beginning his junior year in high school.

I found myself drawn to the music of Iris Dement, a singer-songwriter Steve had introduced to me a few years earlier, after hearing her on public radio. "She has your kind of voice," he'd said. These days, I listened mostly to Cajun music, but Steve was right: something about her quirky, country-flavored singing appealed to me.

One particular song of hers, "Our Town," haunted me. In her drawling voice, steel guitar keening in the background, Iris Dement sang a tale of a woman preparing to leave her small town. Her history unfolds, against a loping rhythm that sounds like a Cajun shuffle: her first kiss, her first love, the bar where she met her man forty years ago, her babies, her parents' graves. All of it is rooted there, in the fading town she's decided to leave.

As I listened to her sing, I felt she could be telling my story. Uprooting yourself from the place that has become a part of you, leaving behind pieces of yourself, in search of—what? Better opportunities, perhaps. You take it on faith.

Sometimes, I found that listening to a sad song helped me feel better. But this one only magnified my sadness and sense of isolation. After a few minutes with Iris, I'd have to slip into the bathroom to cry. Then I would dry my eyes and give myself a fierce pep talk: "Get hold of yourself. No one else is all worked up about this, not even the boys." Then I'd remind myself: "You moved a few times, as a kid. And you survived."

It was true. No one else saw this move as a major upheaval. Steve had been absorbed in his own midlife quest, and now he had the satisfaction of finally succeeding. Many of our friends sounded impressed, even envious, as though we'd fulfilled some universal dream of moving to California. Even those who would never do such a thing themselves claimed to admire our "bravery" in taking such a big step. And the protests I'd expected from Alec and Nate never materialized. Perhaps they, like Steve, had grown tired of the school they'd attended since they were toddlers.

But instead of finding this reassuring, I ended up feeling even more alone with my feelings, wondering what was wrong with me.

Soon after Danny's spring visit to Chicago, Steve flew to the West Coast for an interview that turned out to be mostly a formality. So it was settled: we would be moving to California. I sent Danny a note right away. When we flew out in May to look for a house, I called him from the French Hotel in Berkeley, where we were staying.

"I'll come by and holler at you guys," he said. He sounded happy to hear from us.

I went downstairs to the open-air coffee house on North Shattuck Avenue to wait for Danny. He seemed such a dashing figure that day, as I waited among the latté drinkers, watching him approach.

He drove up in a car that struck me as flashy, although it was nothing more than a midsized American sedan, a couple of years old, clean and well kept. What was I expecting—that he would ride up on a horse, or appear at the side of the road, hiking along with an accordion on his back, like some French-speaking vision from one of the songs that filled my head?

He was all dressed up in a three-piece suit. Through the rear window of the car, I glimpsed a wide-brimmed, western-style hat. We hugged in greeting. I noticed he smelled slightly of aftershave. I pulled back, startled. This was not the image I carried from those summers at music camp, when Danny favored casual attire: slacks and loose shirts, topped off with one of those billed caps sported by all the men.

Danny was a striking-looking man, although it had taken some time for this to dawn on me. One of my single friends had remarked on it when he visited Chicago. She refused to believe that I'd never noticed "that look" she claimed to see in Danny's eyes. I'd protested. "His eyes? I'm too busy studying his hands!"

But my friend was right. Danny was a broad-shouldered man nearing sixty—who could have passed for forty. His chiseled cheekbones, straight black hair, and piercing dark eyes reflected the part of his heritage that was, as he put it, Indian. He never had much use for politically correct terms like "Native American" or "African American"—and he didn't usually bother to spell out what went into the rich, complex lineage of a Louisiana Creole.

I led Danny back upstairs to my family, into a two-room suite the French Hotel brochure described as "Euro-style." I introduced him to Alec and Nate, who mumbled noncommittal adolescent greetings before they turned back to the television screen. We moved on to the adjoining room, where Steve opened the bottle of wine he had bought for the occasion.

Danny spoke easily about his life in California. He had lived all over: briefly in Los Angeles, then in San Francisco, and now in Fairfield, a town halfway to Sacramento. He had even lived in Berkeley for a time, and he often played there. He pointed out to us that we were across the street from Chez Panisse.

"I've played there lots of times, on Bastille Day," Danny said. "I've been knowing Alice Waters for years."

Steve and I had read about the renowned restaurant, but didn't realize we were sitting in the heart of Berkeley's so-called gourmet ghetto. And we were too ignorant to be impressed by Danny's casual reference to the establishment's founder, the high priestess of California cuisine.

After an hour of visiting, Danny had to head off to a family celebration. "A child's birthday party," as he put it, with a touch of formality. Before he left, he had one final suggestion.

"You guys doing anything tonight? There's a band you could go hear. A new zydeco group, Tete Rouge. The accordion player, Ed, he learned from me. He's pretty good. He's a red-haired guy. Guess that's how they came up with the name."

The words were off-hand, but you couldn't miss the pride in Danny's voice. We told him, with apologies, that we just didn't have time, but we'd be sure to see this new band after we moved to California.

The hour with Danny had left me off-kilter. I was used to seeing him at music camp, a magical but slightly unreal place that allows you to step out of ordinary time. Now, I had suddenly glimpsed Danny on his home turf, a cosmopolitan setting where he was obviously at ease. More than just miles separated the West Virginia mountains from the San Francisco Bay Area, and I was having some difficulty making the shift. Danny sensed this, and later he'd tease me about it.

"Remember that first time you saw me in California?" he'd say, with that characteristic twinkle in his eyes. He always did like to keep people off balance.

So in the midst of my unrest, I tried to take comfort in one thing: I was moving on to something better musically, whatever else might be in store in California. In the past year, the Cajun scene in Chicago had begun to feel diminished. Attendance at the public dances had fallen off, and they began to happen less frequently. Everyone had started to move on, and Steve and I weren't sure where we fit.

Increasingly, I looked outside the local Cajun music scene for sustenance—to visiting musicians, to our own trips to Louisiana, and to music camp. I threw myself into guitar classes at the Old Town School of Folk Music, and I felt the pull of other music communities.

It was as though I had come to live in two worlds. I had my regular life, anchored by my familiar world of family, work, and friends. I had constructed this life in Chicago, slowly, over the past thirty years. But now I was preparing to step away from it.

I also had this newer music world I had come to inhabit. It was an alluring "other life" that had crept in unannounced, claiming time and place, slowly filling in the empty spaces I didn't even know existed. I'd tried to domesticate the music life, to share it with Steve and the boys, to strike a balance. Mostly, I had succeeded, but sometimes it still seemed to call to me like a secret lover, a link to a hidden life. The music offered a path to a private, shadowy side of myself I couldn't reach any other way.

Now everything had suddenly reversed itself. The stable life, the orderly rows in my garden, had started to disappear. And the other life, the delicious mystery of the music, was emerging as the point of stability, perhaps even the core of the new life in California I was about to enter.

But I needed them both: the orderly rows and the wilder flowers in between. The ordinary and the transcendent. Each depended on the other.

Even though I had moments of giddy excitement at the thought of entering Danny Poullard's orbit in California, I couldn't abandon myself to those feelings for long. No matter how inviting the music community in California might be, I had no guarantee of finding a place there. And not even the music I loved could make up for the sadness of leaving home—and the uncertainty of starting life over in an unfamiliar place.

Part Two   Danse de Poullard

Twelve First Jam at Danny's

Steve and I sat in slow-moving freeway traffic, heading north from Berkeley toward Danny Poullard's house in Fairfield. The heavy August air magnified the oppressiveness of rush hour. Since I hadn't started my new job, at a mental health agency an hour south of Berkeley, I hadn't faced the frenzied Wednesday night rush that would soon become part of my weekly routine. Still, I felt impatient and keyed up, unable to shake that queasy mixture of excitement and anxiety.

I had been waiting so long for Danny's weekly jam sessions to get started again. At least it felt like a long time, even though we'd been living in California for just over a month. But when you have just driven across the country and settled into a strange new place—well, the experience of time is altered.

I thought back a few weeks, to our introduction to the local music scene. We had arrived in Berkeley just in time to attend a special celebration: a dance and "roast" honoring Danny for his contributions to the Bay Area Louisiana French music community.

We had learned about this months earlier, when an out-of-state music friend contacted us with the news. A group called the California Friends of Louisiana French Music (CFLFM) had begun to organize an event honoring Danny. It would be held at Ashkenaz, the renowned world music club in Berkeley where we'd first seen him play a few years back. We got in touch with the president of the CFLFM, a dancer named Jim Phillips, who filled us in on the details. Don't tell Danny, he instructed us. They wanted to surprise him.

Ashkenaz, it turned out, had just reopened, following the shocking death in December of the owner. A disruptive patron, angry at being expelled, had returned and shot David Nadel, the much-loved human rights activist who founded the club in the early seventies. For a time, the future looked uncertain. But then a group of supporters reopened the club as a nonprofit community arts organization. So the "roast" for Danny Poullard would also celebrate the return of Ashkenaz.

When we approached the club, I felt excited at the thought of seeing Danny again—but also tentative. I hadn't heard from him since we arrived in Berkeley ten days earlier, even though I had left a couple of messages on his home answering machine. I'd tried to push aside my disappointment at the lack of response.

"Danny won't be here today." The man at the door took our money, then handed us a program. "He's in the hospital. Got a bad infection from a spider bite, last week when he was in West Virginia."

West Virginia? It took a moment to register. While we were driving across the country, and then waiting in a series of motels for the moving van to arrive, all our music friends were at Cajun-Creole week at Augusta. I'd been too preoccupied to think much about it.

Danny had tried to ignore the spider bite, I later heard. But after he returned home, it got worse, until he ended up hospitalized and on IV antibiotics—where he remained for a week. Such a strange parallel to Steve's own cat bite disaster, during our final month in Chicago.

The organizers tried to make the best of it at Ashkenaz. They even set up a phone hook-up to Danny's hospital room. Still, the celebration was festive, and—even without the guest of honor—it served as the first step in our introduction to this new music community.

The CFLFM had invited all sorts of dignitaries and honored guests. The former mayor of Eunice read a proclamation from the lieutenant governor of Louisiana. Marc and Ann Savoy had flown in, to honor Danny and take a turn playing.

Danny's family sat at a special table up front, to the side of the stage. His mother—tiny, spry, white-haired—and two brothers had come from Texas, where most of the family lived. Danny's wife, Ruby, looking stately and beautiful, was there. I spotted a daughter holding a baby grandchild, along with several other little girls decked out in ruffled Sunday-best dresses.

People passed around a microphone on the dance floor and told funny stories about Danny. On stage, a rotating line-up of musicians took turns playing and telling their own tales. Aside from Marc and Ann, they were local musicians, although some had Louisiana roots.

Danny's Protégés: that's what the printed program called them. I read my way down the long list, smiling when I came to Harton's name. How nice, I thought—he's been gone for at least five years, but they've included him. Then a bigger surprise: my own name. I felt touched and honored—but I had a nagging sense of not belonging on a list of real musicians.

I recognized the name of one of the emcee's—Miss Freida, a Cajun woman who had been a friend of Harton's. She was a storyteller and an accordionist—and something of a character, he said. No wonder they'd been friends.

When I figured out who she was, I walked over to introduce myself. She was a pretty woman, around my age, with the outsized charm of a Cajun Minnie Pearl. "Well hello! I knew y'all were coming out here." Like she'd been expecting me. It turned out she'd heard all about us, too, from Harton.

"Would you like to play? Or say something about Danny?"

"Oh, no." I was surprised—but flattered. "Thanks for inviting me, though."

"We'll talk later, all right?" Another tune was starting, and Miss Freida had already been claimed by a dance partner.

I looked out into the sea of bodies, remembering our first visit three years earlier. Once again, I was dazzled by the vibrant, diverse crowd—and seduced by their sweaty harmonious energy. But this time I could recognize some of the dancers. I spotted Freida. And there was Jim, the CFLFM president—a hearty guy in cowboy hat and boots, constantly in motion, whether he was on or off the dance floor.

I thought I recognized a few other people, too, from the excursions Steve and I had already started to make into the Cajun-zydeco scene. The previous Sunday, we'd danced to a zydeco band at Bobby's Back Door Cajun Barbeque, a jumping place in Richmond with the familiar, gritty ambience of a Chicago blues bar. A few days later, we'd taken the boys to a restaurant called Caribbean Spice, where a Cajun band was playing. Despite the strangeness of our circumstances—living out of suitcases—I couldn't help feeling like the proverbial kid in the candy shop.

I noticed a couple who looked familiar. Then it hit me—I'd seen them on a video Harton has shown us back in Chicago, a homemade affair filmed at a Catholic church dance. My attention had been on Danny and his accordion. But Harton kept his eyes on the dancers. "Look, there they are! Robbie and Shirley are the best around. Everybody back in California wants to dance like them." He'd inclined his head toward the middle-aged Creole couple gliding across the small screen.

Seeing them now, in person, I could understand what Harton meant. Surrounded by hundreds of serious dancers—including some flashy ones—this couple stood out. Not because they did much of that athletic foot stomping and twirling or indulged in any intertwined-thigh maneuvers. They were too subtle for that, completely in harmony with the music—and with each other. Shirley, ladylike and refined, balanced her husband's bolder steps. Harton admitted he had tried to pick up some moves from Robbie.

I encountered them later, as they helped set out food for the vegetarian potluck in the back room. I introduced myself to Robbie, explaining I had recognized them from a video. If he was taken aback, he didn't let on. He'd smiled when he learned of the connection.

"Oh, of course! Harton. How is he?" His manner was courtly.

He and Shirley, I would soon learn, were close friends of Danny's, founding board members of the CFLFM, and arbiters of the local dance scene. Although they were welcoming to a fault, they insisted that newcomers respect their Louisiana culture. Shirley had issued edicts for dancers, including this one: Ladies Don't Stomp!

Danny came home from the hospital a few days after the big Ashkenaz celebration, and he resumed public playing almost immediately. When we finally caught up with him, his response did not disappoint me.

It was a week after the roast, and Danny was playing with the California Cajun Orchestra at Ashkenaz. He spotted us on the dance floor, planted in front of the stage, and smiled down at us from on high.

"These are my friends Blair and Steve. They just moved here from Chicago."

People standing nearby smiled and clapped. One or two even came over to say hello.

Danny invited us to his next gig, at a ranch party up in the hills somewhere. It really was a horse ranch, owned by a Creole family. They'd set up an outdoor wooden dance floor surrounded by bales of hay, along with a barbecue. The CFLFM had a cultural booth, and we saw a few familiar faces there.

One man who was busy videotaping set down his camera and came over to say hello, when he spotted Steve's Sheryl Cormier t-shirt.

"Y'all know Sheryl?" he drawled, extending his hand. "My name is Elton. They're friends of mine. She and her band stayed with me last time they played in California." He was from Louisiana originally—someone else who'd been part of the Creole migration, as I'd learn later from Danny. Cousin to another man who'd asked me to dance, our first night at Bobby's Back Door.

I was starting to feel this was one big neighborhood, where chances are you'd know somebody who knew somebody else or was maybe related. It was a whole different way of relating to people—and I liked it.

Danny seemed to be keeping an eye out for us. And he'd always notice when someone asked me to dance. "Oh—that guy. He always goes after the new women. But don't worry. I had my eye on you. I don't miss a thing from up there on stage." He wanted to make sure we met the right people, introducing us to anyone who might be standing around. "These are my friends—they just moved here from Chicago" is how he always put it.

Friends? Even though our relationship had been evolving in the direction of greater ease and informality, I still felt more like his disciple. Danny had been my once-a-summer mentor, and now he was taking me—Steve too—under his wing. It was disarming. And unnerving.

It hadn't been easy to develop a relationship with Danny. During my first Augusta class, we didn't connect at all. I'd been my usual reticent self, and the class had been particularly large. There was considerable interest in this new teacher who was said to have a unique approach to the Cajun accordion. His style was different from the other instructors, whether Cajun or Creole or "Améri-cain," because Danny's story was different.

Danny, a Louisiana-born Creole, had moved to California in the early 1960s, joining a migration that began in the 1940s. Many people from Louisiana, Creoles in particular, had moved west during those years, drawn by wartime economic opportunities and the promise of a more open social environment.

Danny never played music when he was growing up in Louisiana or Texas, even though he came from a long line of musicians, and his father, John, was an accomplished accordionist. When Danny was young, his father had stopped playing, after getting shot on the way home from a dance. John Poullard didn't pick up the accordion again for years—and he discouraged his children from playing.

Danny didn't pick up the music until after he'd lived in San Francisco for some time, when he was into his thirties. But once he decided to learn, he was determined to master the accordion, even though a cousin taunted him that he'd never make it.

Danny learned from others in the Louisiana expatriate community, musicians who played for house parties and Catholic church dances. He started out on electric bass, then eased into the accordion. He listened to recordings, trying to match what he heard. And eventually he was able to learn from his father, who had finally resumed playing, after Danny had grown up and left home.

Danny told stories at Augusta of practicing for hours, wearing out the grooves in his LP's, then going to work the next morning on three hours of sleep. Sometimes he'd even call up his younger brother Ed in Texas and ask him to play one of the old family tunes over the phone, so he could get it right. Danny was determined to learn—and to learn it all.

He ended up mastering the traditional Cajun accordion styles—the classic versions of Cajun dance hall tunes from giants like Lawrence Walker and Aldus Roger and Nathan Abshire. But he could also play that distinctive, old-time Creole sound that had been passed down in his own family. He had bridged the two traditions, Cajun and Creole, in a way few others had.

So Danny remained an intimidating figure to me. He'd been hard on himself, and he was equally demanding of his students. By the end of the third summer at Augusta, he decided to lay it out for me. He had some definite ideas about how I needed to change my approach to the accordion.

For starters, Danny corrected the position of my right hand and

The Poullard Family in Crowley, Louisiana, 1984. Photo copyright © by Chris Strachwitz. Seated, left to right: Danny Poullard and Edward Poullard. Standing, left to right: unknown, John Poullard, Clarence LeDay.

arm and told me to shorten the thumb strap. Use a rubber band, he suggested, offering me one. The idea was to bring my hand nearer to the button board, my arm closer to my body, in order to have more control of the accordion.

"I wonder why none of your other teachers bothered to tell you this," he'd remarked. It was a pointed observation, a question left hanging in the air.

I did as Danny suggested, but these sudden changes made me feel awkward and unnatural. I'd been playing for six years, but now the accordion felt like an alien instrument. I was in unfamiliar territory—like being forced to use my right hand, rather than my left. Instead of more control, now I had none at all.

"I feel like you're telling me I have to start over from the beginning." I sounded more plaintive than I intended.

Danny just looked at me and smiled. "That's right."

He also convinced me that I needed to simplify my playing. "You make things too hard for yourself. A lot of you guys do that."

Many of us were getting ahead of ourselves, Danny explained.

We were trying to "jump all over the keyboard," to add octaves and chords or "blends" before we had mastered the basics. To Danny, "the basics" meant being able to play a simple version of a tune, one note at a time, with feeling, rhythm, and embellishment—everything that gave it that unmistakable Louisiana flavor.

It was true because we all felt such urgency about learning. In myself and in others, I could see that tendency to apply the standard formulas for adding layers of complexity to a tune prematurely, without having the right foundation.

You did not even need all ten buttons to do it right, Danny would say, trying to make his point. "Listen," he'd say. "I'll play a tune on just these four buttons—or just these three."

He'd let his hand hover over the middle buttons—5,6,7—home base. And he'd play a whole tune that way, with more energy and feeling, more Louisiana spice, than seemed possible, with just those three buttons. I listened, watched, taped it all.

"That's what you have to work on," he'd said, the last summer I had seen him at Augusta. And he left me with one final piece of advice: "Blair, you have too much going on in your head. You just need to play!"

It had been a year since Danny had "re-programmed" me, as he called it, a year since he'd heard me play the accordion. What if I didn't measure up? I worried about it, as we made our way through the slow-moving rush-hour traffic. To add to my uncertainty, I had no idea who else would be at this jam.

Danny's jam sessions were something of an institution. In the Bay Area, they had been popular among aspiring musicians for some time. But once Danny began teaching at Augusta, where people from all over the country gathered, his jam sessions became even more widely known.

There really wasn't anyone, even in Louisiana, who did what Danny did: regularly share his music with anyone who wanted to learn from him. I'd heard the sessions were held in his garage once or twice a week. I also knew Danny did not accept money for this. His reward was in helping preserve his Louisiana French culture, and in the almost parental pride he took in all those musicians in the Bay Area's Cajun and zydeco bands he had personally shaped.

Danny had given us directions when we saw him at the ranch

party, but we still managed to turn off at the wrong exit. We eventually found our way to North Texas Road, and from there it was just a few blocks to his house. In some ways, that remains my clearest memory, the one I am certain comes from that evening and no other: approaching his house for the first time.

I had no idea what Fairfield was like. But I had imagined Danny in a small town, with a bit of a rural flavor. Mostly, I pictured the garage: a weathered, comfortable old place, set off behind the house. Inside, I imagined a group of people gathered in a respectful circle around Danny. He probably lived in a comfortable, sprawling ranch house with a country feeling, simple and airy. Like some of the people we'd visited in Louisiana: Harton and his father, the Millers, or the Cormiers.

Instead, we found ourselves turning off the highway and into a middle class suburban subdivision, with winding streets named for flowers, matching split-level houses with attached garages, small neat lawns with decorative statues, and a grassy park-like area with children playing baseball. It was like any number of communities that sprang up all over America in the sixties and seventies. It felt familiar to me. Too familiar.

I felt a twinge of disappointment. I had spent much of my early life in suburban settings that looked not too different from this one. But I had left for the city, in search of a life that was different. Had this wild, passionate music that I had come to love really brought me back?

When I took a closer look, I had to admit that this was not like returning home. This was California, not the Midwest. The place was different, the people were different. And Danny's household was certainly different.

Danny greeted us warmly at the front door to his split-level home. "Hey! You guys made it. Come on in."

We passed briefly through the house, too quickly to take much notice of the surroundings, and then into the attached garage.

It felt like entering a cave. My eyes strained to adjust to the changing illumination, until shapes started to emerge out of the shadows. I saw immediately that the garage was crowded, very crowded. There were no cars inside—just Danny's motorcycle, and even that was a tight fit. Gradually, I took in more: clothing, chairs, refrigerators, saddles, toys, instruments, festival posters on the walls. This was Danny's domain, a setting in creative disarray. Weeks would pass before all the details registered.

It turned out Steve and I were the only ones there that night—another surprise.

"I tried to call up this guy Mark, but he can't come tonight." Danny sounded apologetic.

Attendance had dropped off recently. Danny tried to explain. One guy had recently married, so he'd stopped coming regularly. And then the most recent group of regulars had formed their own band, so now they were often busy with practices and gigs.

I thought I heard a little regret in Danny's voice, along with the pride. Maybe I was thinking about my own teenage sons, and anticipating the future.

"It must be like when your kids grow up and leave home, and they don't come back to visit."

Danny agreed, looking sad for a moment, but then he took out his accordion.

We had brought along an offering of red wine, and Danny was well supplied himself. We knew by now he preferred wine to beer, the more typical choice back home in Louisiana or east Texas, where Danny's family had moved when he was a teenager. But he'd adapted to California ways; he'd lived here since he was a young man just out of the service, the South left behind him.

It was a long night, where everything flowed: the wine, the conversation, and the music. Instruments passed back and forth: Steve on fiddle and guitar, me on guitar and triangle. Danny played accordion, guitar, a little fiddle. We wouldn't get home until two in the morning.

I remember watching Danny play the accordion, studying his hands. Maybe if I watched closely enough, I could figure out how he got all that sound out of that little box.

Danny's fingers danced lightly, moving all over the button board. No need for him to follow the "less is more " advice he doled out to his students. The graceful, almost delicate movements of his fingers were a little incongruous, compared to the appearance of his hands.

Danny had large and powerful hands, work-roughened, with fingers as thick as small sausage links. He had built a career around those hands—but not just as a musician. "I always had a job," is how Danny put it. He was proud that his music was a hobby—his passion, but not his livelihood.

Danny had started out as a meat-cutter, working in packing plants in San Francisco. Eventually, he a got a good job with the government, working his way up to supervisor of the food services at first one, then another, military base in the Bay Area.

"At the Presidio they actually wanted me to wear a suit and tie!" His tone suggested that this was probably the most unreasonable demand an employer might make. Danny had recently retired from his last job. But his hands still looked like they knew what to do with a knife.

I felt completely filled up by the sound of his music. It was a feeling I'd had many times over the past three years. Although I had fallen in love with Cajun music before I'd ever heard of Danny, I had come to feel that there was something distinctive about his sound. Perhaps it was some echo of the old-time Creole style of his father. I couldn't analyze the difference, but I knew how it made me feel.

I had tried to explain all this to Danny the previous summer, when I wrote to him after we returned home from Augusta. I thanked him for what he had taught me and assured him that the awkward "re-programming" had been well worth it. However, I also wanted to tell him what his music meant to me.

"When I listen to other people play," I wrote, "it's like riding on a fast train, moving steadily along. But listening to your music is like being carried along in a boat, rocking on the waves—surging forward, then falling back a little, then surging forward again."

Danny never wrote back. I didn't really expect it. But after we had been living in California for a few months, he finally brought up that letter.

"It made me feel like crying," he confessed. "After I read it, I had to take a walk around the park across the street."

Danny's surprising admission almost made me cry. He was a man who rarely lost his composure. He told me this story on two separate occasions, as though he wanted to make sure I didn't forget it. Later, Freida would tell me he'd even shown the letter to her.

But on that first night, sitting in Danny's garage, wrapped in his music, I hadn't yet heard that story. I still saw him as an invulnerable mentor, and I couldn't understand his treating me as a welcomed guest. I'd always tended to idealize my teachers, no matter whether they were high school French teachers, professors, psychoanalytic supervisors—or accordionists.

Danny had this strange way of knowing what you were feeling, without much being said. Toward the middle of the evening, he stopped suddenly, looked at me closely, and demanded: "What can I do to make you think of me as your friend?"

He was smiling as he spoke, but also a little challenging. It seemed like a serious question he was posing, one that needed an answer. I didn't really have an answer.

We continued to play. Then, well into the evening, he put down his accordion.

"Blair, why don't you play?" Danny looked at me, waiting.

It was the moment of truth, the one I had been anticipating and fearing all evening—especially once I realized it would be just the three of us in the garage that night.

I picked up my own accordion, trying to remember everything Danny had shown me about the right way to position my hand in the thumb strap.

I started with a waltz. Since it was slower, I figured I was less likely to trip myself up. Then I took a deep breath and launched into a two-step—always more of a challenge for me. Finally, I stopped, trying not to appear too concerned with Danny's reaction.

There was a brief chasm of silence.

"You sound great." He was smiling. Beaming.

It was a clear pronouncement, a judgment that left no room for anything from me but a simple "thanks."

I was surprised, relieved—and very happy. This was the most positive endorsement I had ever received from Danny, and I let the feeling wash over me.

He considered a moment, then added, "You're even doing better than one or two of my California students." He smiled with a satisfaction that I didn't quite understand.

Perhaps it was Danny's way of reassuring both of us that I had benefited from his teaching, even though it had been sporadic and long distance. Or maybe he just wanted to spur me on.

It would be a long time before I felt it again—such whole-hearted approval from Danny. He could be tough on people. He rarely offered direct praise, at least to someone's face. It just wasn't his way.

On this night, though, there was no more room for doubt and worry in Danny's garage. I was a voyager who had finally found a safe harbor, a place to rock gently on the water before venturing out again. I felt safely contained, but free and expansive at the same time. The music kept on swirling around us and through us as the hours wore on, the laughter flowing as freely as the wine. Time stood still, boundaries dissolved, and the world dropped away. We rode the waves of sound that whole night long.

Thirteen Musical Chairs

I was sitting in Danny's garage at the regular Wednesday night jam session, trying my best to stay out of everyone's way. Dennis, our old friend from Chicago, sat to the right, playing my accordion with exuberance. Every time he opened the bellows, I got jabbed in the side. I tried to shuffle my chair to the left, but I ran into Maureen, leader of a popular local Cajun band—perched on a high stool, looking good in her short dress and pastel tights. She sounded good, too, on her latest instrument, a fiddle, while she waited for her turn on the accordion. I tried to back up a little, but felt something pressing into my back. It was impossible to widen the circle. Such hard work, trying not to take up too much space. I tried to compress myself—easier with a triangle in my hands, more of a challenge when I switched to guitar.

Space was always at a premium in the garage, even with the Poullard family cars permanently banished to the driveway. Usually, the only vehicles parked inside were Danny's motorcycle, along with the ride-on toy car belonging to the little girl of the house. But on this night, even the Harley had been moved outside, because Danny was anticipating a bigger crowd than usual.

When Steve and I first stepped inside the garage that evening, with our three Chicago friends close behind, we could see Danny had made some serious preparations. He had cleared a large area of the floor and had arranged a dozen chairs in a neat circle. The usual assortment of plastic glasses, along with a few bottles of red wine, sat on the wooden accordion case positioned in the center of the circle—Danny's version of a coffee table, jam-style.

Creating a clearing in Danny's garage was like pushing back the vegetation in a tropical rainforest. An optimistic act, but the effect would be temporary. Outside the perimeter of the circle, the obstacle course remained, threatening to engulf anyone who entered: Racks of clothing, in storage for some unknown purpose. Piles of clothing, in transit to somewhere. A couple of working refrigerators. Kids' toys. Tack from horses long since sold.

When Danny invited someone to the garage, he'd often say: "Don't worry about bringing an instrument. I have whatever you need." That was the truth. They were everywhere—on the floor, in boxes, on storage selves, on overhead racks. You never knew what might materialize from Danny's collection.

Accordions predominated. Most were single-row Cajun accordions, in a range of keys. But Danny had a few others: the triple-row and piano accordions, in case he wanted to venture into zydeco and Tex-Mex. Even a tiny child's toy Cajun accordion, made in China, like the one we'd bought at a gas station in Louisiana. He owned several guitars—acoustic and electric, a few fiddles, a bass or two, several triangles. Probably a few other instruments I hadn't yet seen.

Finding a place in Danny's garage was never a simple matter. Late arrivals might end up wedged into an uncomfortable spot or perched on some awkward surface—like an accordion case, pressed into service when the available chairs were filled. I sometimes found myself sitting on the periphery of the circle, feeling uncomfortable. And very peripheral.

Finding a place musically could be even more complicated. The chairs were visible, at least—unlike the complex set of rules, roles, personal relationships, and conflicting expectations that determined what happened at a jam. After exploring this hidden terrain for close to three years, I was still finding my way.

Finding a place used to feel easier. We had moved to California at a time when jam attendance had fallen off. Sometimes no more than the three of us—Steve, myself, and Danny—holed up in the garage.

Most nights, a fiddler named Mark, a gentle soul who lived nearby, joined us. Ed, a warm, sturdy man with a long red pony tail—leader of the zydeco band Danny had urged us to see when we first visited Berkeley—sometimes stopped in to visit or maybe play a little accordion. He and Mark were both seasoned musicians, adept at multiple instruments and many styles of music. But they were also tolerant and accepting, and we couldn't help but feel at ease around them.

Their chairs were empty now. First Mark, then Ed, had died suddenly, about a year apart. Mark in his mid-forties, Ed a little older, seemingly in good health. Danny had been close to both men. He sometimes cried when he spoke of them, late at night, when there weren't too many people around.

But there was a natural ebb and flow to life in the garage, something I failed to understand at first. After our first six months in California, the jams began to get bigger again. Danny's spirits rose whenever new students arrived—and especially when old protégés drifted back, with their talk of gigs, shifting band line-ups, venues, recordings. It was shop talk from a world I envied, but feared I'd never join.

I enjoyed the music and camaraderie when the garage was full. But sometimes I couldn't help but miss the more intimate times I remembered from our first months in California. Now and then, I caught myself feeling displaced. Then I felt guilty. I knew Danny's gifts deserved to be shared, and I could tell he was in his element on nights like this one, surrounded by students and admirers. It still amazed me, the way he gave away his music so freely. The price of admission was nothing more than an honest desire to learn and perhaps a bottle of red wine.

Steve and I had made a point of arriving early, because we knew finding a place would present a bigger challenge than usual. We'd heard that a former jam regular who had moved away might be visiting tonight. A few newcomers were also expected. Sure enough, Danny was just finishing up a session with a new accordion student when we arrived. Someone else was about to enter the fold.

Gradually, the empty chairs filled up. The air became saturated with sound, mournful waltzes and rocking two-steps, simple tales of love and loss sung in Louisiana French. Eventually we were an even dozen, filling the garage with our talk, gossip, laughter—and the quieter currents that remained unspoken. As always, Danny sat at the center, presiding over it all. It was easy to forget we were in a suburban subdivision in Fairfield, and not somewhere back in Louisiana or Texas.

On this night, I had a simple goal. I had been excited when our old friends from the jam group in Chicago—Denise, Earl, and Dennis—decided to visit. I felt lucky to be living in the midst of this

Jam session in Danny Poullard's garage, Fairfield, California, 2000. Photo courtesy of Denise and Earl Thompson.

vibrant Louisiana French music community, and I wanted to share as much as I could with them. Above all, I wanted them to experience the most important part of my new musical world: Danny's weekly jam sessions. I also wanted my friends—especially Dennis, a fellow accordionist—to have the chance to be heard.

I planned to set my own needs aside for the night—if I could. But I had grown more self-assured since we'd left Chicago, and I could finally admit it: I also wanted a chance to be heard myself.

Although my problems with self-confidence continued to surface, I did know my playing had improved—thanks to the immersion I'd undergone these past few years in California. An authentic Louisiana-inspired sound surrounded me, and I couldn't help but soak it up. Steve and I heard live music at least twice a week, between Danny's jams and the dance venues in the Bay Area. It was like a year-round Augusta.

But something else was different, beyond the sheer quantity of the music. I now had a single, coherent accordion sound as a model. Danny's music dominated most of my serious listening: the live music that fueled our dancing, the weekly jams, the tapes I poured over during my solo practice sessions, the music in my earphones when

I took the long train ride to work. I treasured my homemade tapes from his garage, crude though they were, because I believed they gave me the best and purest accordion sound I'd ever heard.

Just like a child growing up in a traditional culture, I absorbed the music naturally, from a few people close at hand. In the old days in Louisiana, I might have had a father or uncle who played, neighbors who made music, or the regular band at the local dance hall. Now, I had the constant example of Danny's music—and his presence—to keep me on the right track.

Despite my growing confidence, I still wrestled with conflicting needs I couldn't always reconcile: a deep desire to play—eroded by self-doubt; a need for recognition—undercut by a wish to hide out; an appreciation of others—tempered by envy and jealousy. The unseemly gumbo never stopped simmering. Making music had opened me up in ways that nothing else ever had, and I didn't always like what it exposed.

In the last few weeks, I had been working on myself, trying to cultivate an attitude of Zen-like detachment about these jams. I told myself things like this:

"Whatever happens will happen."

"Roll with the punches."

"Check your ego at the door."

"Making music is not a contest or a race."

"The other musicians are not your rivalrous siblings."

"Remember, you can always write about it later."

These little mantras, while not original or profound, at least made my musical life less turbulent.

As the jam unfolded, I took pleasure in watching our visiting friends play, garnering appreciative comments. Dennis beamed like a schoolboy at the praise from Danny, who had been his teacher at Augusta. It was easy to forget he was a classically trained pianist in his late fifties, a professional musician and teacher himself.

I wondered if I'd ever play with that kind of confidence. I felt the sharp, inevitable pang of envy.

After his first few tunes, Dennis offered the borrowed accordion back to me.

"No thanks. Why don't you keep going? I get plenty of chances to play." I was trying hard to do the right thing.

So Dennis continued. I knew the accordion would eventually make its way around to me, after I had deferred to several others. I would play a few tunes and then quickly pass it along to someone else, not wanting to overstay my time.

But for now, I tried to hold on to my place on the warped kitchen chair—wedged into a small space, trying to avoid flying elbows, bellows, and fiddle bows. Listening to the music that made my spirit dance, drinking red wine, enjoying the camaraderie. I tried to concentrate on maintaining an even rhythm with triangle or guitar, a steady background role in support of the others.

But it was hard work to keep trying to contract myself, to refrain from taking up too much space in the crowded garage.

There was another choice open to me, but I couldn't see it. Or perhaps the path was clear, but I wasn't ready to take it. When you are wedged into a circle so tightly you can hardly breathe, and you can't back up—you have to move forward. It's the only way, even if it means breaking away. It was a paradox, but I was just starting to face it: sometimes you have to leave the circle in order to enter it fully.

So much of my life in California had come to revolve around this music—and around Danny. He had been my foundation, my anchor in this new place. But sometimes the harbor felt confining, rather than safe. And much of the time I was still tossing on stormy seas.

It had been so different in Chicago, when Cajun music was an unsettling new passion, calling to me from somewhere outside the life I was leading. I had to reach out to discover it, and then work to incorporate it, striking a balance with all the other parts of my life. But when I came to California, the music had already staked its claim, so I established my new life around it.

In some ways, I clung to the music like a lifeline. As I'd feared, the move had been difficult for all of us. But I never anticipated such a strange and disturbing series of events to unfold during our first year—grim islands, large and small, in the midst of the sunny California landscape.

Steve started his new job with the painful knowledge that his new boss—and former mentor—had just been diagnosed with the terminal illness that would take her life the following year. A dark cloud also hovered over the new school year for Alec. In August, just before the start of his junior year, four Berkeley High students met violent deaths. Alec told us about the altars set up in the school courtyard, a multicultural memorial to four lost children: Latino, Laotian, black, and white.

Since money was tight, we decided to rent out the studio apartment at the back of the house. Our next-door neighbor, a social worker, recommended a young man she'd taken under her wing. He struck us as pleasant if offbeat: a casually employed earthquake retrofitter who also bought and sold vintage Pez dispensers. But our new tenant came and went at odd hours, drank too much, stopped paying rent on time—and eventually disappeared. When we finally entered the abandoned apartment, it looked like a crime scene—debris piled three feet deep, rotting food, pornographic videos, drug paraphernalia.

Alec felt lost at Berkeley High, so after a few months we enrolled him in a small independent school. He remained in California for just one unhappy year before returning to Chicago—where he moved in with my mother and completed senior year at his old school. From there, he'd headed off to college in New York. Nate had continued to struggle, and we hoped his recent transfer to the smaller school Alec had briefly attended would help him.

My own professional life had proven difficult to reestablish. The small agency where I found a position left me with a "sink or swim" feeling, and it had taken time to develop a stable practice. My work life felt compartmentalized, distant in both miles and feeling from the essence of who I was.

For me, the Louisiana French music community provided a point of stability—and a much more satisfying focus than work. Steve and I had an excess of riches at our disposal, between the local bands and the touring musicians from Louisiana. The monthly Cajun-zydeco calendar featured live music at least six nights a week.

Serious dancers followed the circuit. Ashkenaz in Berkeley, Bobby's Back Door in Richmond, Eagle's Hall in Alameda, and DeMarco's in Brisbane all had Cajun and zydeco bands, once or twice a week. Weekends brought special events like church dances, house parties, and festivals, along with other venues. Steve and I could have gone out every night of the week, but we had to be selective.

I always scanned the new monthly calendar for Danny's dates,

Danny Poullard playing in Brisbane, California, late 1990s. Photo copyright © by Chris Strachwitz.

then circled them and posted the calendar on our refrigerator. He performed with two groups: his main one, the California Cajun Orchestra—the CCO—along with a newer band, called simply "Danny and Friends." Steve and I rarely missed a gig. If we showed up late, Danny always glanced at his watch and said, "Hmmm, took you guys awhile to get here."

From the beginning, whenever we went out, Steve and I saw people we recognized. It was comforting, especially at first, to be able to count on an exchange of friendly greetings, even if the conversation never went much deeper. Little by little, we got to know people—mostly other musicians, but also dancers.

Within the first year, we became involved with the California Friends of Louisiana French Music. We started out attending the monthly CFLFM jam sessions, presided over by Danny. Then I began to submit regular articles to the newsletter. By the second year, I became secretary, after a friendly ambush at Bobby's Back Door, when a couple of the organization's officers recruited me.

By now, most of my personal relationships seemed to revolve

around the music scene. It was the closest thing to a community I had found in California—stronger, at least for me, than anything that had evolved from either of our jobs.

Still, I was feeling restless on that spring night in Danny's garage. The effort to stay on the sidelines, to not take up too much room—it was taking a toll. So much pressure. Sometimes I feared I might implode—or explode.

I needed to step back or step forward. I had to channel all that energy and frustration in a more productive direction. I just wasn't sure how to do it.

At least I had made a start. A year ago, I had started to put together my own band. Not because I felt driven to perform publicly. But after almost three years of nights like this in Danny's garage, I couldn't deny it: I needed something of my own.

Fourteen   Sauce Piquante

The parish gym was nearly empty when Steve and I walked in with our instruments on a gray afternoon in March. We saw little evidence of the festival we'd been expecting, aside from some Mardi Gras decorations scattered around.

KP approached us, straining under the weight of her electric bass and amp. Looking a little wan, as though she really did belong home in bed, nursing her cold. I felt a twinge of guilt for talking her into this.

"So where is everyone?" I figured maybe she'd know, since she'd arrived ahead of us, as usual.

"I heard most people left after the parade at noon. They'll be back later, for the evening dance."

Oh.

We passed through the gym and into the chilly parking lot. I scanned the craft displays and concession stands, shaking in the wind, until I finally spotted Shirley, over by the CFLFM booth. She had invited us here, to play at the annual St. Edward's Mardi Gras Festival her cousin helped organize. The warmth of Shirley's smile reminded me why I'd wanted us to do this. Just a little informal music, she'd suggested, a nice addition to the CFLFM's cultural display. No money was involved, but maybe it would provide some exposure to my fledgling band, along with a chance to contribute to the community.

I noticed another CFLFM member, decked out in beads and devil's horns—and with a corrugated metal rubboard already in place, covering his chest like armor. Not exactly what I'd anticipated. But we could probably use some rhythm support—especially since our new drummer couldn't make it, and we were "between guitarists" at the moment.

Shirley scurried away to find us somewhere to sit. She returned with low, sling-backed fabric chairs—with arms, not ideal for playing music, but I didn't have much choice, since I hadn't mastered the art of playing the accordion standing up. I sank down, immediately off balance, fighting against the strange sensation of being sucked into the collapsible chair.

A biting wind swept across the parking lot, and I imagined the rain couldn't be far behind. I pulled out my accordion and studied my song list, a slowly expanding collection of waltzes alternating with two-steps. We had just enough material for two short sets, sometimes a stretch for the two-hour dances the band had started to play last fall, but more than enough for today. So far, we'd had three public gigs, for a struggling Cajun dance club at a VFW Hall near San Jose, where the dancers barely outnumbered the musicians.

I started with "Lovebridge Waltz"—always a secure beginning. I could hear the familiar sound of Steve and KP joining in on fiddle and bass, along with the harsh scratching of the rubboard. Two couples started to dance on the pavement, between the booths. I began to work my way through the list, waltz followed by two-step, trying to sing. But the rising wind threw my voice right back at me. I heard the desultory bursts of applause after each tune. But I couldn't get comfortable. I kept leaning forward in the too-low chair. I couldn't feel the music.

Then my nose began to run. I alternated between playing an accordion lead, swiping awkwardly at my nose during the fiddle break, then playing again. Funny, I'd felt fine when I awoke that morning—even excited, looking forward to the first meeting of my new creative writing class and then music afterward. I had pictured a perfect day. But now I felt tired and sore all over.

Maybe I'd caught KP's cold at our last band practice. Pumping the bellows felt more difficult by the minute, especially with that heavy ache in my left shoulder starting to blossom into radiating pain. Then I put it together: I must be having a reaction to yesterday's tetanus shot.

The rain started falling, with a few sprinkles turning into heavy drops. We relocated inside, to the gym. Although much more comfortable for playing, the big church hall seemed to swallow up our unamplified sound.

"We could play up on the stage—the sound might carry better," someone suggested.

"No, I don't think so." I quickly vetoed that idea. "We'll be fine just playing down here on the floor, in front of the stage." I wanted to make sure no one confused us with the real band. We were just lagniappe, a little something extra, the appetizer before the main course.

The evening dance featured local accordionist Andrew Carrière, along with whatever band he'd put together for the occasion. I had to smile when I pictured him: a brawny, good-looking man with his trademark ponytail and those sleeveless vests that highlighted his massive arms. He had recently retired after years as a welder for the U.S. Navy, though he could just as easily have passed for an ex-linebacker. People sometimes compared him to Aaron Neville because of the physical resemblance, but also because he'd been known for his singing before he took up the accordion.

Andrew was a close friend of Danny's and around the same age, although he too could pass for someone younger. But he had a different style. Where Danny was cool and contained on stage, Andrew was brash and booming, dancing around with his accordion, light on his feet, working the crowd.

Andrew tended to burn himself out quickly on stage—the only sign of his age. Partly because he often welcomed a break, partly because he was a warm-hearted man, he had a practice of inviting other musicians to sit in. Lately, I'd started to surprise everyone—and myself—by accepting these invitations.

"Miss Blair!" Andrew would yell from across the room. "Want to play? We'll get you a chair." He knew sitting in meant just that, at least for me. Sitting down, so sedate in comparison to him, as I carefully played my one or two songs.

"All right!" he'd invariably say afterward. "You're really coming along!" Andrew was so encouraging—and he also talked openly about his own struggles, even though the music was in his blood.

Andrew came from a well-known musical family back in Louisiana—his father was the famed old-time Creole fiddler "Bébé" Carrière, and several cousins led popular zydeco bands. For years, he sang and played rubboard with Danny's band. But the accordion was something else again. He'd been over forty when he decided to learn. "Danny thought I'd never get there," Andrew confided with a laugh. And just like me, he was left-handed. So in some ways, I felt we were kindred spirits—and he never intimidated me, the way Danny sometimes did.

Andrew had already warned me: I should be prepared to play a few numbers with his band tonight. I had even been looking forward to it. But now I doubted I'd last that long.

I barely felt up to finishing out the afternoon, for the two or three couples who seemed interested in dancing. Most of the sparse crowd remained sitting down—eating gumbo, boudin, jambalaya—listening casually. They were probably too busy eating to dance—or maybe they were uninspired by our music.

I couldn't blame them. No question I was out of sorts, just like KP. Maybe she should crank up her bass. The rubboard player did add some energy, but I missed our drummer. Steve's fiddle, without amplification, seemed like a faint echo. My singing sounded anemic. I couldn't find the beat with my accordion. And my arm kept throbbing.

I spotted a tall, striking Creole man in a cowboy hat, taking a place at one of the long tables, balancing a plate of food as he kept an eye on the two solemn little boys at his side. They looked like miniature versions of him, turned out in matching hats, jeans, and cowboy boots. I recognize this man—their grandfather?—as a regular presence in the local dance scene, although I didn't know his name.

The man watched us closely as he ate, unsmiling. I began to feel self-conscious—as I often did, when playing in front of Louisiana people. Partly because they could be a tough, discerning audience, since they grew up with this music. But also because I knew that some disapproved of outsiders trying to play—even though so many of us did, especially in California. The nagging question was always there for me—especially at moments like this one, when I watched the man in the cowboy hat studying us, with his penetrating dark eyes and unchanging expression.

When we took a break to eat, Shirley put on some recorded music, and I heard the sounds of a popular zydeco band from Louisiana fill the hall. I started to tap my foot, as I ate my jambalaya. I couldn't help but respond to the pounding, syncopated sound; heavy drums and bass, flashy electric guitar riffs; bluesy accordion. Not much need for the delicate strains of a fiddle—or even for the French language, at least with some of the younger bands.

"I bet everyone is relieved," I griped to myself. "Finally they get to hear what they want. The real thing, even if it's just a recording." Kickass dance music. Not a pallid version of the old-time traditional stuff no one likes anymore—and played by outsiders, on top.of it. I'd fallen into a dark funk.

But then I remembered: it was also the Louisiana people who appreciated the simple, traditional music we tried to play. Like Elton, who'd just come up to us and said, "You know, what you guys play is what I grew up with. There wasn't any 'zydeco' back then. It was just French music, Creole music. And you don't play too loud, either. I like that."

Then, in the restroom, a sweet-faced church volunteer approached me to compliment the music—and tell me about her daddy, who used to play the fiddle with a band in Louisiana. Now he was gone, and she had inherited his fiddle.

"Well, you should play it!"

"I know," she said. "I start lessons next week."

And Shirley, so protective of her culture, encouraged me from the beginning, when she first heard me starting to play at the CFLFM jams. She'd always say: "You know, I can actually understand your French when you sing—and that's not true of everybody."

Those jam sessions, held by the CFLFM every month or two, helped newer musicians start to connect to the rest of the community. I'd met KP at one of the jams about a year earlier. At the time, I had just started trying to form a band.

Funny, the way starting a band—once unthinkable—had come to seem possible, expected, part of the natural progression if you spent enough time trying to learn to play—and if you were one of Danny's protégés.

And it didn't hurt that I had my very own fiddler at home.

Steve and I had been playing together for seven years by then. More nights than not, we pulled out our instruments after dinner. So there we were: an accordion-fiddle duo, the core of a band. I

The author and her husband Steve Tabak, 2008. Photo courtesy of Susan Richard.

figured all we needed was a guitarist to complete the picture. I had visions of an acoustic trio along the lines of the Savoy-Doucet Band. I'd just started to look for a guitarist—so far, no luck.

But then this slender, pretty blonde I'd been running into at the CFLFM jams approached me. She played the electric bass—and she told me she'd love to get together sometime. I didn't know what to say, because I hadn't given any thought to adding a bass player, at least not right now.

But I liked KP immediately, so I had a quick answer: yes. She was a high school English teacher, around my age, with a son getting ready to go off to college. She was fairly new to the bass, although she had played piano and sung in choirs when she was younger. We kept discovering other points of connection: we worked in the same

South Bay town, had both grown up in the Cleveland suburbs, used to attend Presbyterian Sunday school.

So just like that, I had a band. The three of us started to get together for regular practice sessions. It reminded me a little of our days with Harton, but we'd become more focused now. And there was one other big difference: I was in charge. I never questioned my role, since the accordionist usually functioned as the bandleader. And of the three of us, I was the most grounded in the music. I began to put together our repertoire.

KP had a serious, methodical approach to her music. I liked that. She also had a boyfriend, a more seasoned bass player, who helped her work out arrangements for our tunes. We began to make progress. But we really needed a guitarist.

It wasn't easy to find a guitarist for a traditional Cajun band. The role of Cajun rhythm guitar struck many musicians as too limited. A whole night of two- or three- chord songs, played in the same couple of keys—well, it got to be monotonous. And especially with the simple, no-frills accompaniment favored by traditional players: often just an alternating single bass note followed by a brush across the remaining strings. Bass-chord, bass-chord. Boom-chick, boom-chick. More complex styles might involve bass runs—a progression of single notes leading from one chord to the next—or a few extra grace notes here and there. Or some guitarists might substitute bar chords. But overall, it was nothing fancy from the standpoint of many guitarists, especially if they were used to playing lead. Might as well be playing drums, some said.

But Cajun guitar was more subtle, and more difficult, than people thought. Even guitarists who played other kinds of simple, traditional music—old time, country music, bluegrass—had difficulty with the particular rhythm of Cajun music. Without much exposure to the music, and preferably some experience dancing, a neophyte could easily overlook the distinctive Louisiana lope—syncopation, back beat, or whatever you chose to call it. And sometimes the timing of the chord changes, simple though they were, took new musicians by surprise. Cajun music seemed to break the rules. "These sure are crooked tunes," musicians coming from outside the tradition often remarked.

I'd spread the word about my guitarist search, mentioning it to anyone who might have a lead. At the suggestion of Danny's band mate Suzy, I posted a request on the Internet message board of a local folk music society. One man who responded was someone I already knew—one of Danny's protégés, a talented multi-instrumentalist who performed with a couple of bands. Marty had just one question for me: "So, do you have any gigs yet?" Well, no. The idea was to find someone who would work with us to develop as a band. Then maybe I'd look for gigs.

We'd tried out a few potential guitarists, but no one had worked out. A few came to our practices. One even played a couple of gigs with us, until—by mutual consent—we parted ways. I kept finding guitarists whose true musical interests lay elsewhere: in classical, bluegrass, salsa. Either they chafed at the perceived limitations of Cajun music—or they allowed these other styles to creep in, altering our sound in ways I didn't appreciate.

For someone to be happy in the role of Cajun guitarist, especially with a band just starting out, I figured he—or she—would have to possess a deep love for the music and the traditions behind it. It might also help if the guitarist had other musical outlets, like singing or playing one of the other instruments.

Danny appeared to have a proprietary interest in the evolution of my band. After we lost one guitarist, he reminded me he'd seen it coming. "I told you to fire his ass!"

Then one night he had an idea. "I might know somebody who could play guitar with you."

"Great! Do I know him?"

"I think so." He smiled.

"Who is it?" I was getting excited.

"Me."

"You??" I thought he was kidding. I was a little bit flattered, but mostly disbelieving. "Danny, how could that possibly work? You're already so busy, playing accordion in two bands."

Danny admitted a third band would have to be lower priority, and he could never be sure of his availability too far in advance. But he made me promise to hold off on finding a guitarist for our next gig.

"Don't get someone else until I tell you for sure I can't make it, ok?"

Well, ok. I felt a little stuck, though I figured we could manage to play a dance with accordion, fiddle, bass—and our new drummer, a woman KP had found for us.

But I was a little stung when Danny completely forgot about our gig—and then compounded the error by asking Steve to play fiddle with his own band on the same night. After that, Danny was willing to concede that I needed to keep on trying to recruit a regular guitarist.

Danny was also responsible for the band name. Four months earlier, he had dropped by our house, as he sometimes did, in search of red wine and a visit. But I was keyed up—after months of practicing, we suddenly found ourselves facing our first official public gig. It had come about unexpectedly, after we hosted a meeting and one of the people there noticed the instruments scattered around the house. He'd been trying to build up a dance scene in the South Bay, near San Jose. Perhaps we'd like to play?

And the next thing I knew, I'd agreed to audition with a brief opening set for the regular band this man had just booked, at the VFW in Campbell. If all went well, we could play for the next dance.

For our trial run, I'd come up with a name on the spur of the moment: the Burning River Band. It was supposed to be an inside joke, a reference to the polluted Cuyahoga River in Cleveland, the hometown KP and I shared.

We passed the audition. But I thought we needed a better name for our official debut, when we'd get to play a full dance on our own.

So I had spent the previous night poring over Louisiana guidebooks and dictionaries, looking for inspiration. No luck. Then I turned to my Cajun cookbook collection. The good names were already taken: filé, gumbo, jambalaya, tasso, crawdad. Nothing else sounded right.

Danny didn't seem to get the joke about the day the Cuyahoga River caught fire. But he agreed with my own assessment: Burning River was not a very good name, at least for a Cajun band.

He had another idea.

"How about this: 'Sauce Piquante'? It sounds much better."

How funny. Danny had hit upon one of the many names I had considered, and then discarded, when I'd scanned my cookbooks. But now, hearing the words spoken aloud, from his mouth, they had a completely different flavor. They sounded right.

"Sauce Piquante," I said, trying it on. "That does sound better. You're right."

The break was over. When I picked up my accordion I felt different, better. More energized. Maybe the jambalaya had fortified me—or perhaps it was the couple of encouraging comments we'd received. And I noticed a few more people arriving.

I began to play, letting myself feel the music, two-step and waltz, rising and falling, fast and slow.

"Can you play a shuffle?" Shirley asked me. "I want to lead everyone in a line dance."

That was a great idea. A shuffle was always a crowd-pleaser, with the slow tempo of a waltz, coupled with the one-two count of a two-step. But it was the syncopated rhythm, the heavy backbeat, that got even reluctant dancers out on the floor. You could do partner dancing, but these days most folks preferred to do the more communal line dance. Even though it wasn't exactly traditional, line dancing—whether the Electric Slide or the Harlem Shuffle or some other variation—had become wildly popular in Cajun and zydeco circles, as the dance of choice whenever the band played a shuffle. I'd seen a whole roomful of people—fifty, a hundred—dancing in sinuous waves, perfectly synchronized.

I even knew the ideal shuffle: "Black Top Blues." I'd learned it from Danny, although it was a signature tune of Octa Clark, a renowned—and now elderly—Cajun accordionist of Scottish descent. Just one problem: It was my only shuffle. And I'd already played it once, maybe twice.

But Shirley wasn't concerned. "It will be fine. Just play it again. No one will notice." Good point. No one had been listening very closely—and besides, much as I loved the music, I had to concede that a lot of these tunes did sound alike.

Shirley grabbed her cousin and they dragged a few other people out on the dance floor. She demonstrated the basic step, in slow motion. First, to the right: step-together-step-pause. Then to the left: step-together-step-pause. Then back: step-together-step-pause. Then the oh-so-cool rock step: forward, back, forward, followed by a quarter turn to the right. Then you start over again.

Shirley nodded to me, and I kicked off "Black Top Blues." No words to this one, just the accordion, followed by the fiddle break, then back to the accordion. KP kept up a nice solid bass line, and I was glad we had the raucous percussion of that rubboard to add a little edge. We began to get into a nice swinging groove. Not quite "in the pocket" like Mr. Octa, but not bad for the likes of us.

I noticed more people on the floor, trying to enter the line smoothly. I loved watching the dancers. The flashy ones, who kicked high and twirled. The subtle ones, who just shifted their weight from side to side, a low movement in the hips more than the feet. The ones who shimmied and shook, knowing everyone was watching. Each dancer separate, everyone doing a solo. But they were all together, too, riding that same rhythmic wave, feeling that same current, a vibration passing from dancer to dancer—and between the dancers and the musicians.

We were all one, rising and falling, locked together, in perfect harmony, each feeding on the other's energy. Finally, it was starting to happen today—almost at the end of the gig. But at least it had come together. We'd arrived at the place we'd been searching for all afternoon.

Steve was trying to get my attention. He signaled to me, nodding, shaking his head. A pantomime I finally understood: he didn't want me to pass the lead to him. I needed to play the accordion straight through. We were in the groove, we'd finally caught the wave, and we couldn't afford to let the energy drop. So I pressed on, played the accordion without stopping, in unison with Steve. I kept pumping it out, past my fatigue, even farther than I needed to go. Because I didn't want to stop.

Finally, I ended the tune. KP looked drained, and she confirmed what I suspected: she needed to go home. It was time: I spotted Andrew and his entourage entering the gym, ready to set up for the evening dance. He waved.

Shirley said, "Wait—I want to introduce you all before you go."

She led us closer to the now-seated dancers, and said: "This is one of our up-and-coming bands. Sauce Piquante. We'd like to thank them for donating their time today."

We shifted awkwardly as she introduced us each by name. The small crowd applauded—with some vigor, this time around. A couple of people asked if I had a card. I was surprised—but yes, as it happened, I did. I had a few with me, and a whole box at home—fresh from the printer. The band name, my contact information, and a leaf design done up in red—so I hoped it might pass as a chili pepper.

Then the tall man in the cowboy hat walked in my direction. He seemed to be passing out fliers. He looked at me with that piercing gaze, hesitated a moment. Without smiling, without a word, he handed me a sheet of paper.

It was an invitation to his birthday dance next month.

I knew it was probably a public event, open to anyone—but I figured we'd just passed a test.

"Thanks," I said.

Fifteen   In the Blood

"She looks good for seventy-seven, doesn't she?" I had to laugh at myself, showing off my own mother.

"Yes, she does," Danny agreed. He had just set down his accordion to take a break.

I had introduced them as soon as we walked in. Now my mother stood a little distance away from us, talking with Steve and one of our music friends.

Danny peered at her more closely.

"I can definitely see the family resemblance," he concluded.

I felt my usual mix of contradictory feelings: satisfaction, chagrin, and rueful self-acceptance. I'd finally made my peace with the short, sturdy Eastern European look the women in my family seemed to share: broad face, high cheek bones, a Slavic droop to the upper eyelid. It didn't lend itself to glamour, but at least we aged well.

My mother was visiting from Chicago, spending a few days with us before she joined up with a tour group to China. "I've always wanted to see the Great Wall," she'd confessed. We thought she might enjoy this small outdoor festival at Kermit Lynch, the Berkeley wine merchant not far from our house. This time around, the theme was oysters and Cajun music.

I had been a little concerned about showing up with my mother. Not that she didn't like Cajun music. In fact, she had become something of a fan over the years—she had even taken an Elderhostel trip to Louisiana. And I wanted her to meet the man who had become such an important mentor to me.

But she had a way of paying compliments that turned into something else. What if Danny asked me to sit in? She might listen attentively, tell me I sounded great—and then offer to buy me a metronome, the way she had one recent Christmas. Or perhaps she'd repeat her remark that she loved the sound of my accordion—even though it wasn't "a very feminine instrument."

Danny had a similar propensity for speaking his mind. Maybe he would chastise me for holding back when I played, and then start quizzing my mother about my childhood.

I took my turn, singing and playing the accordion, and then Steve sat in on the fiddle. My mother complimented our playing, appeared to like Danny, and thought the crowd seemed nice. The musicians, at least. She had her doubts about some of the dancers. Like that one middle-aged couple, locked close together, denim-clad legs intertwined, undulating to the music.

"The dancing—it's a little sexier here than in Chicago, isn't it?" Luckily, she didn't say this too loudly. "It's just zydeco, Mom," I said. She looked skeptical.

After the festival ended, Danny joined us at the house, playing music and drinking red wine. My mother, a non-musician, listened with a smile on her face, bouncing around on the balls of her feet, staying on the outskirts. I knew what that meant.

"Mom—would you like to play some triangle?"

I'd just taken a risky step. The triangle is a small but penetrating instrument. When played wrong—as it usually is, at first—it can throw off an entire roomful of musicians. Inexperienced triangle players provoke plenty of cringing and eye rolling at jams.

"I'd love to!"

My mother picked up the triangle I held out to her and sat down with us. I picked up the guitar, and we started to play. I held my breath.

I heard the sweet, wild sound of the accordion, fiddle, and guitar, twining together in the familiar dance that never failed to move me. But now there was a new sound: the sharp, clear ring of my mother's triangle, rising above the other instruments.

I listened. And I realized she sounded just fine—at least to my ears. It had taken me some time to master the triangle, and Steve still refused to go near it. I couldn't quite believe my mother had picked it up, just like that.

Danny cocked his head, listened. The real test. I knew he wouldn't hold back, even for a woman in her seventies. He looked at me.

"She's got it. Your mother's got rhythm."

"I guess so. You know, her father played the button accordion."
I shared this fact proudly—and so casually no one would have suspected how recently I had discovered it.

Danny smiled at me. "Well then, it's in your blood, too."

In the blood. I liked the sound of that, especially since I was a late-in-life musician.

I had never considered music making a part of the family legacy—until the last few years, when the accordion story finally began to unfold. When it did, it came out in bits and pieces. Like so much of my family's history.

The first clue had surfaced five years earlier, when we still lived in Chicago. I was at my mother's house, going through our old family albums. Most of the photos looked familiar, even though I hadn't seen them in years. My parents as high school sweethearts, back in Cleveland. The beginning of college—my mother at Kent State, my father at Harvard—until World War II interrupted. My father in the army. Their wedding. Baby pictures. My father, in cap and gown, holding me, a laughing two-year-old, with his mortarboard tipped rakishly on my head. Then the surprise. The photo that brought me up short.

In this photo, I am not quite four. I look directly into the camera, beaming, in my robe and pajamas, my feet planted apart. I am playing a toy accordion.

I took the photo home and put it up on the refrigerator, in one of those plastic frames with a magnet on the back. I liked looking at that bold little girl, smiling down at me. She was giving me a sign, I sometimes imagined, or maybe a blessing. My father had captioned the photo: "Christmas"—and then the year. His familiar, angular handwriting tugged at me. He had died eight years earlier.

The discovery of the photo gave me a feeling of surprise and delight, because I had no memory of ever having a toy accordion. Not that accordions—toys or real ones—were a rarity in those days. But I hadn't imagined the seeds of my own accordion playing had been planted so early.

I'd finally stumbled onto a clue that could help explain my powerful attraction to the Cajun accordion. I had always wondered why the music resonated so strongly for me. My love for the French language played a big part. But I had never managed to explain

The author with her first accordion. Photo from the family collection.

those vivid accordion dreams that began to haunt me, or the obsession that followed, soon after my first visit to Louisiana, ten years
earlier.

As it turned out, there was even more to the story. Alec was on
the right track, when he'd quipped that I might have found myself
playing polkas instead of Cajun music, if we'd visited Milwaukee instead of New Orleans for my birthday.

I began to unearth this part of the story not long after my discovery of the accordion photo, when I began to read a book—by
a professor in Milwaukee, no less—about old-time ethnic music
in the United States. Whole chapters were devoted to the Slovenian
community in Cleveland, where my mother grew up. I was in-

trigued to learn that this community, more than any other, sh
the American polka tradition.

My feelings about this were complicated. Like many outsiders
drawn to Cajun music, I had always taken pains to distinguish it
from polka. Polka was almost a cliché, an example of what not to
do, for musicians and dancers alike.

On the other hand, it seemed only right that I should try to ex-
pand my horizons to include the music of my own heritage. I had already listened to a fair amount of Celtic music—mostly Irish, some
Scottish—back in Chicago. I enjoyed that.

But Slovenian music? For one thing, it was hard to find. There
was plenty of "polka music" around. But American polka had
melded the music of many different countries—Poland, Germany,
Czechoslovakia—and often ended up sounding very homogenized,
and with English lyrics that were less than inspiring. "Roll out the
barrel, we'll have a barrel of fun." "You can have her, I don't want
her. She's too fat for me." This music seemed heavy-handed, corny.
I wanted to find the real thing: traditional folk music, sung in Slovenian.

I finally found a few CDs and tried to listen with an open mind.
I couldn't pretend the sound itself captivated me in quite the same
way that Cajun and Creole music did. But the idea of Slovenian
music had started to touch me—because of the stories I read about
Slovenian immigrants in that book.

They were mostly country people, longing for home, pining to
hear songs in their mother tongue. In America, they had hard lives,
toiling in factories and mines and farms. They were sustained by
their close-knit communities, by the Catholic church, and by good
times with family and friends. Maybe they played their music in
working-class clubs in northern cities and not in country dance
halls in south Louisiana. The sound might have been different, but
the impulse behind it was the same. I began to see my Slovenian
ancestors in a new light.

I wanted to talk about this with my mother. But I hesitated. She
had not exactly encouraged us to embrace our ethnic roots—not on
her side of the family, at least. She had always maintained Slovenian
culture had nothing of value.

"You should just think of yourself as Scottish—like your father." That was my mother's brisk suggestion when the subject of ethnic identity came up. My father's family was definitely Scottish; he'd been seven when the family left Glasgow to settle permanently in the United States.

My parents came of age during the Depression, in adjoining inner-city neighborhoods on Cleveland's East Side, where it wasn't unusual to be poor or to be part of an immigrant community. But from my mother's standpoint, there was a particular shame associated with being Slovenian—why, exactly, was never made clear, at least when I was young.

My mother and her three siblings were all bright, ambitious kids who worked hard to leave their Slovenian identities behind them. They anglicized their hard-to-pronounce last name, went to college, married people who seemed more American than they were, and became successful. Not much different from any other minority group in a rush to assimilate, and trying hard to never look back. My parents' story reminded me of the Cajuns and Creoles in Louisiana in some ways—but those French people stubbornly resisted the push to blend in.

Finally, I took a chance. I told my mother what I'd learned about the Slovenian community from that book. I even read passages aloud to her, bracing myself for what I thought might be a negative reaction.

But my mother laughed and cried as the memories came back. She knew the names of all those polka musicians. She'd danced with a few of them, she informed me with girlish pride. Johnny Vadnal, and the others. When she was even younger, she used to hear Frankie Yankovic, the future Polka King, practicing his piano accordion, while she and the other kids were outside, playing baseball. They felt sorry for him, she said.

She confessed that she'd loved going to those dances in the local Slovenian Hall. She even sang in a children's chorus. But then she decided she had to make a choice. She left that part of her life behind, in order to move ahead—to my father, to a good education, to the kind of life she aspired to.

But now my mother had confirmed what I had always suspected—letting go of the old ways so completely had carried a cost.

However, the most startling revelation was still to come. A year or two later, my mother shared it, in that offhand way she reserved for important but loaded information.

"I think my father used to play a button accordion."

Oh.

This discovery did not give me a heart-warming sense of re-embracing my ethnic roots. It was far more complicated, more bittersweet—because this was the only positive thing she had ever told me about my grandfather.

When I was in my twenties, my mother finally decided to break the silence about her family. I learned only then that my grandfather had been an alcoholic. He was an angry, bitter man who abused his wife and terrified the children. True, he'd had a hard life. Orphaned in the influenza epidemic, he'd been passed around to various relatives until he left the Old Country and took the boat to America—all by himself, as a boy of eleven.

More troubling stories came out, little by little, as the years passed. My grandfather used to sneak women into the house. Once, while he was drinking, he'd pointed a gun at his head until my grandmother wrestled it away.

But for me the most painful revelation had to do with my grandmother—a warm, loving woman my mother adored. She was also an alcoholic, a quiet one, like her own mother before her. They'd all had such hard lives. My mother's generation finally broke the sad cycle.

But my mother managed to share the facts about my grandfather's accordion in a straightforward way. She didn't remember much, just the presence of an accordion around the house when she was very young. A small button accordion, she thought, not too different from mine.

"Isn't there some kind of air button in back?" my mother asked me suddenly.

An air button?

There certainly is. But how could my mother have known that, if her memories of the accordion were so dim?

You can't see the air button from the front of the accordion—because it is hidden in the back. You use the air button to let air escape, so you can move the bellows without sounding a note. You need it when you have gone as far as you can in one direction, and you have to make a change.

This is something you discover in playing the accordion. Most of the time, there is a comfortable in and out, an easy contracting and expanding of the bellows that feels as natural as breathing. But sometimes you realize you have traveled too far in one direction or the other—stretched beyond your limits, or contracted as far as you can go. Either way, you have run out of space. No movement, no air, no sound.

So you stop, open up. A moment of hesitation, and then you quickly reverse direction. You resume playing.

And you find yourself back at the beginning, at the place where you began.

Sixteen   Return to Augusta

I looked up from my accordion and spotted Jean, smiling as she made her way through the festive crowd. It was Wednesday, the night of the midweek Cajun-Creole class party, and Halliehurst porch had filled up with clusters of people—eating gumbo, dancing, making music.

Jean was a tall, pretty woman, with reddish hair and fair skin. She managed to be self-possessed and folksy, all at the same time, a disarming combination. I felt immediate pleasure as I watched her approach, accordion in hand.

The familiar clouds of self-doubt came a half-beat later. I had been holding my own in this jam, enjoying a confidence that still felt fragile. Now I would have to work harder at it. Jean was good. She'd had her own Cajun band for years.

She and I had reconnected—with a warmth and ease that surprised me—at the start of the week, even though four years had passed since our last meeting at Augusta. The move to California had interrupted my regular summer pilgrimage to music camp, but I'd finally found my way back to this magical place, where the Appalachian foothills echoed once a year with the sounds of Louisiana.

"Hey, girl!" Jean would say, in her North Carolina drawl, when we ran into each other during the week. Sometimes she'd just wink. Or she'd offer a cheery "Don't you look pretty!" as we shared a mirror in the college dorm at night.

But the very best thing about Jean was her musical generosity. When she'd heard me play again, she made a point of saying how good I sounded. She was too tactful, too southern, to speak the real truth: "Hey, girl, you finally learned to make something that resembles music!"

She had even passed along what Danny had been saying about me, behind my back. "He's so proud of you," Jean said.

If she hadn't told me, I wouldn't have known, because Danny

was so sparing with direct compliments. My new life in California had been a three-year musical immersion, thanks to him, allowing a kind of growth that could not have happened otherwise. It felt so good to know that he could see it, too.

In response to Danny's urging, Steve and I had finally joined him at Augusta this year. He'd been pushing the idea, with a kind of insistence I didn't completely understand. "One of these days we'll go back," I kept assuring him.

But earlier in the year, I had been forced to re-think my assumptions about time. In January, I got up on the morning of my birthday, ready to celebrate, undaunted by a mere number. A few hours later everything shifted, when I learned about the sudden death of red-haired Ed, Danny's friend and accordion protégé, the day before. The news shocked me, since he had been a vigorous man—and just a year older than I was. I resolved to stop putting things off. "One of these days" could turn into "never again" in an instant, for any of us.

This was especially true for Danny. For all his vitality, he had a history of serious heart problems, going back almost twenty years. He'd been relatively healthy in the time I had known him—ever since his last "roto-rooter," as he put it. He always tried to sound nonchalant, when he made a passing reference to his health. But the worry was always there.

So I'd signed up for Augusta as soon as the new catalog came out, thinking I was doing it for Danny, more than for myself. But as soon as Steve and I drove into campus on Sunday afternoon, I felt the rightness of coming back—along with the excitement, tinged with anxiety, I always associated with the beginning of music camp, even though I'd been coming here for years. The mix of feelings had been particularly strong the very first summer—when Jean and I had met in a beginning accordion class.

I smiled back at Jean, shifting as we widened the circle to include her. There were ten of us, with our accordions, fiddles, guitars, a triangle. Other groups had formed up and down the length of the porch, which wrapped its way around three sides of the turreted Victorian mansion that served as the centerpiece of the small college campus.

In Cajun music, accordion takes the lead. And in this circle, the role had fallen to me—so far. Now I was preparing to share. But I wasn't ready to roll over and play dead. So I launched into another tune, the only way I knew to push back the clouds of doubt that hovered, ready to envelop me just as surely as the mists rolling in off the West Virginia mountains at night.

I did force the clouds back, but the details of that night on the porch are still half-hidden. I played, Jean played, and then we played together. We negotiated all this without words. Sometimes we took turns, sharing the accordion leads, as we alternated with the fiddles, led by Steve. The steady rhythm of the guitars backed us, along with the ringing accent of the lone triangle.

Other times, Jean and I joined forces. We both sang, alternating verses, our French words floating out into the evening air. She knew how to harmonize, so on some tunes she sang along, taking the high road, matching her words to my own.

I was playing to Jean, playing to the gathering crowd. I could hear their laughter and feel their eyes, enjoying us as we enjoyed each other, cutting up. We were a couple of high-spirited women, feeling like young girls together, but making music like we meant business.

Gradually, I found myself entering an elusive musical space I had reached only a few times before. The waves of sound flow all around, radiating outward and inward, filling up your empty spaces. Everything begins to vibrate, flowing together with a synchronized perfection that almost stops time. Rhythm lock. It's as though everything in the universe is inhaling and exhaling together.

It is such a shimmering, transcendent place, a trance you hope will never end. You want to hold on to it, to come back again. But there is no road map to follow, any more than you can choose to reenter a dream.

As we kept playing, I traveled even farther into that musical space. I had a new feeling of abandonment and exhilaration, a sense of being both playful and powerful. I was walking on a high wire, balancing the need to stand out against the desire to just dissolve into the pulsing waves of sound we were all creating together.

I started to play "La Valse de Cherokee," a tune that always felt more rhythmic and propulsive than other waltzes. Maybe it had to do with the words. Instead of the usual chronicle of heartbreak and loss, this was a story about abandoning yourself to the good times.

After the first accordion break, I sang a verse: "Oh, mignonne, s'en aller chez Baieonne, on va couper des cherokis, et faire bouillir des écrevisses." *Oh darling, let's go to the redhead's place. We'll cut firewood, and boil up some crawfish.*

The accordion lead was passed around, with that fluidity that is so much a part of jams. Finally, I decided it was time to end this tune, to claim it as my own. So I jumped in, and took the final ride on the accordion. I ended with a small flourish—opening the bellows, then closing them steadily, making a three-step ascent up the scale before resolving firmly on the high octave. The final twin notes rang out, lingering in the air.

I looked up. Then I saw Danny, standing on the edge of the crowd, a little to one side of me, discreetly watching and listening. Our eyes locked.

"All right, Blair!" He said it firmly, his own way of punctuating the experience, marking it for himself, for me, and for anyone else who could hear. He started to say something else, and then stopped himself.

Danny was smiling. He was pleased. I could tell. But he also seemed surprised.

The next morning, he hailed me on the way to breakfast.

"You sounded good out there on the porch last night."

"Thanks." I knew this was high praise—and the first direct compliment of the week. "I surprised you, didn't I?"

"You sure did."

Then, Danny asked a question that seemed playful.

"So how much did you have to drink?"

I figured Danny was teasing. So I replied in kind, with mock-indignation.

"Not much at all. Less than some of those nights in your garage."

Simple banter, but it happened to be the truth. I'd had one beer at the party on the porch, nothing out of the ordinary. I figured it was the end of that conversation.

The memory of that jam session carried me through the rest of the week—all the way to Friday night. Traditionally, the final evening at Augusta was quieter than the others, with a hint of melancholy. Despite the universal fatigue after a week of round-the-clock music and too many late nights, people wanted to hold on for just a little longer. Letting go meant the sadness of good-bye and a return to day-to-day lives that now seemed a little too ordinary.

This year, I didn't feel the same sense of loss that leaving Augusta usually evoked in me. Finally, I had a musical life back home that offered me more than I could have imagined, everything I needed—a community of people, friends, even a band, and most important, a teacher and mentor.

Steve and I ran into Danny when he was preparing to head back to the instructors' dorm. It seemed early, not much past midnight, but I knew his flight was earlier than ours.

"We should probably say good-bye now," I told him.

We hugged, then Danny drew back, holding me at arm's length. He seemed to be studying me—with a beaming, if slightly amused, appraisal.

"You had the best time this week, didn't you? I think you even had a better time than I did—and that's saying something!" He laughed.

I basked in the feeling, like a child who sees herself reflected back in the gleam of a parent's eye. It is more than just gaining approval for what you have done. You feel that someone is sharing in the pleasure of who you are and what you are becoming.

"I did have a wonderful time," I said. "But best of all is that for once I don't have to say good-bye to you. I know I'll see you soon, in a week or two."

"Isn't that nice?" Danny agreed, with that smile still lighting his face.

The next time we spoke it was by phone, back in California, less than a week later. I was still warmed by memories of the week in Augusta and lifted up by a feeling of confidence and renewal.

Danny's memories of my good times seemed as vivid as my own. "Every time I looked at you, I could tell," he said, laughing into the phone. He was not shy about taking credit for what had happened. "I've pushed you musically, and put you in a lot of awkward situations," he reminded me, "and now it's paid off."

This was the beginning of an unfolding conversation Danny and

I would have over the next weeks. He knew he had witnessed something happening to me, an essential moment when everything shifts and then realigns. But it wasn't enough to have seen it. He wanted to understand it, to explain it—for both of us.

During the first post-Augusta jam session in his garage, he took great delight in reminding me—and everyone else—about how different I had appeared, when he'd first met me at music camp, six years earlier. I braced myself, as he started to launch into his story. I'd heard it a few times before.

"Back then, Blair was so shy she always sat in the back of the class, hiding behind her hair. She always held back. Always wore black. But not any more!" His laugh was almost a cackle, as he threw a knowing look in my direction. The eyes of a rascal. "Les yeux canaille," just like in all the songs.

"That's not true!" I protested. "Not the part about wearing black. At least not in the summer." I couldn't challenge Danny's basic point: I'd gone back to music camp a changed person, after three years in California.

The more serious conversations took place at the end of the evening, when just Steve and I remained. The most important changes Danny had seen weren't in my appearance, of course, but in my music.

"You played as though you had a point to make," he said. "You played like you wanted to be heard." I nodded and smiled. He was right. I couldn't deny it. I'd had something to prove at Augusta—to myself and everyone else.

Danny went on. "You surprised a whole lot of people. Everyone was talking about it. You shocked Charlie. He wanted to know what I'd done to you."

For the first time, I made a confession: I had been worried about going back to Augusta. Afraid my newfound skill and confidence would just evaporate in the West Virginia air.

Danny looked puzzled. "But it's been awhile now that you've been . . ." He trailed off, hesitated. "What's that word I want?" He looked at Steve as though asking for help, then settled on "reprogrammed."

This was a side to Danny I hadn't seen before—searching for the right word. Normally, he didn't worry too much about what to call things. But he was trying to understand the changes he had seen in me—especially that pivotal Wednesday night on Halliehurst porch. How strange that it was Danny, and not I, who was still struggling to find a label. For once in my life, I was not preoccupied with attaching words to an experience. It fell to Danny to try to name it for both of us.

Over the next few weeks, he kept coming back to that night, circling around it, too perplexed to let it go. He made continuing jokes about drinking, wisecracks that I looked almost like I was "on something."

One late night in the garage, Danny was still pondering it.

"It was almost like someone—having a climax."

A climax? I was startled into silence. I wasn't certain Danny even realized he had spoken aloud.

I was shocked by Danny's directness—but not by the idea itself, the connection between music and sexual passion. In fact, I'd heard it before, from another teacher.

It was during my final year in Chicago, when I signed up for a guitar class at the Old Town School of Folk Music. I'd been learning on my own and figured I could use some formal instruction. Beyond that, I was searching for something more fundamental: a music community and a mentor, even if it meant looking outside our small Cajun music circle.

I fell under the influence of a roguish Irish-American musician named Jim DeWan. "I'll be your spiritual guide," he'd deadpanned to the class, by way of introduction. He was well equipped: he had a degree from the University of Chicago Divinity School, deep musical convictions, an edgy sense of humor, and a bad-boy persona he wore with relish.

One night, as Jim was trying to teach us the fundamentals of rhythm guitar, he became exasperated. He wanted us to learn by watching him and by trusting our ears, to feel the music inside us, to let our arms move freely. But the class—mostly adults, thirty and beyond—would have none of it.

Jim watched us as we strummed along methodically, eyes fixed on the chord progressions in front of us, studying the flight plan. We examined the guitar strings, surveying the terrain, before taking careful aim with our picks. We circled slowly, in preparation for a cautious landing—like a flock of timid birds, afraid to get their feet muddy when they touched down.

Overseeing this lifeless exercise proved too much for Jim. He bellowed:

"Hey, where is the passion in all this? You guys need to find it! That's what music is all about—feeling passion, and then making other people feel passionate."

He waited a beat, then added, "Why do you think people who play in bands are always getting laid?"

That got our attention. The room fell silent. A couple of people crossed and uncrossed their legs. Somebody cleared his throat.

But I was smiling. At that moment, I began to understand something that had been eluding me: the source of that intense anxiety I felt when making music in front of other people.

And now, in Danny's garage, the picture had become clearer still. The fundamental fear was not that I would look incompetent, or not measure up to the next person. The deepest anxiety stemmed from what happens, if you allow it, when you open yourself fully to music. You are filled with passion, flooded with feeling, no longer in complete control. It takes trust and courage to allow someone else to see you in that state. Making music with others is an intimate act, a kind of sharing of the self that doesn't come easily.

But I had allowed it to happen on the porch in West Virginia that night. Instead of fear, I felt freedom and exhilaration. Danny knew it, even if he couldn't find the right words to describe it.

There was no mystery, at least to Danny, about what had brought me to this point. He admitted to feeling proud when other people at Augusta commented on my transformation.

"I felt kind of puffed up." He expanded his barrel chest in illustration, straining the buttons on his shirt, laughing at himself.

What had he done to me? Lots of people at Augusta had asked.

Danny finally repeated his answer for me, that Wednesday night in the garage, savoring it in the re-telling: "I just held her feet to the fire!"

And there it was again: the twinkle in Danny's dark eyes, the knowing smile, the sharp thunderclap of his laugh. The kind that always rang out suddenly, from somewhere deep inside, pulling everyone along with him.

I laughed along with Danny. Not that there was much choice. His laughter was a wave of sound that drew you in close to him, making you feel you were sharing a tantalizing secret—or perhaps that you were his accomplice.

But I had been more than his accomplice. I had managed to surprise Danny himself during the week at Augusta. I still couldn't explain what had happened that night on the porch or why I had ventured into a new musical space. All I knew was that the experience was real and fully mine—just like my music. Finally, I had started to claim it as my own.

Seventeen   Singing Higher

"You need to sing higher, Blair."

It was Danny's latest piece of advice. Even though he didn't sing much himself, he had definite ideas about every aspect of the music—including this one.

He'd first made the suggestion in the summer, and he continued into the fall, repeating it regularly at the jams. Eventually, he revealed how he'd reached this conclusion: by hearing me sing at the Augusta student showcase.

"Don't be afraid to push yourself," he reminded me.

It was just one sign of Danny's growing seriousness that fall. It came out in little ways. He was starting to correct people when they referred to his Wednesday sessions as jams—they were workshops. Or he'd make critical comments about students who didn't practice enough. It was a little disconcerting, this air of urgency.

He also wanted to help my band get better—starting with Robert, our new guitarist, who had just played his first gig with us. I'd first met Robert at one of the CFLFM jams, when he'd shown up with an electric guitar and amp. Initially, he met with a rebuff by Danny, who took him for one of those middle-aged rockers who wants to dabble in traditional music, and not someone likely to adapt to the no-frills style of traditional rhythm guitar Danny favored.

But Robert felt the pull of Cajun music for a deeper reason: his own Acadian roots. He'd grown up in Maine, with French as his first language, and he had started out playing guitar in the family band. He kept coming around, and in the spring he approached Danny about coming to the garage jams. After a few months had passed I realized he was serious, if hardheaded—and I invited him to join Sauce Piquante.

Danny was also pushing himself. He wasn't feeling well—he even canceled two jams in a row. The next time we saw him, though, he downplayed the health issues. He'd seen his doctors and insisted he was his usual self. I tried to push my worries away and concentrate on the music.

As it turned out, Danny wasn't the only one who thought I should sing higher. Robert had told me the same thing. He went a step farther and offered me the name and number of a voice teacher he'd worked with.

"Thanks," I said. The slip of paper, like the idea itself, drifted out of sight.

I did love the distinctive sound of traditional Cajun singing— high, piercing, bordering on nasal. A sound that carried over the noise of a dance, even in the days before amplification. Aside from this practical advantage, the traditional style was emotionally compelling. It was an arresting sound, when men pushed themselves to sing at the top of the range, the voice almost breaking, catching in a half cry. No wonder people sometimes called it "the heartbreak key."

But the suggestion to try singing higher myself was daunting— and puzzling. Even with a microphone, my voice didn't always project as well as it should. At jams it was even more frustrating, like trying to sing underwater. Singing higher, I assumed, would involve even more strain.

But I did start to sing higher—at first for practical reasons, after encountering a few tunes too low for my voice, at least with my customary C accordion. So I tried them with my D, and was surprised to discover the small shift, to a key just a step higher, made a big difference. I continued to experiment, and I found even more tunes that sounded clearer and stronger in the higher keys.

One night at band practice I took out my D accordion, determined to see how far into this new territory I could push my voice. Song after song, I tested the waters in the higher keys—and it worked. It wasn't just that my voice sounded better. I felt better—and very different, as though I had crossed a barrier and entered a new place, an unexplored terrain that until now I had just been circling.

I felt light headed, free and floating. Then I noticed a strange vibration, almost a buzzing sensation, centered between my eyes and nose. My voice was starting to have an independent existence— carrying me along, instead of the other way around.

I found myself singing, shaking my head in surprise, and smiling all at once. Robert must have known something was happening, from the way he grinned back at me. At the end of each song, he'd offer a firm "Yeah!"

Afterward, I felt exhilarated. I tried to explain to Steve and Robert how I'd felt, but I struggled to find the right words. I felt invigorated, but a little off balance, as though someone else's voice had been coming out of me. I wanted to experience this again. If singing higher was the answer, then I was prepared to make the shift.

"What was the name of that voice teacher?" I asked Robert. "I think I must have misplaced the number." Maybe I would give him a call, after all.

I'd begun to wonder what kind of voice was best suited for Cajun singing—especially for women. There were so few examples. I knew of only two women vocalists who had recorded a significant body of work: the renowned Cléoma Falcon, and in recent times Ann Savoy.

For women, I didn't believe the answer was simply to sing as high as possible. I'd heard some vocalists approach the music in that way—with a sweet high soprano that sounded beautiful and impossibly ethereal. But it seemed to lack the raw passion of the men's singing.

There was something critical about the quality of the voice, independent of pitch. I turned to books, seeking answers, but my research left me feeling confused by all the unfamiliar terms and categories: head voice and chest voice, pitch and register, vocal placement, timbre.

One idea began to make sense to me: resonance. It was easiest to visualize in relation to a musical instrument. I could imagine plucking the high E string on a fine handmade acoustic guitar, and comparing the sound to a cheaper model—or to an unamplified electric guitar, or even a child's toy plastic guitar. The note, the pitch, might be the same, but the quality of the sound would be completely different.

Guitars—like other acoustic instruments—have a chamber that allows the sound to resonate. The quality of the sound depends on the size and shape of the chamber, as well as other factors, of course: the wood used to construct the guitar, the material and gauge of the strings, other subtle differences.

When singing, you become your own instrument. The sound of the voice is created by air passing through the vocal cords, causing them to vibrate. The quality of that sound depends on how it is amplified by the body's resonating chambers.

It was intriguing, if a little odd, to think about my body in that way—as a series of empty spaces, waiting to be filled up with sound. It was easy to imagine my mouth as filled with sound. But to think of sound as rising into my nose and sinuses? Expanding in my chest, and rumbling down in my abdomen? I had even seen fanciful pictures, a woman's body curved in the shape of a violin, just to make the point clear. Apparently trained singers could learn to focus their voices in such a way that different kinds of resonance were produced.

One morning before work, I tossed a few books into my briefcase. I was determined to figure this out. Once on the train, I pulled out a slim paperback called How to Sing, by a man named Hewitt, originally published in the mid-seventies. The cover promised a "practical, easy-to-follow manual." Most of the book consisted of vocal exercises.

The author dispensed with the more complicated classification schemes I'd encountered in my reading. Instead, he wrote simply of using "higher resonance" and "lower resonance." Higher resonance depended on using the spaces behind the nose, while lower resonance was produced by the spaces below—mouth, throat, and chest.

A voice with higher resonance didn't really sound nasal, according to the author—it was bright, narrow, and focused. The goal was a "brilliant, pointed" voice that could cut through other sounds and be heard.

Higher resonance sounded like what I was after.

I read further, as the author described what should happen if a student followed the written instructions and paid attention to the feeling of the moving air, to the sensation of the sound itself. The singer should feel "a good buzzing behind the nose," "a 'shattering' sensation—like the tinkling sound when you strike a triangle"—and hear "a brilliant, ringing sound." It was, he said, "a sensuous and powerful sensation."

That was it! He had captured the experience I had drifted into that recent night at practice. The thought of recreating this was exciting—too exciting to wait until I got home to try one of the exercises. I figured I would just have to be discreet. Besides, I had seen much stranger happenings on the train.

So—very discreetly—I gave it a try: took a deep breath, began to hum, tapped my nose and cheeks to direct the air upward, smiled slightly, opened my lips and sang a vowel sound.

"Hmmm—Ahhhhhhhhhh."

I made the sound quietly, just enough to determine the exercise worked. Then I stopped, content to wait until I was off the train to continue. I had a fifteen-minute walk to the mental health agency where I worked—ample time for more experimenting.

I always looked forward to my brisk morning walk, even though the path wasn't particularly scenic: across highways and through shopping malls and parking lots, the Mission Hills rising with an incongruous beauty in the distance. On this morning, though, I barely noticed my surroundings, as I passed by the drugstores, Indian markets, video outlets, and fast-food restaurants that lined the route. I was concentrating on my breath. Over and over, I kept it up: breathing, humming, tapping, and singing a single tone, one vowel sliding into another.

"Hmmm—Eeeeeee—Ahhhhhhh."

Yes! It felt the way it had the other night, but even better, since I was walking outdoors, in the clear morning air. It was such a heady feeling, as though I had captured the energy of some living thing. I worked to channel the sound, to contain it, to direct my breath up and out. It felt like riding a wave.

I tried to do it quietly, under my breath, when I passed other people. But I didn't much care if they were staring at me. After all, they were part of that same steady humming, that same universal vibration.

The steady tone I produced felt strong and powerful, and it seemed to link me to something I couldn't quite recall. Like someone chanting. But what could it be? As far as I could recall, I'd never chanted anything before. And then I realized what it was. It reminded me of hearing the "She'ma" in synagogue—chanted slowly, as people seemed to do in California, extending the first word as long as possible, letting the swelling sound fill the air.

In Hebrew, "she'ma" means "hear" or "listen." For Jews, it is the opening to the prayer that affirms their central tenet of faith. She'ma Yisraeil: Adonai Eloheinu, Adonai Echad. For Christians, it is a familiar verse from the Old Testament: Hear, O Israel: the Lord is our God, the Lord is One.

Why was I thinking about this, in the middle of a parking lot? It certainly wasn't the first time I had sensed the connection between music, even secular music, and spirituality. But I had never experienced it so intensely and so improbably: trying to find my voice, searching for higher resonance, and then a few startling moments of transcendence. This path was taking me to some unexpected places.

Eventually it led me to the teacher Robert had recommended. But it took a few more months before I finally scheduled a lesson. I was reluctant to make the call for a variety of reasons. Mostly, it came down to fear.

In my own mind, I was a Cajun accordion player who sang French tunes with a fledgling dance band. In other words, deep down, I didn't presume to consider myself a real singer. It's not that I didn't take the singing seriously. I'd worked hard to learn all those French lyrics, and I loved telling stories through song. In fact, it had come to feel surprisingly natural. But whenever people complimented my singing, I didn't know how to take it. I figured it was my command of French, rather than my voice itself, that made an impression.

I also had my doubts about how good a match this particular teacher would be. Robert had told me a few things about Craig, and I'd done my own research. His credentials sounded far too impressive for someone at my level, and his musical interests seemed, well, different.

Robert had repeated the name of Craig's vocal group in reverent tones. The Edlos had quite a reputation, and not just at the local level. "The Bad Boys of A Cappella" were all classically trained singers, with backgrounds in opera and musical theater. But this group was something else entirely. Their website showed four men in zany costumes, performing in various themed variety shows: Holidays, Country Music, the Sixties. Craig was "the tall tenor."

I listened to the sound clips. Those beautiful, soaring voices and intricate harmonies certainly fit with the Christmas carols. But I didn't know what to make of the country yodels, sixties classics, parodies, special effects—or the original songs about garbage men and shopping malls. It was like a barbershop quartet out of Monty Python.

I finally called Craig to schedule a lesson. Fortunately, he wasn't wearing a costume when I arrived at his doorstep on the appointed day in early December. In fact, he appeared to be quite normal, especially by Berkeley standards—tall, and with the kind of boyish good looks some men carry into their middle years.

In fact, everything felt comfortable and oddly familiar: an inviting older home in a neighborhood not far from my own, cats clustering at the door, a couple of kids, even a therapist wife. But this wasn't a social call. It was a voice lesson, with a personable stranger who—through no fault of his own—intimidated me as soon as he opened the door.

I walked in with reservations, figuring this might well be a one-time consultation. Then I could tell Robert I'd given it a try, and that would be that. I laid out my modest goal: a stronger voice when I sang with my Cajun band.

But there is only so much talking you can do at a voice lesson. Eventually, the inevitable moment came. I walked over to the piano, where my new teacher sat waiting, and prepared to sing. I stood there fidgeting, wondering what strange vocal acrobatics Craig had in mind. He had quite a bag of tricks, as it turned out, along with an encouraging smile, and eye contact so steady it was disconcerting.

I felt awkward and exposed, standing there without my accordion. I couldn't figure out what to do with my hands. Clasp them in front of me? Rest them on the piano, bracing myself? I did feel faint, at times—whether from anxiety, or from reaching for higher resonance, I couldn't be sure.

Craig put me through some simple vocal exercises. Not only was there no French to hide behind, there were no words at all.

First this: Eee—Ayy—Ayy—Aah.

It was a simple sequence of four notes, up and down again. Craig demonstrated, then I was on my own. I repeated the sequence, following the sound of the piano, a half step higher each time, higher and higher, pushed beyond what I thought were my limits, then slowly down again. I stared at the keyboard, hoping that would help anchor me. Was that really my voice? It sounded so thin and wavering.

There was more.

Craig explained that singing should feel natural, like an extension of speaking, or like a cry, a call. He suggested another exercise.

"Imagine that you're calling out to someone, trying to get their attention across a crowded room. Like this."

"HEY! OVER HERE!"

I jumped. Craig's voice was like the crack of a gunshot, cutting through the air. What would his neighbors think?

"I don't really do that." I was apologetic, but firm.

"You don't yell? Ever?"

"No, not really." Yell to get attention? In my family, we didn't even raise our voices.

Craig seemed more amused than perplexed. He tried again.

"Well, what if one of your kids wandered into the street?"

At least I could get into the spirit of that one. I gave it a try.

"Stop!!"

That was a little better, though I sounded more panicked than commanding.

After listening to my voice, Craig had some concrete suggestions: Keep your mouth pursed and your jaw relaxed. Connect the notes, and sustain them at the end. Sing through the line.

Then, there were the images. Imagine sniffing a rose. Imagine inflating a balloon, and slowly letting the air escape. Imagine sending the sound out, rather than up, when you are reaching for a high note.

As for Cajun singing, Craig thought the key element was what he called "forward placement" of the voice. You could achieve it by imagining you were sending the sound through your nose.

And here was a surprise: Craig turned out to be well acquainted with the sound of traditional Cajun music. Much earlier in his musical life, he'd spent some time touring the Gulf Coast with a well-known Texas R&B singer, playing saxophone in her band. For a short time, he even played with Clifton Chenier, the King of Zydeco. He'd been around Louisiana dance halls, knew the sound well, and definitely had an appreciation for it.

"It sounds like this, right?" And then he let loose with a high, piercing "Heeeey" that would have done Iry LeJeune proud.

I left the first lesson with a promise to call soon. I liked Craig. But I wasn't sure about committing to regular lessons—or to a relationship with a new teacher.

My reflections were cut short by troubling news I received the next day. Danny called to tell me he was scheduled for an angioplasty in a few weeks. He was afraid, he admitted. So was I.

I ended up calling Craig to schedule another lesson, for the following month. I left the second session singing under my breath, the next date already scheduled, my uncertainty resolved. With the third, a month later, I shifted to an every-other-week routine. I was already starting to notice some changes in my voice. By then, those sessions with Craig had begun to feel like a stable point in my musical life, with an importance that went deeper than just Cajun singing.

It's not that the anxiety ever disappeared. It just diminished. Or perhaps it simply became more manageable. In fact, those lessons raised my anxiety—because I had to go back to the beginning,and re-experience all the old fears that had kept me silent for so long. Every session with Craig brought me face-to-face with self-consciousness and inhibition, forcing me to fight the battle I thought I'd already won, when I'd finally started singing six years earlier.

Craig's voice had joined the growing chorus, telling me I held back too much, that I lacked musical confidence. I'd heard it before. But with him, getting past my inhibitions wasn't just a complication or a side issue. It became the very core of our work together.

Craig had an uncanny ability to identify all the subtle ways my self-consciousness manifested itself in my singing. There was my tendency to chop off the note at the end of a line, rather than sustaining it, a habit my friend Harton had first noticed. I had difficulty hitting high notes, especially at the start of a song. I had assumed these were technical problems, stemming from a weakness in my voice that I hoped might improve with training.

Craig's diagnosis was a little different. He would catch me in the act, then say: "I know what just happened there. You had it perfectly. Then you heard yourself, and thought 'Oh-oh, this is me singing. But I don't do this.' So you pulled back—and lost it."

Craig didn't miss a thing. It was unnerving, no matter how re-assuring to know he was paying such close attention to my singing. I might not have been able to tolerate it if the discomfort hadn't been balanced by a few other things. Most important was Craig's will-ingness to take me as I was and help me reach the place I wanted to be—a place he knew and valued, in a way I had not expected. He was enthusiastic at even the smallest signs of change.

I was also intrigued by the way he used image and metaphor—and humor. It was a creative, playful approach to teaching. In spite of myself, I began to relax. I even started to enjoy myself.

Finally, I was touched by the way Craig talked about his own teachers and mentors. He was still in contact with every one of them, he said, going all the way back to his high school band in-structor. In fact, at the end of one lesson he suddenly asked, "Want to see my bassoon?" He went off and came back with the case. When he opened it up, he took out a pair of reeds, cradling them gen-tly in his hands. "My teacher made these for me," he said. "Thirty years ago."

I liked the way Craig told stories about his teachers and passed along advice they'd given him. He seemed like a kindred spirit, in ways I would not have suspected. I knew he would understand why Danny was so important to me.

During one of our early lessons, Craig shared an exercise from one of his first voice coaches—an older woman, still teaching in New York. She had created it for him, and now he was passing it along to his own students.

The exercise was designed to help the student learn to sustain the sound—to sing in a connected way, with one tone flowing smoothly into the next. Italians called it legato singing. Singing through the line, as Craig put it.

I liked this exercise. For one thing, it actually had words—in En-glish, of course. Later, Craig would give me an assignment: to come up with a version of my own—in French.

The words had been selected for their sound quality. Together, they made a sequence of pure vowel sounds, one flowing into the other, the consonants no more than a slight interruption in the steady stream of air.

The meaning of the phrase was secondary, at least to a voice teacher.

But since I never found meaning to be secondary, the message was also important to me. I happened to appreciate this one: See Day Arise So New.

Eighteen Orphan's Waltz

Steve and I were a little late getting to Danny's—as usual. By the time we arrived, the Wednesday night Cajun jam session seemed to be in full swing. We thought we could hear the faint sounds of fiddle and accordion filtering down the driveway as we approached the familiar suburban split-level.

Danny lived in a middle class subdivision in Fairfield, close to Travis Air Force Base, a good forty minutes northeast of our house in Berkeley. It was farther than that, in more ways than you could count, from the small settlement in Louisiana where he'd been born, or the rural community in east Texas where his family moved when he was a teenager. Now and then Danny talked about it, what he'd faced as a young Creole boy in the segregated South, growing up in the forties. But mostly he kept the stories to himself.

Steve rapped on the door of the attached garage—hard, so his knock would carry over the music. Finally, the garage door rolled up.

"Hey, you guys." Less force behind Danny's greeting than usual. "I thought maybe no one was coming tonight." He looks so tired, I thought.

We stepped into the cramped garage and weren't at all surprised to find Robert, along with his Martin D-28 guitar. He'd become a regular in the last year, and six months ago I'd invited him to join our band.

We hadn't expected to find him alone, though. From the sounds drifting outside, we had assumed the crowd was larger. But it turned out Danny had been playing along with a CD—trying to deliver yet another rhythm lesson to Robert before everyone else arrived. Most weeks at least a half dozen aspiring Cajun musicians showed up, often more than that. But tonight it would be just the four of us.

Steve pulled out the bottle of red wine he had brought. I produced a six-pack of no-alcohol beer and braced myself. The last time I tried this, Danny had laughed at me.

"Why do you want to drink that shit, Blair?" he had demanded. "It tastes like water."

But this time Danny didn't laugh.

"It's German," I said, offering him a bottle. "It tastes better than you might think."

"Thanks." Danny took a cautious sip. "Hmm. Pretty good. My doctor says I can't drink at all now."

No one seemed in a hurry to play. Danny got heavily to his feet and headed into the house. As he left, he handed me, without explanation, a sheaf of papers.

I began to examine the pages and realized they came from a website dedicated to Kate Wolf, a Bay Area folksinger who had died of leukemia fifteen years earlier. I was familiar with her story, although I didn't know her music well. It was a touching tribute—an attempt by her family and friends to preserve her music and her memory. But I did wonder why Danny had shown this to me. His tastes were certainly eclectic—his latest passion was Tex-Mex—but this didn't strike me as his kind of music.

"That's wonderful, what her husband and kids are doing, to make sure no one forgets her," I said to Danny, when he returned. I offered the papers back to him.

"No, you can keep those," he told me. "I thought you might like to have them."

"Oh—well, thanks." I put the story of Kate Wolf into the bottom of my accordion case, still wondering what the point was. We said no more about it.

We went back to listening to the CD, talking around it. Danny played along intermittently, now and then drawing our attention to the solid, loping rhythm. Robert was impressed and said he'd like to find a copy of the recording, called "Mémoires du Passé." He had never heard of the band—the Lake Charles Ramblers, featuring an accordionist and singer named Jesse Legé.

I felt restless and on edge. I found the sound of the recorded music oddly irritating. It's not that I didn't like "Mémoires du Passé." I even had a signed copy at home. But tonight, the music of the Lake Charles Ramblers felt like an intrusion.

Normally, I would have spoken up. I would have offered to lend Robert the recording and told him the whole story—how I had come to know Jesse at music camp that summer. When I asked him to sign the CD, I felt like an aging schoolgirl at a rock concert. But a kind of edgy lassitude had settled over me, so I said nothing.

I felt too restless, too confused by all the competing sound in the air. I couldn't get comfortable, even with just the four of us in the garage. I shifted my chair around and bumped into something on the floor.

When I looked down, I saw a doll in a box, one of those costume dolls meant mostly for display. She wore a frilly dress, and she smiled at me through the window, her box tipped to one side. She looked cast aside, protected and imprisoned by her plastic dome. The jostling of my chair must have activated something, since I heard a faint sound when I leaned over. The quiet doll's voice couldn't make itself heard above the music. Despite the fixed smile, her voice seemed to register a quiet protest.

I felt like asking Danny to turn off the recorded music. "I'd rather be listening to you" is what I wanted to say—but I didn't. I just waited, until he finally turned off the CD. Then he sat there with his accordion on his lap. Robert was poised with his guitar, with the coiled energy of a teenage boy, all set to launch himself at the first sign from Danny. Steve had his fiddle out. I had my tape recorder ready, my accordion at my feet.

"So—any requests?"

Requests? I felt at a loss. I couldn't really tell the truth—that I didn't care what Danny played tonight, I just wanted to be near him.

Danny had an enormous repertoire. There was a story that he once drove to a gig in Los Angeles and played the whole time—round trip—without repeating a song. He did it to win a bet, he always said. I'd heard this story a few times, like a lot of Danny's stories, but I didn't mind the repetition. In fact, I welcomed the predictability. These stories were like parables, so I figured they deserved repeating. I never doubted their emotional truth, even if the facts might be open for debate. I happened to believe this one, though.

"Do you really keep all those tapes?" Danny asked me suddenly.

"Of course I do."

"Our bedroom is overflowing with tapes," Steve added. Almost four years' worth. He had been after me to do something about the piles of tapes on the nightstand. I did my best to keep them labeled, sorted, in some kind of order. But it felt like a losing battle, as futile as trying to keep order in Danny's crowded garage.

I used to tape everything: songs, stories, conversations, the clinking of wine glasses. I felt every moment was precious, and that I had to preserve it all. As time passed, I'd become more selective—or perhaps just more jaded. Sometimes I brought my tape recorder, but never turned it on. Or I might record, but forget to label the tape afterward. This alarmed me, as though I might be letting something important slip away.

I had been trying to come up with a request for Danny. Finally, I had one.

"How about that combination of 'Bayou Noir' and 'Back O'Town Two-Step'? I know I taped it awhile back, but now I've finally started working on it. I think it might help me to hear you play it one more time."

So now Danny had a mission. He launched into the first tune—and we were swept along. I watched his fingers, wondering—as always—how he managed to coax that rolling, pulsating sound out of that little box. His hands were massive, scarred, after all those years of working as a butcher, even though he'd ended up a manager, sitting behind a desk.

Listening to Danny play, I kept waiting for the moment of transition, what Robert called a modulation, that tantalizing shift to another key. I never got tired of hearing it, that deep resounding chord, played with two adjacent buttons on the push, signaling the moment when "Bayou Noir" was shifting into "Back O'Town Two-Step."

Danny finished with a dramatic flourish. He cast his eyes my way.

"You got that down now, Blair?" He grinned at me, in the old way, with the look that meant: "I dare anyone to top that!"

I laughed back, impressed all over again—and relieved at the flicker of his old cockiness.

"Sure thing, Danny. I've got it—right here on the tape." It was a predictable exchange between us, a playful ritual by now.

"Well, that's good—you think maybe you'll actually play it one of these days?"

Finally, the tension had eased and the music started to flow more freely, even if the atmosphere remained more muted than usual. Danny played a couple more two-steps in a row—"Fond du

Culotte," or "Seat of the Pants," and then "Old-Fashioned Two-Step." In between, we talked about who recorded different versions of the tunes, and we continued to debate the merits of no-alcohol beer.

Then Danny started to play a familiar-sounding waltz. He launched the tune with the accordion, then Steve and Robert jumped on in. At the end of the first accordion lead, he looked over at me.

"You sing this one, Blair?"

"I think so. Orphan's Waltz, right?"

Danny gently corrected me. "Valse d'Orphelin."

Good, I thought. It was a waltz I knew and loved. I'd listened to a few variants of the tune, with different titles, but I preferred the earliest one, recorded in the 1920s by the legendary Creole accordionist Amédé Ardoin. When I listened to those old recordings, I could hear a staccato urgency to Amédé's playing and a high, keening wail in his singing that no one else seemed to have matched. It sounded as though he knew what was in store for him.

Amédé Ardoin died sick and alone in an asylum in Louisiana. There were different stories about what led to his decline—poisoning by a jealous musician, or maybe syphilis. Some said it was the beating he suffered at the hands of a few Cajun men who were offended when a white woman at a dance offered him her handkerchief, to wipe the sweat from his face.

I began to sing the familiar words. "Mes parents ils son presque tous morts. Çela qui restent il y en a plus un qui veut me voir." *My family is practically all dead, and the ones who are left don't want to see me.*

After the first two lines, I stumbled unaccountably and drew a complete blank on the third line. What had happened? I had sung this song many times before.

I waited out the empty space, letting myself feel the silence, and was relieved when the final line in the verse came to me: "Et mes misères faudra je les prends comme ça vient." *I have to take my miseries as they come.* I finished out the last verse, then listened as Steve picked up the plaintive melody on the fiddle.

Then Danny came in on the accordion, pulling the others along with him. I sang the second verse, without hesitation this time. *Good-bye to my family. I've been an orphan for so many years. When I'm sick I have to go to strangers. I have to take my miseries as they come.*

Danny took his final authoritative ride on the accordion and brought the song to a close. After a moment of silence, two conversations erupted. I got caught in the middle.

Robert, on my right, had some encouraging words about my singing. "Yeah. All right! You're holding on to the notes, extending them out now. You've been listening to Craig, I guess!"

He had that last part right. Craig, Robert's old voice teacher, was always pushing me to sustain the note, especially the final one in a musical phrase. Don't let go too soon, especially at the end.

Robert, stubborn in so many ways, was quick and generous in his praise of other musicians. I appreciated his encouragement, but I had more interest in the conversation going on to my left, between Steve and Danny.

I strained to make it out. It sounded like Danny had tried to sing "Valse d'Orphelin" at a recent gig, but discovered he couldn't manage it. "That's the last time I'll try to sing that song," he said.

So when Robert finished talking, I murmured into Steve's ear. "What was that about? The song was too high?"

Turns out I'd misunderstood.

"It was the words," Steve said, keeping his voice low. "Danny almost lost it when he sang the words, and he began to think about—well, his situation."

"Oh—the words." My voice trailed off, because suddenly I began to get it. I thought about the sad story. Alone on the road, abandoned by family, having to rely on the kindness of strangers.

And the way I had faltered at the third line—now I knew what had triggered my inability to give it voice. I just couldn't bring myself to sing "quand je suis malade." *When I am sick.* Because it wasn't just some imagined character in a song who was sick, or even Amédé Ardoin. It was Danny.

Not that Danny was alone and abandoned. He lived with his family, surrounded by friends, students, and admirers. But he was sick, very sick—and he had just started to talk openly to us about his declining health.

He'd had an angioplasty three months before, in January. Ever since then, his doctors had been working to stabilize him, trying to figure out what to do next. They had a new plan now: to get him healthy enough to qualify for a heart transplant.

It was frightening to think about, difficult to talk about. But it was impossible to sing about it—especially in a song like "Orphan's Waltz" that evoked the feeling of loss so powerfully.

For me, it was especially hard to accept the reality, and not only because of my closeness to Danny. In the time that I'd known him, he had always looked robust and vital—and much younger than he was. Even though I knew his history—a heart attack in his forties, a shaky period until he stabilized—I'd never seen it myself. So I'd been able to overlook his vulnerability. Until now.

These days, Danny's health was often on my mind, even when I didn't realize it. I'd started to have recurring dreams about my father again. Ten years since his death, and he still came and went in my sleep. Sometimes the dreams were prompted by anniversaries, or by other reminders of my father, and sometimes by other losses. I'd been wondering what had triggered the recent dreams. Now I knew.

The sadness in the garage hung heavily. Danny launched into a series of fast two-steps, as though to raise our spirits. But it seemed impossible to escape the sense of time passing and pending loss.

I listened to Danny's accordion, and I couldn't help but be lifted up by the music—sweet, raw, heavily syncopated. Although the songs sounded familiar, I couldn't name them.

"A couple of those were my old man's tunes," Danny said, when he took a pause after playing.

That explained it. Danny's father had been a master of that old-time Creole style accordion. It went all the way back to Amédé Ardoin. Unfortunately, John Poullard never recorded his music. I remembered when he'd died, toward the end of the first week Danny taught at Augusta, that summer seven years ago when I'd met him.

But John Poullard had passed his music down to his sons, and now they were beginning to record his tunes. A couple of the grandchildren also played, I'd heard. So the music hadn't stopped.

I watched Danny become more tired, more short of breath, after each song he played. I felt alarmed, as I watched the struggle. So hard to watch—and impossible to know how to respond. Should I insist he stop playing? But Danny didn't take it kindly when anyone told him what to do. Or perhaps I could offer to take a turn on the accordion myself, to give him a break. But I didn't want to seem pushy. And he'd probably see through it.

"Hey, Danny, you think it's time to bring down your fiddle?" Steve asked.

"Great idea!" I chimed in, relieved at the familiar suggestion.

Steve had just the right touch in managing tricky situations like this. Sometimes he would ask Danny to play the fiddle as a way of helping me ease into the accordion. Tonight, though, something else was going on. Just like me, Steve knew he needed to take a break from the accordion. But he had figured out a way to do it, without making Danny lose face.

Danny considered for a moment. "Oh, I don't know. I haven't been playing too much fiddle lately. Might sound like crap."

"Oh come on, you know you sound good." Steve kept pushing.

Finally, Danny let himself be persuaded. Steve took his favorite fiddle down from the overhead shelf, crammed full of an assortment of stringed instruments. After tuning it, Steve passed the fiddle over to Danny.

So then I picked up my own accordion. To my surprise, I had started to feel like playing. I chose a song I'd been working on lately, a lively tune called "High Point Two-Step." Danny played it two ways: the standard, straight, Cajun version, and the more syncopated old-time Creole way. I'd been trying to do it Creole style, and attempted to slip into it as the song progressed.

I liked to sing this one, too. I'd recently learned the simple words. Only later would it strike me how sad they really were, as mournful as any waltz: *Oh, every night baby, I'm here thinking about you, wondering where you are. And I'd like you to come back, darling, even if it's just one more time, before dying.*

There was such a sad undercurrent to this music. Even when the rhythm made you want to dance, the words, if you let yourself feel them, made you want to cry. It was the paradox you couldn't escape.

I glanced over at Danny. He looked too drained to continue, even with the shift to the fiddle.

"So, Danny—maybe we should call it a night?"

"Oh, we can play one or two more. Then we'll quit."

So I led off with a couple more tunes. Even though the desire to play hadn't been with me earlier, now the accordion in my hands brought me comfort.

As I played, I looked around at the garage. I'd been doing that all night long, trying to remember how I felt when we first started coming to Danny's jams. It felt like a long time ago, not just four years. I studied my surroundings as a stranger might, trying to memorize the details.

The garage had changed in the last few months, because Danny had embarked on some home improvements. He was proud of his handiwork—but I couldn't get used to the changes. The garage did look neater, because he'd been forced to clear out everything before laying down the wall-to-wall carpeting. Some of the piles of clothing had disappeared, and the rest neatly packaged in big plastic trash bags. It looked as though somebody was preparing to move.

But I wasn't sure I liked the new look. Danny's garage used to feel like a dark cave, a haven from the world. But now it resembled a suburban rec room. For one thing, the lights were too bright. And I missed the old cement floor—it stood up better to wine spills than the greenish carpet. The fancy new automatic garage door made me jump, the way it shot open as soon as Danny hit the button. It was better when Robert sat between Danny and the old door—supposedly so he could roll it up. But all of us—even Robert—knew the real reason: so Danny could keep an eye on him, to make sure his guitar rhythm was in the pocket.

Danny himself mentioned one other drawback, earlier in the evening. He'd cocked his head, listened closely. "You know, the accordion sounds different in here now—muffled. Must be the carpeting that absorbs it. It kills the sound."

Something else Danny noticed. After the remodeling, the garage was insulated better, so the sound of the music barely reached the outside, with the door closed. I couldn't tell whether he considered this an advantage or not. But it made me sad, to know the wild sound that used to ring out so freely into the night air had become muted and contained. Turned in upon itself. Voices becoming stilled.

"Well, I guess it's about time we stop."

Finally, Danny decided to bring the evening to a close. As always, it was his call. We packed up, helped him stack the chairs and collect the empty bottles.

I hugged him good-bye, as usual. But I held on a little longer this time. I wondered if Danny even noticed.

It's important to hold on, especially at the end, I thought.

And I am not ready to let go yet.

Nineteen Mon Coeur Fait Plus Mal

This Wednesday night there was no jam at Danny's. He had a gig at Ashkenaz with his side band, Danny and Friends.

So instead of hurried Chinese take-out, our usual fare on jam nights, we'd lingered over one of Steve's home-cooked meals. The band didn't start playing until 8:30, and Ashkenaz was just five minutes away by car—much closer than Fairfield.

We had just finished clearing up when the doorbell rang. I was pleased, though not surprised, to find Danny at the door. He often dropped by on his way to a gig.

"I thought it might be you." I gave him a hug and ushered him inside.

"So would you like—a no-alcohol beer?" It still felt unnatural to offer him anything but wine.

"Sure." A pause. "Do you have any French bread?"

Red wine and French bread. That's what Danny always looked for when he stopped by. Sometimes he would share a meal with us, but usually this was all he needed.

Red wine and French bread were staples at our house and easy to find in the neighborhood. We lived just around the corner from Berkeley's Hopkins Street shopping district, a collection of small shops with a European flavor. Like Barcelona, our visiting Chicago friends had thought.

The intersection was anchored by the Monterey Market, a local landmark with a breath-taking array of fresh produce, along with a judicious selection of natural foods and groceries. A cluster of smaller shops radiated out from the crossroad: a bakery, a coffee-tea-cheese shop, an open air café called Espresso Roma, a butcher shop, a fish market, a Chinese restaurant, a liquor store. You could find most of what you wanted, and everything you really needed, right here.

But tonight, unaccountably, we had no French bread. And the nearby shops had just closed. I apologized—and Steve seemed mortified. He began to rummage around for something to offer instead.

Danny and I sat down at the dining room table. He looked weary.

"So how are you?" It was no longer a casual question.

"My mother is dying." He said it simply, with no introduction, no preparation.

"Oh no." The sadness of this happening now, on top of everything else, was too much to bear. I was shocked, even though I shouldn't have been. Steve joined us in the dining room.

Danny's mother was in her eighties. With a failing heart. Just like his.

A year ago, she had been hospitalized, close to death, and Danny flew home to Texas. But his mother rallied. He saw her again over Christmas. She lived on her own, with most of her ten other children close by, in Beaumont and Houston.

She was called Dorcena. Danny had named a song for her, one of his father's, an old-time Creole tune he'd recorded with the California Cajun Orchestra. He called it "Danse à Dorcena." Dorcena's Dance.

I knew Danny had a close relationship with his mother. He stayed at her house whenever he went home to visit his family. They always talked until late into the evening, he said. A bittersweet image, one that always made me hope my own sons would do the same for me, when I got old.

Danny had been trying to arrange a flight to Texas—tomorrow, he hoped. He didn't feel up to playing at Ashkenaz tonight.

"Danny—have your doctors given you permission to travel?" I raised this cautiously, because I already suspected what the answer would be.

Well, not exactly. They had tried to discourage him, although they hadn't absolutely forbidden it. Even if they had, it wouldn't have mattered. Danny needed to be in Texas.

We felt so helpless. Steve resumed his search for bread. It was the least we could do. He found some pita, but it had gone bad, so he kept looking.

Danny had someone else on stand-by for the gig tonight, one of his local protégés. He planned to play for the first hour, at most. Then he'd turn the accordion over to André Thierry, a gifted young Creole musician everyone figured was destined to be a zydeco star.

We continued to talk, the sadness in the air hanging so heavily we could almost touch it. Steve finally located some Italian rolls in the freezer, the best stand-in we had for French bread. He heated them up. It was one thing, at least, we could do for Danny.

Then, abruptly, Danny became my teacher.

"So, have you figured out what I mean by playing 'light-fingered'?"

This was Danny's most recent piece of advice. In the last weeks, he had been watching and listening to me, then saying: "No, play light-fingered!"

Danny was sparing in his feedback, so I knew this was important. He had been repeating this advice with growing urgency.

Just one problem: I wasn't sure what he meant. I knew very well how leaden and heavy-handed my playing sounded compared to his. So perhaps he was speaking metaphorically—make it sound light. Or, he might be giving me concrete suggestions about how to use my fingers.

But I couldn't focus on the subtleties of accordion technique, at least not right now. So I just said, "Well, yes. I think I'm beginning to understand a little better."

"Good," he replied.

Before too long, Danny looked at his watch.

"Time to go. I need to get over there for the sound check."

He was never late for a gig.

"Okay, we'll see you over there later."

Later that night, when Steve and I walked in the door at Ashkenaz, we discovered a fair-sized crowd had already gathered—impressive for a week night. Dancers were on the floor, music was in the air. And on the stage, Danny. Looking and sounding the way he always did—confident, completely in charge, gazing out over the dance floor as though it belonged to him.

The quality of Danny's music didn't suffer much when he wasn't feeling well. He would give it his all—until he ran out of steam.

Then he'd have to stop. I kept waiting for him to give the nod to André, who waited on the sidelines, ready to take over.

But it never happened. Danny kept on playing. He seemed to have received an infusion of the old energy, the music lifting his spirits as the night wore on.

There wasn't much for André to do—except enjoy the music, just like the rest of us. Eventually, Danny invited him up, midway through the evening, to sit in for a handful of tunes, before he reclaimed the accordion. The master giving one of his students a chance to shine. Just like any other evening.

Except, of course, it wasn't.

We waited around until the very end of the night, along with Eric and Suzy, who played with Danny in the California Cajun Orchestra. They had been close to him for twenty years. They had been through so much together, watching Danny's health wax and wane. Tonight, they had come to hear him play and to offer support.

By the end of the night, a handful of people still lingered. We sat and talked with Danny. When I hugged him good-bye, I had that now-familiar fear of never seeing him again.

Danny's mother died the next day, before he could arrange his flight. He reached Texas a day or two later, in time for the funeral. He spent just over a week there.

I called him on a Saturday, just after he had returned to California. I wanted to express my sympathy—and to check on him. No jam this week, I assumed.

But I was wrong.

"No, we'll go ahead and have the jam—just like always."

"Are you sure, Danny?"

"Of course. My mother wouldn't want me to stop the music."

WEDNESDAY, APRIL 18, 2001

Another small group gathered in Danny's garage, just six of us. One by one, everyone offered condolences. But he didn't seem to want to linger in sadness, or even to talk much about his time in Texas.

When Danny picked up his accordion, the evening began to

take on some of the high spirits and manic energy I remembered from the past. Three conversations going on at once. Musical debates. Jokes. Danny's cackle after he'd dazzle us with his rendition of a tune. It helped to have Miss Freida there, with her wisecracks and Cajun joie de vivre.

Someone remarked to Danny that he seemed to be having a good time. We all wanted to believe it. He gave a noncommittal reply, but freely admitted he'd felt much worse a few months back. "Back in January, February, I was dying."

Danny's accordion sounded more driving than usual. And even though he rarely sang, at one point he launched into the beginning of a vocal break.

At the time, we were on a little run of country-flavored tunes. He played a song inspired by Hank Williams, belting out the opening line: "I don't hurt anymore."

Originally, Danny had recorded it with the CCO—and sung it— in French:

"Mon coeur fait plus mal." *My heart doesn't hurt anymore.*

Danny kept pushing us, checking us, taking stock, reminding us of where we'd been and how far we still had to go. Like when Freida asked for help with the complicated part of a tune, and he commented, "You should know this by now."

Same thing when I finally saw the light about a tricky little riff he demonstrated. Danny reminded me, "I tried to show you that, years ago. You remember, with just those three buttons?"

"I know," I admitted, "but it's taken me a long time to be able to learn from you. Somebody has to be pretty good already, just to understand what you're getting at." He laughed at that.

Even Steve came in for a backhanded compliment. Toward the end of the night, Danny said to him, "Your fiddle sounds a lot better, now that you've had a chance to warm up."

"It's what I've been trying to get to, Danny," Steve said.

Danny offered a brief explanation, in passing, for his tough-minded stance.

"I might not be going back to West Virginia, so I have to do my teaching here."

Oh. No one reacted to that or questioned him.

This time, it fell to Freida to suggest that Danny might be ready to stop for the night. He agreed, even though he still seemed to be playing with vigor. But he had to perform the next day, he said, so it made sense to end the evening early.

Before we left, I reminded him of the latest CFLFM event, coming up on Sunday. I often got stuck trying to corral Danny for board meetings—part of my job, as the organization's secretary. I'd be apologetic, promise to ply him with wine if he came, and we'd laugh about it.

But this one was different: an afternoon of dance workshops at Ashkenaz. And the current CFLFM president had asked if Sauce Piquante wanted to provide the music. Of course, I'd said, pleased at the opportunity. I knew very well this wasn't exactly a real gig, since we were just volunteers. But it still felt like a big step, to play at Ashkenaz for the first time.

I hoped Danny would come. He had never heard Sauce Piquante play before.

"If you felt like coming, it would be great. And maybe you could sit in with us." I didn't want to push. I knew Danny was still tired, still grieving.

"Maybe. We'll see."

I didn't really expect him to show up.

SUNDAY, APRIL 22, 2001

KP was nervous. I could tell. So could Danny, I figured. She was looking good, as always, in her trim jeans and vest, but she had a death grip on her electric bass. Danny had just joined us on stage at Ashkenaz. He had finally agreed to let me hand the accordion over to him, at least for a few tunes.

I had invited him up earlier, but he declined. "You guys are doing fine. Maybe later."

I worried that he was too tired to play. But maybe he just wanted to check us out. This was his first time hearing my full band—or most of us, anyway. Kathy couldn't make it, so we were playing without drums. Good thing we had a rubboard player.

Sauce Piquante had never appeared at Ashkenaz. On my own, I occasionally sat in with someone else's band—sometimes Danny,

Sauce Piquante, Berkeley, California, 2008. Photo courtesy of Susan Richard.

more often Andrew Carrière. So I felt exposed, and I knew the band was being exposed, in a way that was exciting—and daunting.

We were the newest of the Cajun and zydeco bands in the Bay Area—the name on the pink calendar that probably left more than a few people scratching their heads. Even though we had been playing publicly for a year and a half, our gigs were easy to miss.

Most months, we managed to play at least once—but always in some obscure, out-of-the-way spot. Every few months we played for the VFW dance in San Jose. We'd also appeared several times at a down-home Hawaiian bar in Berkeley, at a couple of church Mardi Gras festivals, and for some private parties. I always felt surprised—and a little worried—whenever I spotted someone we recognized at one of our oddball gigs.

But that afternoon at Ashkenaz I could see familiar faces in the sizable crowd—and I knew we had some discerning listeners. I was relieved to see people dancing. I'd started to have a good time myself.

But the face I had been watching for was Danny's.

"You guys sound pretty good," he said, when he finally joined us on stage.

He was matter-of-fact. Not effusive, but positive. We were doing just fine.

I stepped aside to allow him to take my seat. I handed him my accordion.

"You might have to loosen the thumb strap," I reminded him. His hands were so much bigger than mine.

And now it was time to introduce Danny. I had always hoped to do this: to introduce him as my teacher and to say a few words about what he had meant to me.

It wasn't hard to find the words, because they were familiar by now. Whenever I played in public, I spoke of him. It had become a ritual. I had found a natural way to do it, I thought—by tying it in to a song I was about to play. Usually it would be "Dance à Dorcena," the tune Danny had learned from his father and named for his mother.

But when I spoke to the crowd that day at Ashkenaz, I didn't need to tie my words to a song, because Danny was right there beside me. Finally, he could hear me speak of him.

I realized this moment was nothing new for Danny. The scenario had been repeated countless times over the years, in all sorts of places. He had shaped so many musicians, had sat in with their bands, had enjoyed their words of appreciation.

But this was the first time for me. And I felt so proud to be standing there beside Danny. This, I knew, was the sweetest memory I would carry with me from that day.

So I spoke the familiar words, thanking Danny for everything he had taught me. Then I picked up a triangle and prepared to be swept away by his music, one more time.

Danny looked around at all of us. He sensed the slight current of anxiety.

"It's just like playing in the garage," he said. Nothing to worry about.

Then Danny hit the opening notes of his first song—and we all tried to follow. It was like trying to jump onto a fast-moving train. He looked around as he played, keeping careful track of everyone: Steve on fiddle, Robert with his guitar, KP on bass.

I listened, enjoying the sound from my comfortable background role on triangle. Then Danny nodded at me as he approached the end of the first accordion break. I realized I was supposed to sing. Luckily, he'd chosen a tune I knew. Same with the next one.

After three songs, Danny said firmly, "That's about enough." He handed the accordion back to me.

"So Danny—did you ever imagine the day would come that I'd have a band, and you'd be the one sitting in?"

I was teasing, and we both laughed. But I also spoke the truth—because I'd never believed a day like this would arrive, much as I might have dreamed about it.

But I think Danny knew. "Your time will come," he once told me.

Afterward, he had a few constructive criticisms. He'd had to adjust the angle of my clip-on accordion mic, and he thought the bass was turned up a little too high in the mix. But Danny's overall verdict remained positive.

"Yeah, you guys sounded pretty good."

He would repeat it several times that day and then later in the week. He also made a point of complimenting Steve's fiddling, something he had never done before.

Danny had offered a straightforward assessment—no less meaningful because it was unvarnished. He was a tough critic. Music was Danny's truth, and he never bent it just to be polite or supportive.

Later, I would learn that Danny had spoken to some other people that afternoon, praising our music. "He's so proud of you," one of the other CFLFM board members reported to me.

A local sculptor named Tyler had come to hear us play. He wanted to have some live Cajun music for the opening of his upcoming show at a nearby gallery. He had heard from another dancer that Sauce Piquante was pretty good. He also hoped we might be, well, affordable, as he later admitted, since we were a new band.

Tyler had been following Danny's music for twenty years, so when he spotted him at Ashkenaz he decided to ask his opinion. First, he made certain that Danny himself would not be interested in such a low-key gig.

As Tyler figured, Danny was happy to see one of his students get the job. "They'll do fine," he assured the sculptor.

Then Tyler mentioned the modest sum of money he had in mind.

"Do you think maybe I could get the accordion player and the fiddler for that?" he asked, hopeful but not quite sure.

"Oh, for that amount of money? I think you could probably get the whole band," Danny said drily.

The following day, Tyler called to finalize the arrangements. He told me the story about his conversation with Danny, and we both laughed.

Just after I had sent Danny an e-mail message of thanks, he called me himself. He figured this was the very first gig he had referred to me, and he wanted to make sure the sculptor and I had connected.

"Maybe this will help your band get some more gigs," he said.

But Danny had also called me with a question—a strange one, I thought. He wanted to check on the spelling of a word.

I loved the sound of Danny's voice. He had that characteristic lilt that comes when a southern drawl takes root in a native speaker of Louisiana French. But there was also a quality that was uniquely his own. When he telephoned, sometimes he didn't even bother to identify himself. He would just say "hey," his voice pitched low in my ear. Then he'd pause expectantly.

Normally, I didn't much care for it when people did this kind of thing. I found it disorienting, to have to identify someone's voice instantly. And the presumption of intimacy bothered me. On the phone, I even identified myself to my own mother, just to be on the safe side.

With Danny, though, I never minded, since I never confused him with anyone else I knew. Except maybe our mutual friend Harton—who tended to do exactly the same thing. I never minded too much with him, either.

But every so often Danny's words came out in a way that I didn't completely grasp. This was one of those times. So I didn't understand his question at first.

"How do you spell—*ATTENUATE?*" I echoed him, puzzled.

"No," Danny said. He repeated the word slowly this time, with emphasis.

"*ITINERARY.*"

Then he added, just to make sure I got it, "Like when you're planning a trip."

Now I understood. But I was even more confused. I couldn't imagine what kind of trip he could be planning. Danny wasn't supposed to be going anywhere now.

But I didn't say any of this. First, I wrote the word for myself, just to make sure I had it right.

"Okay. ITINERARY." I spelled it out, slowly, letter by letter.

I gave no more thought to Danny's pending journey, whatever it might be.

"See you on Wednesday," I said.

Twenty   The Last Session

Danny held his final jam session on April 25, 2001. He died two days later. He had been working in his yard, waiting to take his daughter to school, when he suffered a massive heart attack.

I was at home that Friday morning when I received the phone call I had feared for months. By chance, a musician friend had called Danny's house just after the ambulance left. Delilah had the great kindness to call a small circle of other women in the music community who were close to him.

Word spread quickly among the network of Danny's friends and students. His death wasn't confirmed for a few hours. But no one held out much hope. The numbness, the phone calls back and forth, talking to Steve, trying to reach Harton in Louisiana—it all kept my grief in check. I didn't cry until I stopped to take a shower. Alone, under the cleansing water, I began to think about Danny—the loss of his mother so fresh, and now gone himself. Then I wept, for all of us.

The phone call wiped away much of what I might have recalled about our last session in the garage. I had made my usual tape recording, but I gave it little thought in the days following Danny's death. It was such an intense and emotionally difficult time. But Danny would have been happy, I think, to know the music never stopped. We played through our tears, sustained by the music and the community around it.

It started the next afternoon, when Danny was supposed to have played at Kermit Lynch for another one of their outdoor festivals. Steve and I sat in with the group of musicians who took his place—Suzy and Eric, Marty, a few others. We laughed and cried, huddled together on the edge of the crowd, drank good wine, and told funny stories. It was small, intimate. "Like a Cajun wake," someone said.

That night, Sauce Piquante had to play for the Cajun dance club in San Jose. I found it hard to imagine going through with this, but

I didn't see an alternative. And I knew Danny would have expected us to keep the commitment.

I felt Danny's presence, unnerving but steadying, that whole night long. The promoter—rumored to be "born again"—insisted on leading us all in a prayer circle at the end of the dance. I found myself oddly comforted—although I did request a silent meditation, so we could each pray in our own way.

A week after the last session, Steve and I made our usual Wednesday night drive to Fairfield, but this time it was for Danny's visitation and Rosary service. It felt so strange to continue past the turnoff for his house. I was glad to have Harton with us. He'd flown in from Louisiana a few days earlier, and he would spend the rest of the week at our house.

We returned to Fairfield the following day for the funeral mass and interment. There, we could see all those people Danny had touched, the pieces of his life: family from Louisiana and Texas, Pennsylvania and California; his motorcycle club, in full biker regalia; neighbors; members of his church; fellow musicians and protégés; his fans; his many friends. So many communities, diverse and overlapping, claimed a piece of him. Freida spoke, at Danny's request. Harton sang a hymn in Latin, his ghostly voice floating from above and behind us, where he sat sequestered by himself, in the upstairs room usually reserved for the choir.

Afterward, we returned to the house, along with Danny's family and some of his friends. The garage had been closed up—completely filled, I heard, with furniture shifted out of the house to create more space. Guests filled the house and yard, visiting and eating. I had a sudden wish to ask if I could go inside the garage, one last time, just to sit for a few minutes. But I didn't.

On Saturday, a week and a day after Danny's death, the California Cajun Orchestra was scheduled to play at Ashkenaz. Suzy transformed the CCO gig into a memorial dance. She wanted everyone to share in the music. One by one, in large groups and small ones, musicians stepped to the microphone and remembered Danny—in the stories they told and the songs they played. Sauce Piquante was introduced as the final band to emerge from Danny's garage. Harton joined us, to sing one last song for his old friend and teacher.

A few days after the memorial dance, I decided to listen to the tape from the last session. It was a Tuesday morning in early May when I put the cassette into my backpack as I headed off to work. Perhaps I felt ready to listen, with the last of the mourning rituals completed. I was also thinking about the next day, and the reality of our now-empty Wednesday nights.

I did not have a detailed memory of the final session, although I knew what the atmosphere had been like. For the past several months, everyone in the garage had felt the pervasive anxiety about Danny's health and the unspoken awareness that time was short. Danny had been pushing harder, reminding everyone that these were workshops, not just jam sessions. More recently, I'd become aware of his reaching out in other ways, calling people he hadn't seen in awhile, setting things right when they needed to be.

I recalled the last session, though, as more upbeat, even high-spirited. That was the great irony: Danny had begun to look better physically—and to feel better. Able to play full gigs again. He was riding his motorcycle. Ready to hang out at Bobby's Back Door, listening to the band and socializing—as he did the following night, the evening before he died.

A month earlier, I had watched Danny struggle to breathe, not knowing whether I would see him again. But I hadn't left the last session with a sense of foreboding. In fact, I had an eye to the future, for two reasons. I started to learn a new tune—"Gilton," by zydeco master Boozoo Chavis—and I resolved a troubling question about a musical opportunity my band had just been offered.

The issue with the Sauce Piquante gig was simply this: it conflicted with one of Danny's. We had just received an invitation to play at the annual San Francisco Free Folk Festival, a low-key weekend of workshops and performances organized by the city's Folk Music Club. On the same day, a Saturday, Danny would be playing at the Isleton Crawdad Festival—a wild three-day carnival of food and music held each year in a little Delta town near Sacramento, with a dozen or more bands and fifty thousand people in attendance. The two events were hardly in competition. But it came down to respect, I thought. How could I play at the same time as my mentor? I kept waiting for the right moment to broach this with Danny, but it never came.

Finally, at the end of night, everyone else had left. Steve and I remained behind, helping Danny clean up. Time had almost run out. Feeling awkward, I explained the conflict. An ethical dilemma, I felt sure.

Danny listened. Then he threw me one of those looks I knew how to read by now. Disbelieving, a little amused.

"Blair—do you really think anyone else worries about that kind of thing?" He drove the point home by mentioning a couple of his more successful protégés. "You think they worry about it? You should take the gig. It would be good experience for you guys."

Relief washed over me. I knew I had done the right thing—despite feeling a little foolish for having asked permission to do something Danny dismissed as a non-issue.

When we finally hugged good night, I left the garage with a feeling of confidence and clarity.

"I feel like I've just been given his blessing," I said to Steve when we got outside, where Robert waited by his truck.

So I left with a sense of the future, even if it might be foreshortened. I had a new tune to work on, plans for the band, and the belief that I would still be able to share this with Danny. I did not think we were saying good-bye for the last time.

But when I decided to listen to the tape, I was searching for a sign—or some kind of message. Did Danny know the end was so near? And I wondered why none of us sensed this was our final night together.

PREPARING TO LISTEN

I had done this so many times before: sat down on the train, slipped on the headphones; pulled out a pen to list the songs on the cassette sleeve; prepared to let the music carry me back. This was such a familiar ritual, these last four years, traveling to work with the sound of Danny's accordion lifting me up. I had filled almost forty tapes with the music from his garage. Now I would hear the final one.

I never knew what I would discover on a tape, even when I listened the next day. For one thing, my memory of those long Wednesday nights could be uneven. And my recording habits were erratic, although they had evolved over the years. I tried to avoid capturing too much talk, or songs already represented in what I'd begun to think of as the "Danny archives." But I didn't always succeed. I often ended up taping long stretches of conversation. Or I might preserve a fumbling version of a tune played by a student, only to forget to turn on the recorder when Danny showed us the right way.

There never was a clear musical agenda in Danny's garage. What emerged on any given Wednesday was a function of many things: who showed up, specific requests made, what Danny thought might be helpful—and whatever else caught his musical fancy.

Sometimes we could tell where Danny was heading. He might play a string of tunes from some legendary accordionist of the past, like Amédé Ardoin, Aldus Roger, Lawrence Walker, or Nathan Abshire. Danny evoked their presence so strongly it was like touching history. He had an uncanny ability to capture the individual styles of the musicians he admired.

Sometimes Danny played songs by popular young accordionists, like Steve Riley or Geno Delafose. Or he might launch into a series of old-time Creole tunes—his old man's tunes, as he'd call them. Danny could master anyone's style, but he always put his own unique spin on a tune. He was expressive in a way few other accordionists could approach, creating nuances on an instrument that didn't always lend itself to subtlety.

I always loved it when Danny played a song two ways: first "the straight Cajun way," and then in that old-time Creole way, so we could hear the difference. Danny didn't appear to favor one approach over the other. They were variations on a theme, intertwined, each complementing the other. But I usually preferred the Creole version, with the distinctive loping rhythm and the catchy syncopation.

Sometimes the teaching became more explicit. If someone requested help with a particular song, Danny would first play it slowly and simply. Sometimes he might break it down even further, phrase-by-phrase, leaving an unsuspecting student thinking the tune was easy.

Then Danny would start to play at normal tempo. Little by little, the simple demonstration tune would turn into a dazzling, intricate display—constantly shifting into the next higher level, a little different each time through. At the end, we'd all be left shaking our heads.

Danny would smile slightly and say in an offhand way, "Oh, that was just a few little variations." But if you looked closely, you'd see that twinkle in his eyes, a look the songs call "les yeux canailles." Mischievous eyes, sly eyes.

Or one of us would suggest two songs that sounded similar—the same tune with different names, perhaps? Sometimes Danny would concede the point, but often he'd express surprise at our ignorance. "Those two songs? Completely different."

Then, just to show us, he'd play two, maybe three songs back-to-back—tunes that to him sounded as different as, say, a haiku and a sonnet. And someone would whisper to the person who had provoked this lesson, "Don't worry, they sound alike to me, too."

Occasionally, Danny would teach by isolating a particular technique—like the "octave roll." Or some other recurring pattern, one of those quick little runs that showed up in a number of different songs. "Frills," he'd call them. Then he'd play a series of tunes to demonstrate, so we could hear for ourselves. "So that's how you get that sound!" someone would always say. Like discovering a hidden key, or finding some musical Rosetta stone.

But usually the instruction wasn't so explicit. It was learning on the fly, whatever you could pick up by watching and listening. All those nuances, both spoken and unspoken. Ultimately, Danny followed a hidden logic on Wednesday nights, some process of musical free association we didn't always understand at the time. Often I uncovered it only later, when I went back and listened to the tape.

As I sat on the train, preparing to step back into that final night in the garage, not quite two weeks had passed. But it felt like a lifetime ago. All those evenings of music, laughter, conversation—distilled into perhaps fifty hours of recordings. It seemed like so much, and then again, it seemed like nothing at all.

I wondered what I'd discover, when I turned on the tape—and whether it would sound like all the other nights. I would be listening with different ears now, guided by the knowledge I didn't have before, searching for answers to questions I hadn't yet asked.

1. *"Unnamed Fragment of a Two-Step"*

The tape begins in the middle of a fast two-step, an instrumental. Danny opens with a slow demonstration, and then shifts into high gear on the accordion. Although the song is familiar to me, it is not something I play. It is one of those tunes that always prompts me to ask, "What's that one called again?" I think maybe this is a Nathan Abshire tune, but I can't be sure. I've always found instrumentals harder to remember, without words to anchor me.

There wasn't much singing in Danny's garage, even though most of the tunes did have lyrics. Our primary focus was on learning to play. Danny himself sang only intermittently, probably for two reasons: family tradition ("my old man didn't sing") and his heart problems. I liked Danny's voice, but he was always dismissive when we'd urge him to sing. He'd laugh and say, "I sing when I get paid." Now and then, someone decided to sing along—most often, one of us.

2. *"Lovebridge Waltz"*

"Lovebridge Waltz" is one of the first songs I learned on the accordion—and the first one I ever played for Danny. A fitting choice for the opening track of the final tape.

Freida gives an appreciative whoop during the bridge—a more elaborate version than Danny usually played. That must be why I recorded it, since I already had many examples of "Lovebridge Waltz" on tape. *Or perhaps I simply wanted to go back to the beginning, and preserve Danny's playing of this song one last time.*

"Lovebridge Waltz" is a much-loved song by Iry LeJeune, the accordionist and singer who recorded so much of the core Cajun repertoire in the fifties, although he drew heavily from the work of legendary Creole musician Amédé Ardoin, who recorded twenty years earlier. Like so many Cajun songs, "Lovebridge Waltz" tells a story of lost love and abandonment. *But it is also about setting out on a journey, in search of something you have lost.*

In the original recording, Iry opens with his high plaintive wail:

"Hey, 'tite fille, moi je me vois, après, oui, partir, mais m'en aller donc te rejoindre." *Hey, little girl, here I am leaving, setting out to find you again.* Then in the next breath, he tries to convince his black-haired love—and himself—that it doesn't really matter. *Even if you wanted to come back, look, I don't want anything more to do with you.* The memory of her hurtful words will never go away. Then he warns her: some day you'll end up crying, too. *Such a complicated mixture of feelings, after people leave us: sadness, denial, helplessness, anger.*

It took me a year to work up the nerve to play "Lovebridge Waltz" for Danny at Augusta. I'd played it earlier in the day for my other teacher—Eddie LeJeune, who was enthusiastic, and probably relieved, when I made it through his father's famous waltz without serious mishaps. So I approached my first individual session with Danny feeling more confident than usual.

Danny listened closely to my rendition of "Lovebridge Waltz."

"Not bad." He paused. "Of course, the way you're playing it, it could just as easily by Swedish music, or Irish music, or something."

Then Danny proceeded to show me what was missing: the distinctive loping rhythm, that special kind of energy, that marked it as a true Louisiana waltz. We had taken the first step in what he later liked to call my "re-programming."

I have a picture someone took of me that summer in West Virginia, posing with my two teachers. Danny stands in the middle, his arms around both of us. The two men smile broadly, while my own smile is more tentative.

Steve and I had returned to Augusta that last summer to share it with Danny. I also wanted to see Eddie again—but I never guessed it might be his last time at camp. Eddie had a fatal heart attack the following January, three months before Danny died. He had just turned fifty.

3. "The Cricket's Song"

At this point in the tape, Danny is preparing to play a tune called "The Happy One-Step." But before he begins, we are forced to pause for another song: the steady chirping of a cricket.

There were two crickets singing that night—first one voice, then two, coming from some hidden place inside the garage. *This had never happened before, at least in my memory.*

On the tape, we all stop to listen to the sharp, high-pitched chirping. Robert, with his fondness for electronic gadgetry, decides to measure the strength of the sound.

"That's incredible—it's over sixty decibels," he announces. His voice is a little hushed with the wonder of it. We all marvel at it. I comment that the cricket's voice is as piercing, as penetrating, as a triangle. It's a sweet sound, Robert thinks.

But Danny wants the noise to stop. So Robert offers to oblige him. He begins to shift things around in the garage, to see if he can find the cricket. Another man, a recent addition to the garage, joins in. The three men set out on a "search and destroy" mission.

In the meantime, I get pulled into a conversation with Miss Freida, sitting next to me. Like so many Cajuns, she is a natural storyteller—and she is also a speech therapist. She explains that some people can't tolerate sounds falling within a certain frequency, then adds how amazing it is that Danny has such acute hearing after playing music all these years. Then she starts to tell me about her mother's sharp ears and follows with a story about her old uncle back home in Louisiana.

Trying to follow her, I lose track of what else is going on, and I don't pay much attention to the small drama unfolding around us. But now, on the tape, I can see it clearly, as I hear the cricket's fate being decided. Robert starts dismantling parts of the garage, moving piles around. He is determined to root out the offending sound. Danny laughs, says something to egg him on.

"You'll have that cricket's death on your hands," the other member of the search party warns. He's serious, it turns out.

Danny laughs again, and suggests the end is in sight for the cricket.

"It's a dirty job, but someone's got to do it," Robert says cheerfully.

But they can't seem to find the cricket. Danny thinks the cricket is calling to its mate, who is somewhere outside. Someone suggests maybe the cricket is a musician, and he belongs here with us.

Danny laughs, but says firmly, "This is my turf. He can go somewhere else."

They give up for the moment, and Danny gets ready to resume playing.

The cricket's voice can be heard intermittently for the rest of the tape. It is a persistent undertone, a counterpoint to the main melody during the pauses in our music and conversation. It is as steady as a heartbeat. At some point in the evening, the voice of a second cricket joins the first. Danny is none too pleased with this. He is affronted, I think, by the competition.

Afterward, I would remember how much the small, persistent voice of the crickets had troubled Danny. He became so distracted by the sound he seemed to be somewhere else, drawn away from us by a call only he could hear. Was he already beginning to leave us?

At the time, Danny's concern struck me as an overreaction. But now, listening to the tape, I am startled at how loud the cricket's voice really is. Close to deafening. I can hear it now, through Danny's ears, in a way that I couldn't before. What else, I wonder, was he feeling that night that we didn't understand?

Eventually, Robert located the crickets and escorted them safely out of the garage. I felt relieved at their escape. I briefly entertained this thought: Perhaps Danny didn't want to silence the cricket's voice. Perhaps he just wanted to free it.

But then I had to face it: this interpretation, however comforting, was a poetic distortion, a sentimental attempt to make Danny into something other than what he was. Such a hard lesson, to accept people as they are. I struggled with it in Danny's garage. Sometimes it was even more challenging than learning to play the accordion.

4. "The Happy One-Step"

Danny finally forgets about the crickets and begins to play "The Happy One-Step," first recorded by the legendary Cajun fiddler Dennis McGee in 1929. Dennis McGee had a long musical career, with a repertoire extending back into the nineteenth century. He started out playing with accordionist Amédé Ardoin, at a time when crossing racial lines was unusual—and sometimes risky. He kept playing until shortly before his death at the age of ninety-six.

"The Happy One-Step" is beautiful—so spare and haunting— played simply on the fiddle. Attempting a fiddle tune on the accordion—when it's even possible—sometimes means the heart of the song gets lost. But Danny was one of those rare players who could manage it, with his knack for being both hard-driving and expressive on the accordion. On the tape, he manages to retain some of the delicate, lilting quality of the original fiddle version of the song.

There are no words to "The Happy One-Step," although the title suggests it is a cheerful song. I first heard it through the recordings of Marc and Ann Savoy, who often pair it with a mournful waltz. So I've come to think of "The Happy One-Step" as a song preceded by sadness.

There is one arrangement I particularly love—by the Magnolia Sisters, Ann's all-female band. She pairs the tune with one of her favorite waltzes by Dennis McGee and his longtime fiddle partner, Sady Courville. In memory of her two old friends, Ann wrote words to the waltz, expressing how much she missed them.

In the last few years, Ann's lyrics had begun to haunt me. At first, I didn't know why. But then I understood: one day I would be feeling the same way about Danny, and I could imagine myself singing a song like hers. And now, listening on the train, that time has come.

Later that evening, back at home, I will put on Ann's recording, and I will listen to her sweet, clear voice echoing my own loss. I'll smile at her description of Dennis: "toujours jeune et trainaillant." *Always young and rambling.* That's the part that reminds me of Danny.

Then the mournful waltz ends, and there is a moment of hesitation, the moment I think of as a deliberate turning away from sadness. "The Happy One-Step" begins. But it is more bittersweet than happy.

5. *"Tit Monde"*

The next song is a slow, bluesy shuffle called "Tit Monde"— or "petit monde." Literally, "little world." Sometimes translated as "little one." It is a term of endearment in Louisiana French. But it often seems to be an expression of despair or frustration, directed at a lover who is untrustworthy or absent. Sometimes a singer will spontaneously call out "oh, tit monde" in the middle of an instrumental passage, the sound hovering in the air like a weary reproach.

This version of the song comes from Canray Fontenot, one of the last of the great Creole fiddlers. I think back to hearing him at Augusta—and to our visit with him at home in Louisiana, the year before he died. Afterward, I wrote to his wife Miss Artile, assuming she wouldn't remember us. But she did. She wrote back, in careful, spidery handwriting. She sent me a mass card and a copy of the funeral program.

"Tit Monde" is one of the few songs that inspired Danny to sing—or at least start to sing. "Oh, tit monde—" he'd bellow, a broad smile on his face. Then he would trail off, the rest of the words hanging unspoken in the air. Perhaps he didn't recall the rest of the words, or maybe he didn't think they were necessary.

Most singers just improvise the words anyway, changing them as the spirit moves them. Canray started out like this, on one of his recordings:

"Oh, tit monde. Moi, je connais tu me donne les blues, bébé. On as eu pour se séparer . . ." *I know you give me the blues, baby. We had to part.*

On this night, though, Danny doesn't try to sing. He just plays that rolling bluesy lament on his accordion. Maybe he just thought the words. *It hurts to leave you. It gives me the blues.*

6. *"Fond du Culottes"*

"Fond du Culottes" is an instrumental, another one of those ragged-sounding two-steps I associate with the old-time style of accordion playing. I think of it as one of Danny's father's tunes, though an accordionist named Sidney Brown recorded it. But Danny always said, "I play this one just like my old man."

The title translates as "seat of the pants." *Hanging on, making a narrow escape, holding on by the skin of your teeth. What Danny did for so long.*

7. *"Enterre-Moi Pas"*

The next song is "Enterre-Moi Pas"—"Don't Bury Me." It's a traditional two-step, with whimsical lyrics that don't make much sense. There are multiple versions, mostly saying something like this: Little girl, when I die, don't bury me in the cemetery, just bury me in the corner of the yard, in the yard at your daddy's house. Or under the bed. Or by the chimney. Any place but the cemetery.

The Balfa Brothers have a version that is cryptic, even ominous: "O, tit bébé, 'garde ici et 'garde là-bas. Ça qui vient prépare-toi. Prépare-toi je m'en viens te chercher." *Oh, little baby, look here and look over there. Get ready for what's coming. Get ready. I'm coming to get you.*

Sometimes when Miss Freida was around she would sing this one. But on this night in the garage, she doesn't. No one does. *We just listen to this strangely ominous song, a song that seems to be mocking death.*

8. "Gilton"

"Gilton" is one of the handful of zydeco tunes Danny played. Unlike some of his fellow musicians, he refused to change his repertoire simply to take advantage of the greater popularity of zydeco. Although Danny liked the style well enough, he often pointed out that zydeco tunes were much less challenging to play on the accordion.

Mostly, Danny played what he knew and loved best: Cajun music and old-time Creole. But he resisted labels and refused to be pigeonholed. "I play French music," he'd say. Or simply, "I play good music."

On the tape, Freida requests Danny's help in learning "Gilton." Then she plays what she has learned so far. Danny obliges with a slow version, then a fast one. As the conversation resumes, I hear the sound of my own accordion, as I begin to work on the tune, playing quietly in the background.

Now it comes back to me: the way my fingers lightly searched the buttons, looking for the right notes; bending forward, to better hear my first quiet attempts; my surprise, when I realized I was getting it—on the first try. My first attempt at a zydeco tune. Usually, it took me forever to learn a new song.

I looked up and saw Danny. Watching me, with a half-smile. Maybe a little surprised himself.

I didn't realize until after the last session why this new song had come to me with relative ease. "Gilton" was similar to a Cajun song I already knew, a classic two-step called "Les Flammes d'Enfer." The

Flames of Hell. The rhythm was different, but—as Danny always reminded us—the melody was simplified.

The words to "Gilton" are simple, but, unlike many zydeco tunes, they are in French. The song had been recorded a few years earlier by Boozoo Chavis, an exponent of a traditional style of zydeco that remains close to its rural French roots.

Boozoo's lyrics are self-referential, something of a tradition in zydeco circles. The title refers to a popular zydeco club in Louisiana. The lyrics simply repeat the same phrases in varying order. They translate as: "We went to Gilton's. We had a good time. We amused ourselves last night with Boozoo's music. We danced last night to Boozoo's music." When Danny recorded this song with the California Cajun Orchestra, he followed the tradition, changing the last line to: "On a dansé hier au soir de la musique à Poullard."

I resolved that night to work on "Gilton" during the week and to come back the following Wednesday with a polished version of the tune to show Danny. By that time, both Danny and Boozoo had suffered heart attacks, and Danny had died. Boozoo lingered for a little while, and then died about a week later, at the age of seventy. *So they were both gone. And I was left with an unfinished song.*

9. *"Donne-Moi Une Autre Chance" (Give Me One More Chance)*

The Cajun accordionist Aldus Roger was one of Danny's major influences. He had a long musical career and died just a few years before Danny, at almost eighty years old. The next track on the tape is a beautiful waltz he recorded in the sixties. It was written by Johnnie Allan, a major figure in a regional musical genre known as "swamp pop"—a combination of rhythm and blues, country western, and traditional Cajun-Creole. More recently, Steve Riley recorded the song.

It's another story of separation and loss. With tears in his eyes, the singer begs his blue-eyed love not to go. Give me another chance, he begs, I'll never hurt you again. But now, the words seem to evoke another kind of loss. "Aujourd'hui tu veux me quitter parce que il faut." *Today you're leaving because you have to.* "Donne-moi une autre petite chance avant de mourir." *Give me another chance before dying.*

10. "Fifi Poncho" / "Tite Anna"

The next song is a dance hall standard, an instrumental Danny referred to as "Fifi Pancho"—or sometimes "Fifi Fancho." First recorded in 1929 by Joe Falcon, it was popularized some years later by the great Cajun accordionist Nathan Abshire, another of Danny's biggest influences. It is a particularly rhythmic, hard-driving two-step.

But the roots of the song go back earlier, to the rich tradition of unaccompanied singing in Louisiana French music—sometimes referred to as "home music," preserved by women. The melody for "Fifi Pancho" is based on an old Acadian ballad called "Tite Anna," associated with the Cajun ballad singer Lula Landry.

The song tells the strange story of Little Anna, who is being twirled so fast on the dance floor that she is slowly disappearing. All that's left is the bun in her hair and her red ribbon. Soon there will be nothing left of her. Her partner is turning her so fast he is going to kill her. "Ça va venir, il y en restera plus. Il y en reste proche plus. Il y en reste proche plus." *Soon there will be nothing left at all.*

11. "Conversational Interlude"

Before the final song, there is a long stretch of conversation—recorded by accident. We talk at length about the upcoming Isleton festival where Danny will be playing. I start to circle around the difficult issue of whether I should accept that gig in San Francisco.

Robert is starting to get a little restless with all the talk, so he begins to play some guitar riffs, filling the garage with discordant sounds. When the volume passes a certain threshold, Danny speaks up.

"Robert, why don't you put that away and save it for a rock and roll session." Danny's tone is friendly, but he is serious.

Robert laughs, not surprised at the familiar rebuke. He agrees it's probably best that he put the guitar solo back in his pocket and "pull it out when there is someone around who can appreciate it." Someone he can "use it on." Danny laughs along, appreciating Robert's humor—and also glad that he's stopped.

Then Freida reminds us that she will be leaving soon on her

much-anticipated trip to Africa. She will even be going on a safari, she tells us.

Danny gives a knowing laugh. "So what are you hunting for?"

Freida is a good friend, a family friend, and she plays along with him.

"I'm hunting for—" she pauses for effect, "—an animal!"

Their banter becomes even more ribald as they joke about what—or whom—she might find over there. Freida thinks she may end up scandalizing some of her conservative Cajun relatives. It's a thought she seems to relish.

The conversation takes a more serious turn. We talk about racism, a subject that surfaced every so often in the garage. But usually it was late in the evening, with only a few people around.

Robert wonders how people can be so ignorant.

"It's how they are bred," Danny says. "They'll go to their graves like that."

12. "Quoi Faire?"

The final song is incomplete. It begins with the sound of Steve's fiddle, playing quietly in the background, weaving its way into the conversation. Steve has started to play a traditional Creole tune called "Quoi Faire." He is making a subtle attempt to get the music started again, but no one seems to notice. The sweet, lone voice of the fiddle continues a little longer and then stops.

But Freida picks up on it—and she begins to sing, unaccompanied. She sings the opening phrase of the song: "Quoi faire—" and then the tape stops abruptly. So Freida is interrupted, her voice suspended.

The evening continued, and the conversation continued, for some time afterward. We kept talking right up until the last moment, when Steve and I were alone in the garage with Danny, and I hugged him good-bye for the last time. But this is the final moment I have recorded on the tape, for reasons I can't explain.

"Quoi faire—" Freida sings it out, a little stridently. The plaintive question hangs in the air, cut off before anything more can be said. Before the question can be fully posed, much less answered.

"Quoi faire" means "why?" in Cajun and Creole French. There

are probably as many versions of the song as there are singers. It is another one of those bluesy, improvised laments for a lost love.

I've been trying to learn the words, but so far I can't manage any more than this:

"Quoi faire, quoi faire, t'es comme ça? Quoi faire, quoi faire, tu m'as quitté?"

Why, why, are you like that? Why, why, have you left me?

AFTERWARD

The tape had ended. Now I knew. The final session in Danny's garage had been one long good-bye. Thoughts, feelings, and memories flooded me. Everywhere I looked, I saw signs and portents. Some leaped out at me when I read through the list of song titles. Others came as I listened to the tape. More emerged later, in the weeks that followed, when I reflected on what I had heard and what I had written. Endless layers of meaning filled the tape. It was a message in code—unless I had simply imagined it, looking back through the distorting lens of sadness and loss.

But this is what I decided: It didn't really matter, how or when I came to know these things—because I had heard the true message, felt the hidden current, running all through the music. Laughter and tears, love and loss. Holding on and letting go. The mysterious dance of memory linking past and present—and carrying us forward, into the days ahead.

Twenty-One Another Wednesday Night

SIX MONTHS LATER

From the outside, the house looked dark, just like the other small stucco bungalows lining the street. No sound disturbed the autumn air. It was late, at least by the standards of this quiet residential neighborhood on a Berkeley side street: nearly ten thirty on a weekday evening. It was only when I reached the door that I heard the faint promise of music, coming from deep inside the house.

"There must be a couple of people still inside," I thought, "hanging on till the very end." I opened the door and walked in.

In that moment, I crossed the threshold from dark to light, from chill to warmth, from quiet to sound. I had been feeling tense and restless, but now I was filled with a sense of ease and expansiveness. The music called me back into the heart of the house, where I found a much bigger group than I'd expected.

Ten people were gathered in a close circle, shoulder to shoulder, filling the space that usually served as the dining room—my dining room. Although I was in my own home, the space had been transformed. I was enveloped in the sights, sounds, and smells of a Cajun jam in full swing.

I hadn't really thought about what a jam smelled like, until someone recently mentioned the scent of something—maybe the wine?—when she first entered. It was true. There was a kind of rich heaviness in the air, a warm vapor rising up to surround you when you walked in from outside. The red wine was just a small part of it, though. The air was filled with many things: the sharp tang of new accordion bellows; the softer, more complex scent of the woods in the instruments; the dust of the rosin from the fiddle bows. Was it possible that the sound itself had a smell?

Or perhaps the heaviness in the air came from the heat and scent of people working physically together—their bodies close, almost touching, synchronized as they made music. There were always so many men at these musical gatherings. Maybe it was their scent we'd noticed, that other woman and I.

As I looked around the circle I was about to enter, I felt a quick rush of affection for everyone in the room. The level of closeness and the degree of personal knowledge we had of one another—well, it varied. I had known Steve for over thirty years, the rest for four years, at most. But this was the closest I had come to finding a community in California. This was where I felt most at ease.

It was a diverse group, the people who passed in and out of these music circles. We all had day jobs, toiling at many different tasks: writing and welding, teaching and truck driving, healing and repairing, working on computers and on boats. We represented different races and backgrounds, with an age span of close to thirty years. A few hadn't quite finished high school, and some had graduate degrees. We were single and coupled up, divorced and married, straight and gay, childless and not, vegetarians harmonizing with NRA members. Our local Louisiana French music community was rich and varied. But I'd come to believe that it was usually like this with musicians, this crossing of all the divides that so often separate people.

Whatever the differences among us, we had one thing in common: we were locked in an embrace with this music we had come to love. So we were also locked in an embrace with one another, however fleeting. It is a hard thing to understand, until you have made music with other people, and have felt it: That powerful connection that feels so intimate—and at the same time impersonal, linking everyone to something larger, outside themselves.

Steve left the circle to greet me. We kissed and stepped into the kitchen to exchange a few words about our respective evenings. I gave him a quick review of my writing group, and he told me how tonight's jam had been going.

We had hosted our first jam session six months earlier, just a few weeks after Danny's death, with the prospect of all those empty Wednesday nights beginning to loom. We knew that simply playing together, or having a band practice, wouldn't fill the void. But I wasn't convinced that holding a regular jam at our house—or at anyone's house—would feel right, either. Nothing could replace Danny's garage.

But other people had been talking about the need to stay connected after Danny's death, and our house was mentioned as a likely spot. In the end, Steve convinced me we should try it. Perhaps it would feel good, if a group of us could continue to come together each week, to grow and share musically, and to remember past times.

We didn't hold the jams every Wednesday, at least at first. I wondered whether anyone would show up, without someone of Danny's stature to anchor us. But people did come, and momentum had been building lately. So we tried to avoid canceling a jam, even during weeks like this one, when one or the other of us had a conflict.

I could hear someone playing the accordion, and I wondered who it might be. The playing sounded slow and cautious—but solid, like someone in the early stages of learning who was catching on fast. It was time to join the circle. I picked my way through the instrument cases, before I found an empty chair and sat down.

I poured myself a glass of wine, slipped off my shoes, and let the music wash over me. The fiddles and the lone accordion danced together, their alternating leads played out against the steady rhythm laid down by the guitars. I was surprised and impressed as I listened to the handsome silver-haired woman on the accordion. She had been playing for less than a year, and each time I heard her she sounded better.

"You're sounding great!" I said. She looked pleased.

The accordion passed to someone else, this time a younger woman. I relaxed into the waves of sound, happy to be simply listening and visiting. Then came the inevitable suggestion that I take a turn.

"Thanks—maybe later," I told Maureen. "Why don't you keep playing for a while longer? Maybe I'll play some triangle."

Partly, I wanted to be a good hostess. But I was also reluctant to break the spell the music had cast over me—and I feared it would happen, if I took over the accordion. Playing triangle or guitar, I could fall into an easy hypnotic groove and become part of the sustaining background rhythm. I would be submerged in that strong river of sound, deepening the spell of the music.

But with the accordion, it was different. Even though I should be at ease, sitting here in my own home with people I knew, something always seemed to shift once I picked up the accordion and stepped to the foreground. I began to judge myself—and to fear the judgment of others. Something got lost.

"Blair, don't you sing this one?" Maureen was sweetly persistent. She was always so good about that, trying to draw other people in.

It turned out I did know the words to the song she had started to play. And so I allowed myself to be pulled in, grateful for this easy point of entry. I sang for most of what was left of the evening. Sometimes I sang alone, sometimes a couple of us harmonized. The plaintive French lyrics wove their way in between the accordion and fiddle leads. I could feel my spirits start to lift, higher and higher, along with our voices floating out into the evening air.

Finally, I picked up my own accordion, to play the last few tunes of the evening. I listened to the first note ring out and I smiled, steadied by the sound of my own music.

The spell hadn't been broken at all.

Coda: Higher Ground

SEPTEMBER 2005

We've finished the sound check—finally.

"Let's go," I say, after an impatient glance around the room.

I kick off the first set with "Lacassine Special" and then move on quickly to "Quoi Faire." I don't say much in between, either to the rest of the band or to the small crowd starting to fill the bar. I just play my new red accordion—and sing. If I play hard and fast enough, if I try to pierce the darkness with my voice, then perhaps my spirits will be lifted.

"Quoi faire, quoi faire t'es comme ça? Quoi faire, quoi faire tu m'as quitté?"

Why, why, are you like that? Why have you left me? The French words sound plaintive, a counterpoint to the lively, pulsing rhythms of the music. Abandonment by your lover—the eternal story, it seems, in Cajun and Creole music. But the underlying themes are deep and wide: love, desire, abandonment—and the wish for connection, for restoration of something lost. Even though I haven't lost my lover—Steve is at my side, fiddle in hand—the song matches my mood tonight.

The music has changed for me over the years. When I first fell in love with Cajun music, the songs painted pictures in my mind: imagined scenes from times past in Louisiana, exotic stories from other people's lives. But now the music reminds me of people and places in my own life, and it helps me tell my own stories.

I study the unfolding scene around me. Sauce Piquante is playing at a little place called McGrath's Irish Pub, in Alameda, just across the bridge from Oakland, not far from the shipyards. The once-shabby mariner's bar was transformed a couple of years ago into a music club by the new owner, a guitar-playing Englishman who happens to love Cajun music. His blonde Finnish girlfriend sits on a stool, listening, while the Persian bartender breaks into a quick little boogie as he crosses the room, preparing to serve the gumbo he's cooked up for the occasion.

Improbable scenes like this charm me, even after eight years in the Bay Area. Normally, I'd smile, but tonight I'm not in the right frame of mind. We are playing for a hurricane fundraiser, originally billed as a Katrina benefit. But the Gulf Coast has just suffered another devastating blow, a one-two punch, Katrina followed by Rita.

After Katrina, people kept approaching me with expressions of sympathy, as though I had suffered a death in the family. They assumed I must have friends who had fallen victim to the storm. I thanked them and said I felt grateful because the people I knew personally had been out of harm's way. I explained—patiently, as always—that New Orleans isn't really home to my music. It's country music, from the French-speaking communities, Cajun and Creole, black and white, to the southwest: the swamps and bayous, the small towns, and especially the prairies.

But then my thoughts turned immediately to all the people who weren't so lucky, in New Orleans and close by in Mississippi. It was like some terrible dream, to see the city under water, and all those people suffering, displaced. And it did feel personal, because New Orleans had played such a pivotal role in my life. Fifteen years ago, during my first visit to that strange and beautiful city, I discovered Cajun music. The encounter sent me off on a life-altering journey.

But now, with Rita, the second hurricane, I have been touched in a different way. The eye of the storm passed over Beaumont, Texas, the home of two of my musician friends. Ed and Jude. Creole and Cajun. Friends and musical partners. They call each other brother. I can picture them, sitting in their living rooms, working in their shops, playing music, building accordions. Steve and I visited them both in the spring, after our first trip to New Orleans since moving to California.

Ed Poullard lives in the countryside outside Beaumont. With the passing of some of the older musicians, he is now the most prominent living Creole fiddler, a link to times past. He is also a gifted accordionist—like his older brother Danny, my friend and mentor. Danny was the guiding spirit of the Bay Area's vibrant Louisiana French music community, until his death four years ago. I still miss him.

Jude Moreau, a tall Texas Cajun who usually wears a cowboy hat, lives in the small town of Groves, not far from Ed. He plays and

Edward Poullard, at home in Beaumont, Texas, 2004. Photo courtesy of James Fraher.

builds Cajun accordions—including the one I hold in my hands. Jude came to visit us in Berkeley a month ago, and to deliver the accordion, just as Katrina was looming offshore.

My new accordion, a birthday present from Steve, is even more wonderful than I had imagined. I'd wanted something different from my other accordions. Red, I finally told Jude, after many discussions. And wet-tuned, which means the reeds are tuned a little apart from each other, so that the sound echoes, reverberates.

I was afraid this new accordion might not measure up to my dreams. Or perhaps it would appear too flashy, too much of a departure from the more traditional look and sound of my two other handmade Cajun accordions—both of them beautiful instruments, crafted with natural wood. Many steps removed from my first instrument, an austere black accordion, factory-made by Hohner.

But the new accordion is perfect. The glistening lacquer finish is definitely red. "It looks like a candy apple," one admiring friend

Jude Moreau playing at Festivals Acadiens, 2003.
Photo courtesy of David Simpson.

said. The red finish has a translucent gleam, so the distinctive wood grain is clearly visible underneath—curly maple on the front, quilted maple on the sides. Silver metal trim on the corners, ten pearly white buttons, contrasting wood inlay, red bellows. The accordion is almost too beautiful to play. Inside, Jude wrote an inscription: "Handcrafted with love for my dear friend Blair"—and then his name, and a number, #100.

I can't shake off my worries about Jude and Ed. I haven't been able to get in touch with either of them since just before Rita hit the coast. E-mail, voice messages left on home answering machines, cell phones. Nothing works. I even tried posting on an Internet Cajun accordion discussion group. But no word so far.

They must have evacuated ahead of the storm, I tell myself. Ed and Jude both have good sense, along with the resources to take care of themselves and their families. But I need to know for sure.

Sometimes it helps to speak your worries aloud. So after playing those first two songs, I do.

"We're here for a hurricane benefit," I tell the crowd. "And this last one, Rita, has really hit home."

And then I tell my stories: about Ed and Danny; and the story of Jude, who made my new accordion; and a word or two about the Katrina evacuee who is staying with us. Finally, I go back to playing—and to telling my stories in song.

As I play, reassuring news is heading my way, crossing the few seconds of cyberspace dividing the Gulf Coast and California. A message waits on my computer—from Jude. He and his family are safe, staying with relatives in Opelousas. A little later, he sends a second message, saying that he's spoken to Ed, who is also safe.

They have all reached higher ground.

The next day, I will wonder a little at the timing. Perhaps my friends heard my words or music, or sensed my thoughts, across all those miles. Just as quickly, I'll dismiss this as magical thinking. It was just coincidence, surely.

But I've experienced so much in the way of odd connections and serendipity over these last years that I'm no longer so quick to discount such speculation. Or perhaps it's just that I've developed a greater appreciation for magic and mystery, as I've followed my unexpected musical path. It has been a journey to a higher ground I didn't even know I was seeking, all those years ago. I think back to my first trip to New Orleans, and I smile. The time and place seem so far away—and close enough to touch.

Suggestions for Listening

In compiling this list, I have had a modest goal: to provide the written equivalent of a soundtrack for *Accordion Dreams*. These are personal selections rather than a comprehensive discography. But I hope they offer a good starting point for anyone who is new to the pleasures of Cajun and Creole music.

I have included selections by most of the musicians cited in *Accordion Dreams*—and, when possible, I have chosen recordings that include the songs mentioned in the book. Consequently, the albums I have listed may not be the most recent by a particular artist, nor do I claim they are "the best." A number of groups (BeauSoleil, Steve Riley and the Mamou Playboys, the Savoy family) have multiple recordings to their credit, with new albums appearing regularly. I would be hard-pressed to pick a favorite. Also, because this list reflects my musical influences during the period described in *Accordion Dreams*, it does not include a host of newer bands, including young traditional groups like the Lost Bayou Ramblers, the Pine Leaf Boys, and the Red Stick Ramblers.

Following the recordings by individual musicians/groups, I have included a list of a half dozen compilations I have enjoyed, in the interest of providing a more comprehensive overview.

For more information about the history of Louisiana French music, profiles of older musicians, discographies, and traditional song lyrics, there is no better resource than Ann Savoy's *Cajun Music: A Reflection of a People*. For an up-to-date guide to musicians who are currently active, I would suggest David Simpson's excellent LSU-Eunice website: "Louisiana Contemporary Cajun, Creole, and Zydeco Musicians" at www.lsue.edu/acadgate/music/musicmain.htm.

For information about bands outside Louisiana, especially the SF Bay Area, see Andrea Rubinstein's Cajun-Zydeco Web Resources, at www.sfbayou.com. And if you'd like to take a look—or a listen—to my own band, you'll find Sauce Piquante at www.saucepiquante band.com. But I hope you will begin with the traditional sources of this music listed below.

Happy listening!

INDIVIDUAL MUSICIANS/GROUPS

Abshire, Nathan. *Nathan Abshire: The Cajun Legend*. Swallow, 1994.
Ardoin, Amédé. *I'm Never Coming Back: Amédé Ardoin: Pioneer of Louisiana French Blues, 1930–34*. Arhoolie, 1995.
Ardoin, Bois Sec, with Balfa Toujours: *Allons Danser*. Rounder, 1998. Also see recordings by Balfa Toujours on their own.
Balfa Brothers. *The Balfa Brothers Play Traditional Cajun Music, Volumes I and II*. Swallow, 1991.
BeauSoleil. *Bayou Cadillac*. Rounder, 1989. Also see their many other albums.
Carrière Brothers and the Lawtell Playboys. *La-La: Louisiana Black French Music*. Audiocassette. Maison de Soul, 1995. Includes Delton Broussard on accordion.
Cormier, Sheryl. *The Queen of Cajun Music*. Swallow, 1992.
Fontenot, Canray. *Louisiana Hot Sauce Creole Style*. Arhoolie, 1992.
Frank, Keith. *The Creole Connection: The Masked Band*. Louisiana Red Hot, 2001.
Legé, Jesse, with Mack Manuel and the Lake Charles Ramblers. *Mémoires du Passé*. Swallow, 1997.
LeJeune, Eddie. *It's in the Blood*. Rounder, 1991.
LeJeune, Iry. *Cajun's Greatest—The Definitive Collection*. Ace (UK), 1992.
Les Frères Michot. *Elevés à Pilette*. LFM, 1996. Also see their recent album.
Magnolia Sisters. *Prends Courage*. Arhoolie, 1995. Also see their newer albums.
McGee, Dennis. *The Complete Early Recordings of Dennis McGee*. Yazoo, 1994.
Moreau, Jude, and the Bon Temps Playboys. *Retourner au les Vieux Temps*. Louisiana Radio Records, 2002. With Edward Poullard on fiddle.
Poullard, Danny, with the California Cajun Orchestra. *Nonc Adam Two-Step*. Arhoolie, 1995.

Poullard, Danny, with the California Cajun Orchestra. *Not Lonesome Anymore*. Arhoolie, 1991. Winner of the first annual "Prix Dehors de Nous" awarded by the Cajun French Music Association (CFMA) for best recording by a band outside Louisiana.

Poullard, Danny, with Edward Poullard and D'Jalma Garnier. *Poullard, Poullard & Garnier*. Louisiana Radio Records, 2001. Danny Poullard playing in the old-time Creole style; released a few weeks before his death.

Riley, Steve, and the Mamou Playboys. *Ti Galop Pour Mamou*. Rounder, 1992. Also see their many other albums, especially two recent ones, *Bon Rêve* and *Dominos*.

Savoy, Marc, Dewey Balfa, and D. L. Menard. *Under a Green Oak Tree*. Arhoolie, 1989.

Savoy-Doucet Cajun Band. *Home Music with Spirits*. Arhoolie, 1992. Also see their later recordings.

COMPILATIONS

Cajun Dance Party: Fais Do-Do. Columbia, 1994. The earliest commercial recordings (1929–34) by Cléoma Breaux Falcon, Joseph Falcon, the Breaux Brothers, Amédé Ardoin and Dennis McGee, and others.

Cajun Music and Zydeco. Rounder, 1992. Inspired by photographer Philip Gould's book by the same name. An appealing range of modern commercial recordings, alternates Cajun and zydeco tracks.

Cajun Social Music. Smithsonian-Folkways, 1990. Recorded live during a 1975 visit to southwest Louisiana by French folklorist Gérard Dole. Includes Marc Savoy, Nathan Abshire, Nonc Allie Young, and others.

J'ai Eté au Bal, Vol. 1 and 2. Arhoolie, 1990. Music from the acclaimed Les Blank documentary. Covers an impressive range of Cajun, Creole, and zydeco music. Vol. 1 includes a rare recording of Walter Mouton and the original "Allons à Lafayette" by Joseph and Cléoma Falcon.

Legendary Masters of Cajun and Creole Music: Les Haricots Sont Pas Salés. Cinq Planetes (France), 1997. Live recordings with a "house party" feeling by French documentary filmmaker Jean-Pierre Bruneau, from 1972 music sessions in the homes of Cajun and Creole musicians. Includes Cajun greats Dewey Balfa, Nathan Abshire, Dennis McGee,

Shirley Bergeron; Creole masters Bois Sec Ardoin, Canray Fontenot, Bee and Freeman Fontenot.

Music from the Zydeco Kingdom. Rounder, 2000. Compiled by Michael Tisserand, who wrote *The Kingdom of Zydeco*. Like the book, it offers an excellent introduction to zydeco. Includes some early Creole recordings, but gives more attention to the modern zydeco sound.